*The Writing on the Wall*

# The Writing on the Wall

## Women's Autobiography
## and the Asylum

*Mary Elene Wood*

University of Illinois Press   *Urbana & Chicago*

Library of Congress Cataloging-in-Publication Data

Wood, Mary Elene.
    The writing on the wall : women's autobiography and the asylum /
Mary Elene Wood.
        p.   cm.
    Includes bibliographical references and index.
    ISBN 0-252-02098-7 (cloth).  —ISBN 0-252-06389-9 (pbk.)
    1. American prose literature—Women authors—History and
criticism.   2. Psychiatric hospital patients—United States—
Biography—History and criticism.   3. Mentally ill women—United
States—Biography—History and criticism.   4. Women patients—
United States—Biography—History and criticism.   5. Women and
literature—United States—History.   6. Literature and mental illness.
7. Autobiography—Women authors. 8. Mentally ill—In literature.
    I. Title.
PS366.A88W66 1994
362.2'1'0973—dc20                                               93-38401
                                                                    CIP

# Contents

# Acknowledgments

I would first like to thank the Center for the Study of Women and Society at the University of Oregon for the fellowship support that allowed me to complete this book. The following people read parts of the manuscript in its various stages and were kind enough to give me their advice and encouragement: Paul Armstrong, Suzanne Clark, Jay Fliegelman, Estelle Freedman, Barbara Charlesworth Gelpi, Margo Horn, Linda Kintz, Arturo Islas, and Louise Westling. Ann Lane's feedback helped me clarify my ideas for the book. Lois Rudnick's careful reading of the manuscript and insightful suggestions were invaluable in helping me shape the book into its final form. Catherine A. Larson, local history specialist at the Kalamazoo Public Library, went well out of her way to give me useful research assistance. I am grateful to Carole S. Appel, Cat Warren, and Rita D. Disroe for their considerable expertise in preparing the manuscript for publication.

The members of the Feminist Theory Group (Fem Thug) at the University of Oregon provided an environment of fruitful discussion and good eating that enabled me to make progress on this book despite demanding work responsibilities. My colleagues and friends Diana Abu-Jaber, Michael Clark, Amy Klauke, Anne Laskaya, Annie Popkin, Tres Pyle, and Claudia Yukman provided both professional and personal support. I was fortunate to have a friend and supporter in Marilyn Farwell, who read and commented on large sections of the manuscript and was always ready with helpful advice. More than once, Jamie King reminded me that the project was worthwhile. At various points over the last several years, my longtime friends Kathryn Cirksena, Maria Damon, Jesse Gathering, Linda Gardner, Rebecca Mark, and Anna Richert helped give me a sense of connectedness and sanity that made it possible for me to immerse myself in stories of madness and injustice. Rebecca in particular was always there to give me perspective and urge me through yet another set of revisions. I would also like to thank my parents, James and Eunice Wood; my grandmother, Mary Shepro; my sister-in-law, Jordana Raiskin; and my sister, Leslie Wood, for giving me the family support that makes other kinds of work possible. I am especially grateful to my mother, who was kind enough to share her experiences of the mental health system with me and who thus provided the inspiration for this book.

Finally, I owe inestimable gratitude to my friend, colleague, and life partner Judith Raiskin, who saw this project through each of its stages and who read more versions of each chapter than either of us would care to remember. Because of her humor and love, I was able to continue working with often heartbreaking materials. Her constant support is there on every page of this book.

# Introduction

I first began reading autobiographies by women in mental institutions almost by accident. In the middle of another research project, I ran across Elizabeth Packard's *The Prisoner's Hidden Life; or, Insane Asylums Unveiled* on the shelf above the book for which I had actually been searching. When I pulled it down and started reading through it, I recognized it as a text to which Phyllis Chesler had referred in her important 1972 study *Women and Madness*. Soon after, I began to hunt for any autobiographies of this kind that I could find.

In a way, these women had lived through and written about one of my own worst fears: Their perceptions of the world had been denied and disallowed not only by medical and legal professionals but by their own families and friends. This denial had then been enacted violently upon their bodies through incarceration, drugging, sexual assault, beatings, and internalized hatred. Despite all this, they were able to write about these experiences, recreating themselves with the same discursive tools that had been used against them.

I chose to focus on autobiographies in the study, rather than journals or diaries, because I was interested in how a woman institutionalized as insane structured a narrative for public consumption, a narrative in which she would have to convince a skeptical audience of her sanity. I found that even as I researched this project I was anticipating the objections or questions of my own readers who might wonder if these narratives were "authentic" stories of real people or rather sensationalistic fictions disguised as autobiographies. After all, how could an insane woman write her own story? Just as the writers included testimonials to their sanity from judges, doctors, and politicians, I found myself contacting the archives of the asylums in which they had lived and hunting down the newspaper articles they referred to so that I could obtain proof that they really were who they said they were.

While it may be necessary for a researcher to check sources and find out particulars about her subjects, in this case my vigilance and anxiety about legitimating these writers developed in the context of the very assumptions and prejudices against which these autobiographers had struggled. The pages of letters and, in the case of Elizabeth Packard, sanity trial transcripts, were not enough to convince my imagined readers that these women actually had been institutionalized, released, and declared sane; I needed to go to outside sources to confirm this, to the "official" sources to which Packard and the other writers referred with disdain as ignorant of actual asylum practices and conditions.

When I realized I was doing this, I began to question my own motives. Would my desire to prove the authenticity and believability of these writers have been as intense had they not been institutionalized as insane in the first place? I doubt it. And why, given that I saw autobiography and fiction as intertwined, did I so want to establish that these writers really who were they said they were? Wouldn't their stories of incarceration and oppression as women called insane be just as powerful and valid if they were fictional characters?

Of course, I did want my readers to know that such lives existed, were lived, were real. But at the same time, when dealing with the issue of madness, I felt a particular need to be very clear about what was true and what was false, what was real and what was fantasy.

As I recognized my discomfort with the topic of sanity/insanity, I began to see what these writers had been up against. They had to imagine an audience of readers more or less like me—sympathetic, yet skeptical; fascinated, yet afraid. They knew that a woman called insane cannot even begin to enter an argument and be listened to. After all, if they could be "shut up" as mad, perhaps so could the reader. Perhaps the line between sanity and insanity, between inside and outside the asylum, was not such a clear one.

The question of how to describe asylum experience adequately, and how to understand the line between inside and outside, has run like a thread throughout the scholarship on the history of mental science and its discourses. Historical studies of the asylum since the 1960s have often relied on official records of asylum statistics and writings by superintendents and physicians rather than on writings by asylum inmates. Norman Dain, for example, tends to portray the development of the asylum in America as a progressive one, marked by the aspirations of physicians and thinkers who were often stymied in their

genuine care for the good of patients by uninformed general practitioners, opportunistic "medical cultists," and a naive public (*Concepts of
Insanity*, pp. 147–48, 154, 164). The historian Gerald Grob's early work
looks at treatment of mental illness in the light of complex social,
economic, and political forces affecting patients, their families, and
practitioners (*Mental Institutions*, pp. 132–33). His later work, however, tends to represent asylum staff workers as beleaguered, if at times
coercive, and patients as unaccommodating and belligerent (*Mental
Illness*, p. 16).

Other theorists and historians, working largely under the influence
of Michel Foucault, have countered this version of events by looking
at the rise of the asylum more from the patient's perspective and with
a view to understanding the role of the asylum in the context of larger
social forces that worked to perpetuate class, race, and gender hierarchies.[1] More recently, historians have questioned this "social control" model. In discussing the emphasis on custodial care in the late
nineteenth-century American asylum, Constance McGovern states
that "to imply that this very real element of custodialism was an attempt on the part of middle-class doctors to exercise social control
over the lives of their working-class patients is simply too easy and,
indeed, misleading" (p. 16). She challenges "the assumption that the
patients and their families were passive victims of state policies and
institutional programs" (p. 16). In an important article on sex roles
in the treatment of mental illness in the nineteenth century, Ellen
Dwyer maintains that, since families and community members were
responsible for committing patients, "doctors cannot be blamed for
the increasing numbers of men and women in lunatic asylums" toward
the latter part of the nineteenth century (p. 40). While McGovern and
Dwyer go far toward showing the complexity and diversity of asylum
relations, they seem anxious to exonerate physicians from blame and
to portray them as dedicated and caring professionals. In an effort to
draw an accurate picture of asylum reality, for example, McGovern ex-
amines patient records which she claims show "consistency and can-
didness" (p. 5), record regular visits by dedicated physicians, and provide "new evidence" to revise "the conceptualizations of asylums as
custodial institutions or as totally repressive, dehumanizing places"
(p. 4).

After reading the asylum autobiographies I discuss here, I cannot
help but be skeptical about efforts to revise asylum history that rely

primarily on case records kept by physicians and attendants. While I think these can be telling sources, they clearly clash with the renditions of asylum life provided by Elizabeth Packard, Sophie Olsen, Lydia Smith, and Clarissa Lathrop, renditions in which attendants play a much larger daily role in patients' lives than do doctors, in which a doctor's visit rarely involves more than a sentence or two exchanged in the hall, and in which "recovery" involves following asylum rules (e.g., that the patient must leave or enter her room on the attendant's demand or that she may not read books or wear her own clothing) that have little to do with life on the outside. To question the official record, however, is not necessarily to "blame" individual doctors or to think of "social control" in terms of some individuals repressing others. I am less interested here in finding particular villains than in trying to understand the social forces that coalesced so that family members and physicians decided together that a patient should be committed to an asylum for her own good and then denied that what happened in the asylum had little to do with learning to live a meaningful life in the world outside. Rather than exposing asylum officials as bad guys, I want to understand the popular medical discourse that portrays them as developing useful "treatments" even as it reveals their paternalism and denial of patients' subjectivity. I want to understand why Dr. John Gray, superintendent of the state asylum at Utica, New York, could present himself and his work as so beneficial that present-day historians portray him as one of the more enlightened alienists,[2] while Clarissa Lathrop, who was a patient under his care at Utica, saw him and his policies as erasing her sense of self. I wonder too what part the asylum, its professionals, and its discourses came to play in the popular imagination, so that while some lay persons had increasing faith in asylum practices toward the end of the nineteenth century, others distrusted the asylum, believed that unjust commitments were commonplace, and joined asylum reform movements.[3]

In the light of a powerfully emerging, if conflicted, professional psychiatric discourse, Packard, Olsen, Smith, and Lathrop, as well as Jane Hillyer and Zelda Fitzgerald had to develop strategies that would convince their readers to enter their narratives and accept, at least partly, the world that each narrative created.[4] These strategies vary depending on the historical contexts of each text, the genres available to the writer at that time, and the specific psychiatric and other authoritative discourses that might interfere with and help shape each writer's project. For example, the middle-class status of these writers was significant because while it did not keep them from being institutionalized, it did provide avenues for their release. It also gave them a hook back into a society of ordered hierarchies. As each writer discovers, while in the asylum, the tenuousness and constructedness of that ordered world, she learns to depend on her middle-class place in it to guarantee her sanity to herself and her readers as she describes her life both within the asylum and after her release. Throughout the second half of the nineteenth century, the public asylum in the United States became increasingly populated by immigrants and poor people. As women from middle-class backgrounds, these writers both tried to speak for this wider population and sought to differentiate themselves from the lower classes, who at times represent the "really insane" in each autobiography.

On the one hand, the writers' use of class status as a writing strategy contributed to the maintenance of class distinctions. On the other, it also gave legitimacy to their narratives. With the exception of Fitzgerald, whose autobiographical novel approaches her institutionalization obliquely, all these writers take on the task of describing asylum conditions and their experiences in the asylum in the face of massive denial that such stories could be true. While there are many voices for asylum reform in the late-nineteenth century and early twentieth, so that these writers do not speak from completely isolated positions, still they must create strategies that will allow their writing to penetrate the cracks in psychiatric discourse, whose claim to authority in describing mental illness became increasingly powerful into the twentieth century.

■

The mid- to late nineteenth-century asylum in the United States and its discourses were beset by contradictions that the autobiographers could magnify and expose as long as they could maintain their credibility. Early and mid-nineteenth-century asylums had promised to provide "moral treatment," in which patients would be treated humanely in a family setting. With Pinel's famous "freeing" of the insane at the Bicêtre asylum in 1793, physical punishment and restraints supposedly began to be abandoned in favor of this new treatment philosophy. Patients would be provided a paternal superintendent and a maternal "matron" who would help shape their behavior back into normality.

According to this new approach, if treated with calm, kind, and orderly methods, the insane would abandon their madness. "Moral treatment" was the treatment of choice in insane asylums in the United States in the early nineteenth century.

Yet, as Foucault has pointed out, this new system merely introduced a more psychological form of coercion, in which "the asylum sets itself the task of the homogeneous rule of morality, its rigorous extension to all those who tend to escape from it" (Foucault, *Madness*, p. 258). For middle-class women, the family model was less than satisfactory, since it often demanded their submission to male authority, abandonment of intellectual pursuits, and acceptance of domestic tasks as their natural lot in life. For working-class women, while the asylum may have provided needed rest from backbreaking work both inside and outside of the home, its regimen nevertheless served to shape their behavior so that they could return to the domestic and workplace labor they had left behind. Indeed a recurring theme in the autobiographies I discuss, voiced by the middle-class writers who often claim to speak for all those incarcerated, is a complaint about the "occupational therapy" that the writers and other inmates see as poorly compensated labor. The work that the alienists see as having a moral function within the asylum "home" the writers see as exploiting their labor within a tightly controlled marketplace. The contradictory readings of this work-as-therapy reveal that the autobiographers themselves suspect the moral purposes behind the institution. Their questioning of the function of patients' labor ultimately exposes the constructedness of the nineteenth-century split between public and private, market and home.

All the autobiographies I discuss challenge in some way the authority of psychiatric professionals and reveal connections in the dominant discourse between the place of women in the institution and in the family. Thus Elizabeth Packard clearly and repeatedly draws an analogy between husband and asylum superintendent and finds that both fail to allow her spiritual or intellectual independence. Toward the middle of the nineteenth century, this asylum family model began to break down, as most public institutions grew too large to work according to any small-scale family model.[5] As asylums expanded, the "matron" figure began to disappear, to be replaced by a large staff of attendants. The "motherly" influence thus was no longer present even as a pretense as asylums became structured hierarchically, with a male superintendent at the top managing scores of workers. Yet the family-model discourse continued to circulate as superintendents and neurologists, whose field became increasingly respectable in the late nineteenth century, insisted on their paternal relationship to their patients. For male patients, this discourse placed them in an infantilized or feminized position in relation to "fatherly" superintendents. For women, the discourse reinforced their position within the larger society, in which they were largely denied a public voice.

For both men and women, the nineteenth-century discourse of asylum-as-family reinforced the notion, elaborated by Elaine Showalter, that to be insane was to be feminized (*Female Malady*, pp. 3–8). This is not necessarily to say that more women were diagnosed as mentally ill or committed to asylums. Historians have shown the lack of significant statistical differences between the sexes in these two areas.[6] It is to say, however, that to be labeled insane was to be associated with the feminine. As Nancy Tomes has pointed out, women's insanity was often thought to be a danger inherent to the female body, particularly the reproductive system, while men's insanity was attributed more commonly to bad habits, such as alcohol consumption or overwork ("Historical Perspectives," pp. 151, 161). In other words, insanity could result from women's very constitution, their very femaleness, while for men it would most likely be caused not by who they were but by what they did. The association of insanity with the female body, the tendency of asylum "family" structure to cast patients as dependent and submissive, and the assumption that insanity, like other illnesses, rendered patients passive and deprived them of the willpower required of men—all contributed to the association of madness with femininity.

The paternalistic perspective of asylum discourse in the nineteenth century, a perspective implying that the feminized patient was unable to judge the quality or nature of care, helped obscure the violence still intrinsic to asylum management in the United States. According to the autobiographers I discuss here, despite the development of "moral treatment," physical violence and restraint as patient management techniques within the asylum were rarely completely abandoned, but simply moved out of the public eye. Because of overcrowding in understaffed asylums, these violent management techniques—such as beatings, cold water dunkings, confinement in locked boxes, forced drugging, and forced feeding—were relied on as a way of controlling large numbers of patients. For women patients, drugs were used as a controlling mechanism of choice. Constance McGovern has pointed out that twice as many women as men received drug treatment in the asylums she studied ("Myths of Social Control," p. 13). However, nineteenth-century autobiographers make clear that hands-on violence was also used against women patients, as well as verbal threats.

Packard, Smith, and Lathrop all describe the restraining and managing devices, many of which amount to means of torture, used in the "lower" wards—the straitjackets, cold tubs, cribs with slatted lids. They tell of women being raped, then called insane and removed to lower wards if they told anyone. They tell of untrained attendants threatening, dragging by the hair, dunking in cold water, beating, and torturing patients out of frustration, impatience, or for no discernible reason at all.

To all these stories, alienists had answers, most of which referred to diagnoses of the complaining patients or to the unfortunate yet practical necessity for physical restraint.[7] Patients who reported abuses to authorities after their release were seen as vengeful, bitter troublemakers who probably had not fully recovered from their illnesses.

The autobiographers' references to violence within asylum management of patients are echoed by several investigations of state institutions in the late nineteenth century, investigations that were followed with great interest by journalists. One 1884 article, entitled "How to Restrain a Patient: First Break His Jaw Then His Ribs and He is Quiet" (*New York Times*, Feb. 8, pp. 1–6), reports on the investigation of a patient's death at the Utica asylum, where autobiographer Clarissa Lathrop was a patient. Another New York state investigation that drew a large degree of public attention during this period involved the Ward's Island Asylum. In this case, neurologists Edward Spitzka and William Hammond, members of a "Committee on Asylum Abuses" formed by the Neurologists' Society, testified that asylum officials were insufficiently trained in "the new anatomy and physiology of the nervous system" (*NYT*, Dec. 2, 1880, p. 8) and thus were ill equipped to determine treatment of patients. The neurologists condemned the use of restraining devices and encouraged thorough investigation of asylum practices.

To further reform asylums, neurologists and other concerned citizens formed the National Association for the Protection of the Insane and the Prevention of Insanity, which adopted its constitution on July 1, 1880 (Grob, *National Association*, p. 4). In a paper read at its first convention, J. C. Shaw, superintendent of New York's King's County Insane Asylum, proclaimed that when he first took charge he "found a large number of patients in restraint-jackets, straps and seclusion. . . . Some of these patients had been in restraint for months, and even years" (Grob, *National Association*, p. 16). He abolished the restraints and had them burnt, discovering "that there must have been *three hundred* pairs of restraint apparatus, straps, camisades, etc." (Grob, *National Association*, 17, Shaw's emphasis).

Interestingly enough, however, neurologists, such as those who helped form the association, did not necessarily base their criticisms on the complaints of patients themselves, whose stories some saw as "doubtless exaggerated and unfounded (*NYT*, Dec. 2, 1880, p. 8). The most damaging (because more credible) testimony in the 1880 Senate investigation of New York state asylums came not from patients but from the Reverend William French, a respectable missionary who occasionally visited the asylums. French, who had kept careful notes on his asylum experiences, reported on Jane Stevens, who had died from injuries inflicted at the asylum, and Rose McCabe, a nun who had been confined to a filthy room because she awakened a nurse to attend to a distressed patient. During these investigations, asylum superintendents supported the use of physical restraints and denied any wrongdoing, continuing to call into question the motives and perceptions of those giving testimony (*NYT*, Dec. 8, 1880, p. 2).

While the autobiographers complain of drugging and other forms of violence, they claim that patients were especially controlled by threat of removal to the dreaded back wards of the asylum. Asylums were divided into wards differentiated by the "severity" of the patient's illness. The "better" wards were more accessible to public visitors, while the "worse" wards tended to be in more remote sections of the asylum, which visitors from the press or from state legislatures were seldom invited to explore.[8]

Not surprisingly, then, movement among the various wards is one of the primary structuring devices of these autobiographies. Indeed, physical movement from place to place was important to these narratives because where a patient was largely determined the treatment she received. Such involuntary movement represented her powerlessness within the asylum world, given that, according to these autobiographers, she rarely knew when she would be moved, why, or where (until she actually arrived). Her location in the asylum also represented how close she was perceived as being to sanity and thus to release.

■

The control over her life lost in the asylum is regained in the telling of the narrative, as the narrative voice directs reader and story from place to place, often with little warning or explanation. To read these narratives can thus be a disorienting experience. It is through this disorientation that the writers can undermine the readers' skepticism. Disrupting the alienists' presentation of asylums as places of healing and nurturance, of "asylum," this wrenching movement from ward to ward, in which friends are lost and tentative communities disrupted, reveals the patients' experience as terrifying, disempowering, and often violent. Yet the writers must maintain a fine balance in mimicking such disruption in their writing. If they lose the narrative line too much or present a narrative voice that drifts too dramatically, they risk slipping into the category of "insane." This danger is particularly evident in the early twentieth-century writings of Jane Hillyer and Zelda Fitzgerald, who, provided with the experimental examples of modernist writing, are all too aware that their literary experiments as women called insane may be read as madness.

Each writer, then, develops strategies for presenting her narrative as a legitimate one. Nineteenth-century writer Elizabeth Packard describes the abuses she witnessed in the asylum by placing them in a Christian context of struggle between good and evil. This religious narrative provides her with a framework within which her own "witnessing" can be considered legitimate by her readers. Lydia Smith and Clarissa Lathrop adopt the stance of journalists recording evidence from an objective distance. As they try to interrupt the official version of their experience, told from outside that experience by those who think they know what is best for the patient, these asylum autobiographers draw strategies from a grab-bag of generic traditions— slave narrative, captivity narrative, domestic novel, sensation novel, romance, political essay, religious tract, realistic novel, new journalism. I emphasize strategy here, even though such strategizing was not necessarily always consciously planned out, because, with the exception of Fitzgerald, these writers wrote with a distinct purpose—to reform the asylum. Supported by and as part of an organized movement, Packard, Smith, and Lathrop wrote to promote the reform of asylum laws and practices. Jane Hillyer wrote ostensibly to promote the newly discovered wonders of twentieth-century psychiatry and particularly psychotherapy, but within this officially sanctioned purpose she too advocated reform of asylum conditions.

All of these writers were faced with the problem of how to create self-narratives that would be read as legitimate, as sane, when they themselves had been labeled insane. The dominant forms of writing developed throughout the nineteenth century—sentimental romance, domestic novel, political treatise, realistic novel—tended to invoke madness in one breath and circumscribe it in the next, reinforcing the claims of a coherent world. Insanity was that which literary form was not, that which acceptable literature contained or excluded. To make an argument or to tell a story was to spin out a logic. How would these women use these forms to tell their stories without recreating the very categories of sane and insane that had meant their own ostracism and incarceration and that continued to rule the lives of women left behind in the asylum?

This was precisely the challenge faced by these autobiographers, who often do reproduce the very hierarchies deconstructed by their asylum experiences. Yet even in so doing, their texts expose the extent to which the forms available to them are marked by class and gender. Nancy Armstrong has argued convincingly that "genres are rooted in gender" (p. 41) in the nineteenth century. Through the ideology of separate male and female spheres, the middle class could imagine a haven from the competitive environment of a rapidly industrializing society. In accord with this division, writing that created a personal world was gendered as feminine, while writing that involved an impersonal exchange of ideas related to the public world was gendered as masculine. Given that the private sphere was marked as feminine, to the extent that autobiography treated a subjective, inner life, it was engaged in a feminine pursuit, regardless of the gender of the author, even though many male writers claimed this pursuit as their own. When these women asylum autobiographers take autobiography as their medium, they choose a form that is both denied them, given that all writing is in some way public, and marked as apt for them, given its private and thus feminine "nature." At the same time, these autobiographers go beyond the private nature of the genre to challenge the separation of spheres by blending personal narrative with expository sections on psychological and political theory. The threat of these texts is that they actively promote social and political change from within a "feminine" genre.

In the very act of telling their stories, these autobiographers rupture a prescribed narrative, a narrative that says that they are insane, that they have no place from which to write, that writing will make them sicker, that they should live in institutions, and that they should give over control of their lives to husbands, fathers, and doctors.[9] Beneath this prescribed narrative runs an even more powerful one that says middle-class women who do not live as wives, daughters, or mothers within the socially defined parameters of those terms will not be considered full human beings, let alone writers. When these women write—and, specifically, when they write the stories of their lives— they disrupt these narratives with the first word on the printed page. If we see action and experience as themselves permeated with discourse and with resistance to prescriptive narratives, then the question of who is writing, of the *person* who writes becomes very significant.[10]

The genre of autobiography gave these writers incarcerated as insane a way to resist the ideology that would erase their subjectivity. The study of women's autobiography is crucial because it embodies a moment when women have chosen to rupture the dominant narratives that deny their ability to speak from an "I," whether that "I" is consciously illusory or authoritative or both. Most nonfeminist theorists of autobiography have not known what to do with women's autobiography precisely because it cannot be easily codified within histories of autobiography that chart a movement from Rousseau's authoritative self-assertion to a postmodernist self-fragmentation.[11] Women do not fit into such a paradigm because their adoption of an autobiographical project has never come from a place of authority. As Sidonie Smith writes in her study of women's autobiography, "even the rebel whose text projects a hostile society against which he struggles to define himself, if he is male, takes himself seriously because he and his public assume his significance within the dominant order: Only in the fullness of that membership can the fullness of his rebellion unfold. For women, on the other hand, rebellious pursuit is potentially catastrophic" (*Poetics*, p. 9). Even when a woman's autobiography seems steeped in conventionality in terms of its form or its concept of selfhood, it challenges that conventionality by the very fact of its existence.

The tradition of autobiographical writing helps women incarcerated in asylums create an illusion of coherent consciousness even as they also expose that illusion by appropriating other genres and other narrative voices along the way. Their texts challenge us to find the line between strategy and unconscious disruption of conventional narrative. To what extent do they believe they have become coherent and whole, offering these narratives as proof of their mental health? To what extent do they strategize for political reasons through a parody of coherent identity?

While the strategies used operate differently in each text, the rules of autobiography intersect and challenge the generic conventions—such as those in domestic and sensation fiction—that tend ultimately to reinforce the separation of male and female spheres and the institutions of marriage and motherhood. The narratives I discuss here use autobiography to claim that "real experience" is a legitimate place from which to speak, even if that experience itself seems illegitimate.[12] The exception to this may be Zelda Fitzgerald's autobiographical novel *Save Me the Waltz*, which substitutes fiction for autobiography. Yet this move in itself signals a historical moment in which asylum autobiography has come too much under the control of medical authorities seeking to use it as proof of their own ability to cure the mentally ill patient. In Fitzgerald's case, as in that of the other writers, her narrative interacts with the experience that struggles against being contained and defined by conventions, both literary and medical.

The intersection of autobiographical writing and experience is nowhere more apparent than in the letter writing that appears continually in these autobiographies. The nineteenth-century autobiographers I discuss here include as part of the text letters they wrote while incarcerated. These letters both break up the linear, chronological order of the narratives and challenge the notion of a coherent consciousness creating the text. They posit another "I" than that of the narrator, the "I" of the letter writer, which is almost always presented explicitly as a mask, a strategy. At the same time, the writers make clear that these letters were written clandestinely, against the rules of the asylum and in spite of the punishment that would result if they were discovered. Carried secretly from the asylum by other women who had been granted their freedom, they almost always held a plea to those outside for help in gaining release from the asylum.

In terms of the autobiography's content, the letters represent the possibility of bodily freedom and the breaking of a rule that could result in bodily punishment. While women's letters have been forged and intercepted in American literature since the epistolary novels of the eighteenth century, these autobiographies foreground the dangers inherent in the writing and delivery of the letters for real-life women in real-life confinement. As readers, we become intensely aware of the significance that they were written by women institutionalized as insane who were expressly forbidden to write. The conditions of their production give them a power and subversiveness that they would not otherwise have and that carries over into the autobiographies themselves. As letters to the reader that barely escaped interception, these texts call attention to their material existence and the material reality of the asylum world they come from and portray.

■

In chapter 1, I examine *The Prisoner's Hidden Life; or, Insane Asylums Unveiled*—Elizabeth Packard's 1868 story of her involuntary imprisonment in the Jacksonville State Asylum in Illinois—in the light of nineteenth-century concepts of women's rationality. Nineteenth-century medical advice literature in the United States tended to identify women with their reproductive role, describing them primarily in relation to husband, parents, or children and defining them as less rational and less autonomous than men (Smith-Rosenberg, pp. 183–88). Through her writing, Elizabeth Packard rejects her relegation to the private sphere, yet uses the discourse on motherhood to establish her authority. By reformulating concepts of motherhood, she substitutes her writing and political work for her children and thus legitimates her entry into the public sphere. This gesture helps reveal the contradictions within the ideologies of motherhood, rationality, and the separation of spheres.

As she works to legitimate her entry into the public sphere, Elizabeth Packard brings together strategies of spiritual autobiography, slave narrative, political treatise, and domestic fiction. Not unlike the "eclectic" slave narratives that Robert Burns Stepto describes as combining individual story with authenticating documents, often with little or no verbal bond between them, Packard's text interrupts her personal story of asylum captivity with letters declaring her sanity, expository discussions of the wrongs of both asylum and legal system, and stories of others in her position (Stepto, p. 226).[13] While her situation was certainly different than that of an African American slave, the forms of the slave narrative were available to her as possibilities for ways to shape her narrative.

At the same time that she draws on slave narrative, Elizabeth Packard uses the conventions of the sentimental and domestic novels. According to these conventions, a middle-class female protagonist exemplifies the feminine virtues of piety and domesticity by dying if she loses her virginity (in the sentimental novel), or achieving emotional and financial independence despite hardship (in the American domestic novel). Following to some extent the model of Richardson's *Clarissa* and Susanna Rowson's *Charlotte Temple*, the domestic novel pits the heroine's virtue and intelligence against the nefarious schemings of an evil rake who, in his nineteenth-century American incarnation, either dies or is reformed by the heroine's virtuous character. For Packard, the plotting villain provides an appropriate container for the asylum superintendent, Andrew McFarland, whom her audience would recognize as an untrustworthy male character with questionable motives. She herself is the imprisoned Clarissa figure, who, kept confined against her will, must depend on her own virtue, her faith, and her always hampered efforts to communicate through writing to the outside world.[14] This association with the sentimental and domestic novels allowed Packard to present her readers with a familiar situation—a woman's confinement against her will—and to connect that confinement with sexual violation.

At the same time, like the domestic novel heroine, Packard assumes a more powerful position than Clarissa or Charlotte Temple. By joining autobiography with the domestic and sentimental novel, she wrests control of herself-as-confined-virgin and presents McFarland as the often pitiful object of her superior gaze. The fact that the self of classic autobiography is traditionally a masculine (though feminized) one aids her in this endeavor. As she moves, through autobiography, into the position of subject, she assumes the mask of coherent self surveying the world, including the others around her. McFarland may be Lovelace to her confined Clarissa, but she has no intention of dying like the fictional character. Protected by the priority given to self in autobiography, she does not even have to marry him or lead him to see the error of his ways. Without indicating any repentance on McFarland's part, Packard repeatedly outwits his attempted interception of her letters and, through authorship of the narrative, gets the last word. In addition, she appropriates the masculine form of political treatise to place herself on the same intellectual level as McFarland and engage him in debate, which, of course, he always loses.

In chapter 2, I place Elizabeth Packard's work next to that of another inmate at the Jacksonville Asylum, Sophie Olsen, whose autobiography Packard published as part of her own text. Where Packard in many ways allies herself with power within the institution and works for legislative change, Olsen describes incipient revolution among the inmates. While Olsen too presents herself as middle class, she aligns herself more explicitly than does Packard with the body of inmates who plan violent rebellion. This difference reveals Packard's middle-class position within the asylum and makes more apparent the ways that she, in contrast to Olsen, adopts values of individuality, rationality, and scientific thinking that contribute to maintaining middle-class hegemony. At the same time, since dominant definitions of rationality exclude her, Packard defines ways of seeing based not on the individual's ability to know the external world but on the popular faith in God, Spiritualist science, and the legitimacy of personal experience.

The long tradition of spiritual autobiography in American literature provides Packard with a discourse for plotting her inner journey through the asylum. Drawing on a tradition of female religious dissenters, such as Anne Hutchinson, and the jeremiad warning the world of its spiritual errors, Packard allies her own voice with the will of God, who seeks to chastise the sinful ministers and physicians who incarcerate her.

Spiritual autobiography provides her with a tradition in which the self alternately disappears before God (and religious history) and claims its own god-like control of the narrative. As modern readers we need to be particularly attuned to this genre operating within Packard's text. Her claim that she is fulfilling a divine mission in exposing asylum wrongs may appear as a kind of mad grandiosity that fulfills our expectations of a writer declared insane. Yet such a claim finds a place in a tradition of writers who chronicled their relationship to God in just this way. William Bradford and Jonathan Edwards, like Packard, saw their personal roles as paramount within Christian history even as they declared the all-subsuming power of God's will. As a woman, Packard runs the risk of her religious vision being regarded, as was Hutchinson's, as misconceived, but by referring obliquely to the tradition of spiritual autobiography, she nevertheless gives her narrative some legitimacy.

In chapters 3 and 4, I look at *Behind the Scenes* (1879), which Lydia Smith wrote after she had been in the Kalamazoo State Asylum in Michigan, and *A Secret Institution* (1890), which Clarissa Lathrop wrote after she was released from the Utica State Asylum in New York. While Elizabeth Packard grounds her sense of self in her God-given missionary role, Smith and Lathrop find themselves more engaged with a secularizing culture. As their incarceration forces them to reconsider their familial identities, they suffer a sense of rootlessness and powerlessness that is only partly resolved as they search for new sources of identity. Lydia Smith never abandons her nostalgia for a unified family, even as, after her release, she begins to assume a more public identity as an asylum reformer; in the tradition of Harriet Beecher Stowe, Jane Addams, and others, she grounds her reform activities in metaphors of motherhood and womanly nature. In contrast, Clarissa Lathrop, who was an unmarried schoolteacher before her family had her committed to the asylum, asserts her independence after her release and insists on supporting herself economically.

In chapter 3, I address the problem that both Smith and Lathrop seem to be overly suspicious, often to the point of paranoia, in their judgment of those around them, especially physicians, attendants, and family members. This aspect of their narratives could easily lead a twentieth-century reader to conclude that they were indeed mentally ill, deserved incarceration, and wrote their stories in fits of paranoia. Such a reading itself comes under suspicion, however, when we place the two narratives in the context of the wider middle-class paranoia evident in various late nineteenth-century literary genres in the United States and England. Smith and Lathrop rely not only on the conventions of sentimental fiction but on those of its late nineteenth-century relative, the sensation novel. Lydia Smith in particular plays on such familiar characteristics as the plotting family, the undeserved confinement (often in an asylum, as in Charles Reade's *Hard Cash* and Wilkie Collins' *Woman in White*, for example), the impending or already accomplished murder, and the sexual victimization of an innocent young woman. Smith and Lathrop's gesture of taking the reader "behind the scenes" of the asylum world echoes a wider cultural pre-occupation with secrecy and revelation that shows itself in the popularity of English sensation writers throughout the nineteenth century.

Like the sensation novelists and detective story writers selling books quite successfully in the second half of the nineteenth century, Smith and Lathrop emphasize the suspenseful unraveling of narrative secrets. Yet in their version of this form, the secrets are never really revealed; the reader can never be fully satisfied that all has been discovered and the "really" crazy characters packed off to the asylum. For Smith and Lathrop, no final answer comes to reassure the reader that there really is a distinction between sanity and insanity, that stories can provide coherence for self and world, that middle-class fear and anxiety can be alleviated by identifying madness and controlling the mad.

In chapter 4, I discuss the ways that Smith and Lathrop draw as well on the new journalism, which was itself busy exposing asylum abuses in the nineteenth-century United States, and on strategies of realist fiction, which sought to capture the objective facts of a class-conscious, rapidly industrializing world. Next to the traditionally feminine sentimental tradition, they place a masculinist description of reality. The narrative voice in both writers vacillates between the personal feminine and the omniscient masculine. Lathrop especially appropriates the journalistic tone of objective observer, whose own position seems to disappear before the construction of a reality. This position of removed observer contributes to reproducing the idea that some realities are "truer" than others, an idea in which white middle-class reality inevitably takes precedence. As Henry James remarks in "The Art of Fiction," "It goes without saying that you will not write a good novel unless you possess the sense of reality; but it will be difficult to give you a recipe for calling that sense into being. Humanity is immense, and reality has a myriad forms; the most one can affirm is that some of the flowers of fiction have the odour of it, and others have not" (p. 52). In describing a "reality," Smith and Lathrop enter into the very discourse that has denied their view of the world. Still, by appropriating the voice, tone, and stance of the realist narrator, they cross the gender line into the public realm.

In chapter 5, I discuss the shape that twentieth-century asylum autobiography takes given the advent of mental hygiene and the beginnings of psychoanalysis. By comparing Jane Hillyer's 1927 autobiography *Reluctantly Told* with *A Mind That Found Itself*, the 1907 autobiography of Clifford Beers, one of the founders of the mental hygiene movement, I examine the role of gender and class in both the production of asylum autobiography and concepts of subjectivity and insanity in a period when the writing of mentally ill "patients" was itself becoming an object of analysis for medical professionals. Looked at from this perspective, the advent of the "talking cure" brings with it both a space for the female patient's voice and the co-optation of that voice by psychiatric discourse.

Case study narratives as well as experiments in literary modernism contemporary with Hillyer's text help provide her with ways to represent her asylum experiences. Rather than building a case for asylum reform by reporting the facts of what she sees, as do Smith and Lathrop, Hillyer's narrative voice speaks from within her psychic disorientation. Her text is more concerned with the unreliability of memory as a center of consciousness and the connections of sexuality to identity than with the collection of evidence. Read next to Beers' autobiography, Hillyer's exposes the extent to which Beers imposes order on psychic disintegration. Her writing, in contrast, balances delicately on the edge of dissolution and marks a far boundary for modernism's portrayal of a fragmented self.

In chapter 6, I examine Zelda Fitzgerald's autobiographical novel *Save Me the Waltz*, published in 1932. Beginning with representations of Zelda Fitzgerald as a mentally ill woman in both professionals' accounts of her illness and F. Scott Fitzgerald's *Tender Is the Night*, I argue that she had already been so constructed and reconstructed by husband and doctors that the asylum autobiography they wanted her to write only offered her one more set of expectations. The novel becomes a substitute for this autobiography, a kind of allegory in which she can subversively draw connections between the main character's alienation from her own mind and body and the definitions placed on her by family and medical professionals. The novel, as it follows in the tradition of the previous autobiographers, who were able to name these connections more explicitly, reveals the extent to which twentieth-century psychiatry is rooted in the development of the nineteenth century mental institution.[15]

As a public figure occupying a privileged world of socially elite artists and intellectuals, Fitzgerald must actively create a persona and narrative to counteract the versions of her life circulating in the press

and the literary works of others. Before she can create an autobiographical "I," even if that "I" will only be deconstructed, she must
appropriate it from where it is scattered out in the world.[16] This appropriation, estrangement from, and eventual refusal of the coherent "I,"
as well as the implications of that refusal for bodily experience, is a
shadow story behind the third-person narration of *Save Me the Waltz*.
For her a false step in the manipulation of the "I"—given the history
of women's writing and of the regulation of women's sense of identity
through ideologies of "mental health"—could mean the dismissal of
her work and the further questioning of her sanity. This double reaction to her experimentation does in fact show itself in reviews of
her novel and narratives about the lives of the Fitzgeralds.

■

While I do not intend for any of these texts to be taken as representative of women's experience in mental institutions in general, I do
think they can lead us to ask: How was each of these autobiographies
possible? How were these women, defined as insane and incarcerated
against their will, able to write about their experiences and ideas?
What were the cultural, ideological, and personal contexts that allowed such writings to emerge? To what extent did the experiences
of these women lead them to question, or to cling to, the privilege of
their own middle-class position? Perhaps most important, what can
these writings reveal about the ways in which mental science has constructed itself and attempted to define sanity and insanity through
gender? In addressing these questions, I have tried to look at the issues
that each work suggested to me. Thus, since Elizabeth Packard sees
herself as a champion appointed by God to defend women's rights
against institutional abuses, I examine her subversion of the dominant narratives of Christianity and science. Because Smith and Lathrop mimic the narrative conventions of sensation and realist fiction,
I discuss them together in relation to those genres. Since Jane Hillyer
adopts the language of mental hygiene, I juxtapose her work to Beers'
highly influential autobiography, which introduced many hygienist
concepts to the American public. In discussing Zelda Fitzgerald's
novel, I look at the ways the medical crises at the novel's center address
and respond to intensely medicalized conceptions of mental illness in
the early twentieth century. In every case, I have tried to draw out the
thematic and formal peculiarities each writer may or may not have
planned as she searched for ways to write about life in the asylum.

Each of these texts describes a writing voice coming into being in relation to an asylum world and the larger social and legal relationships that world reveals. As each writer tells a story of diagnosis, incarceration, and transformation, she discovers and engages the ways that definitions of "woman" and the "feminine" intersect with notions of madness. She comes to question the boundary she was taught to see between normality and abnormality, legitimate religious belief and mental disease, lay experience and expert knowledge, the inside of the asylum and the outside.

The asylum practices shown in these texts, in which physicians and attendants infantilize women patients, control their communication with each other and the outside world, and diagnose their behavior as disease, are continuous with wider social and legal practices in the United States from the mid-nineteenth century to the early twentieth. These autobiographies suggest that when physicians open and review any letters women inmates send or receive while in the asylum on the grounds that inappropriate correspondence could worsen their illness, such "treatment" coincides with laws that deny women rights to their own property and children and with medical theories that claim middle-class women thrive best when their reading material is restricted to religious tracts and essays on domestic economy.

Similarly, these narratives reveal that the asylum autobiographer's own self-writing is informed by her life before incarceration. Each of these narratives presents the writer's history as a middle-class woman, a history that becomes both more and less obvious in relation to the asylum's hierarchies. In some cases, she suggests that the ward she is assigned to or even her diagnosis can carry more weight with both asylum officials and other inmates than her preasylum class position. Her writing itself, however, tends to invoke a rational discourse based on an education that has taught her to regard access to such an education as itself a sign of superiority. This class distinction seems especially crucial to the nineteenth-century writers here, who were incarcerated in state institutions meant primarily for poor inmates. These narrators often inadvertently reveal the intersections of asylum hierarchies with the dominant cultural notion that those of lower-class or immigrant status were not as mentally fit as those of the middle or upper classes.

Regardless of how each autobiographer writes out her own social position, the asylum worlds we see in these texts are not isolated, romanticized spaces. They are institutions whose practices feed and are fed by ideologies and practices in the "outside world." Even as these autobiographers write about confinement, they ultimately show that the asylum walls are permeable. The players in the asylum world act out the social, medical and legal belief systems of the larger society. Fortunately, what gets through one way can also get through in the opposite direction. These autobiographers write through the asylum walls and show that those called mad can speak their own names.

# Part 1

## Different Visions
### Asylum Autobiographer
### as Middle-Class Medium
### and Revolutionary

# 1

## Elizabeth Packard
## and Versions of Sanity

■   In 1860, Theophilus Packard forced his wife Elizabeth from their home and committed her to the state insane asylum at Jacksonville, Illinois. According to her own account, she had long been battling with Theophilus, a Presbyterian minister, over the validity of what she considered the outdated and repressive concept of innate depravity. Elizabeth held her own Bible discussion groups, where she encouraged church members, mostly women, to question the traditional Calvinist doctrine and develop personal interpretations of biblical passages. Her husband and certain church elders considered her preaching subversive and indicative of an unbalanced mind. With the signature of a doctor and the corroboration of Andrew McFarland, the asylum superintendent, Elizabeth Packard was separated from her four sons and her daughter and made a prisoner of the institution. She would not be released until 1863, after which she would become an active and successful lobbyer for the rights of married women and the mentally ill. To raise money to support herself and her campaign, she published several pamphlets and books, the first of which was her autobiography, originally published in 1867, then reissued a year later as *The Prisoner's Hidden Life; or, Insane Asylums Unveiled.*[1]

She based her autobiography largely on writings she kept hidden in the backing of her mirror in the asylum, out of the sight of asylum authorities, who would examine and confiscate any writing materials they found in inmates' quarters. As Packard introduces her book: "the working of this Institution is so carefully covered up, and so artfully concealed from the public eye, that the external world knows nothing of the 'hidden life of the prisoner,' within. Therefore the journal of an eye witness taken on the spot, is now presented to the public, as the mirror in which to behold its actual operations" (p. 125). Packard does not fail to note the significance of the place in which she chooses to hide her asylum writings; the mirror that she brings with her from home and preserves throughout her imprisonment comes to represent her maintenance of a sense of sanity and selfhood. She can look into it and see the person she has always known, maintaining her need to look as well as be looked at, resisting the attempts of asylum authorities to deny her position as subject and identify her as an insane woman and an object of study.

As her asylum stay lengthens and she begins to record her experiences in journal entries and letters, she comes to identify her writing with the mirror; her journal reflects the "actual operations" of the asylum. By presenting her journal as a record of fact, she tries to separate her work from the "insane" woman whose credibility as a witness would be questioned by her mid-nineteenth-century audience. She hopes that if, by holding up her mirror, she can convince her readers that her experience is objective fact, they will see not only the asylum world but also their own image superimposed on her portrayal of the asylum. She seeks to establish her own sanity as a woman labeled insane and to show that an asylum community of insane women can reflect a world that smugly considers itself sane.

In trying to discover how a woman incarcerated as insane can speak her own experience, Elizabeth Packard engages in the nineteenth-century debate in the United States over what constitutes valid evidence and authority and to what extent women could be considered rational beings. Packard's text questions the growing scientific monopoly on knowledge and cultivates the idea that a woman's personal observation and testimony are sufficient evidence in themselves, proof of a reality whose existence must be respected and recognized. She thus challenges the dominant nineteenth-century American belief that middle-class women are only reasonable, if at all, within the domestic sphere and rarely able to observe and describe the world with the same accuracy with which men can.[2]

An asylum autobiography is the appropriate place for Packard to formulate a redefinition of the female subject, given that in the discourse on insanity and on the nature of the asylum, power distinctions within the larger culture emerge in extreme form. Packard's autobiography shows that in nineteenth-century discussions of insanity, much more is at stake than the good of the suffering patient. Both alienists and patients struggle to define "sanity" and "rationality" and the ways these terms help construct gender and class distinctions. In so doing, the actors in what Packard refers to as "The Great Drama" argue over who has authority to enforce logical systems, not only in the asylum itself but in the legal codes and social mores that intersect the asylum world.

In crafting her autobiography, Packard taps into several generic traditions that establish the authority of a speaking subject. In particular, her text invokes the strategies of spiritual autobiography, captivity narrative, and slave narrative (which itself draws on spiritual autobiography), strategies in which the writing voice presents itself as coherent and sane even as it occasionally disappears into selflessness before the story it tells and the spiritual power it invokes. By comparing her own situation to that of the slave, however erroneous and self-serving that comparison may be, Packard connects her narrative to an autobiographical tradition in which personal experience provides grounds for argument against injustice. By simultaneously drawing on the American version of the sentimental novel tradition, in which a virtuous woman is victimized by an unfeeling rake, Packard's text reaffirms the middle-class womanhood of the writer, whose public presence threatens to identify her as someone who has stepped outside her proper sphere. By drawing on forms familiar to her middle-class readers, Packard recreates and uses the ideology of middle-class femaleness, stressing her piety and maternal feeling, even as she calls that ideology into question. This asylum autobiography thus calls upon and reformulates a variety of forms and strategies that weave themselves throughout the text in an effort to create a speaking female subject— Elizabeth Packard—who is rational yet "feminine," authoritative yet victimized, autonomous yet selfless, politically-minded yet maternal.

■

Packard's work follows the pattern described by autobiography theorist Estelle Jelinek, who claims that in writing the stories of their lives, women tend to create forms that are often nonlinear and fragmentary (Jelinek, p. 12). At first, Packard's form seems scattered and disorganized as she alternates between telling her story in the past tense, offering present-tense journal entries, telling the stories of other inmates, expounding her views on morality and religion, and introducing letters she wrote while in the asylum.

The fragmented nature of the work is complicated by the fact that Packard presents other women's histories along with her own, offering chapter after chapter titled with other women's names as well as several first-person narratives that she appends to her own writings. The longest and most important of these is by Sophie Olsen, who entered the asylum as a voluntary patient in 1862 under pressure from her husband. Packard clearly intended that the works should be read as a whole. In fact, in a later edition of her autobiography, *Modern Persecution*, Packard incorporated Olsen's narrative, which appears in an appendix in the first edition, as a chapter of her book, eliminating the appendix of the first edition. The first-person narratives of other inmates are also important to Packard's autobiography because they provide complementary, alternative visions that rarely duplicate Packard's story but help create a multi-voiced narrative about life within the asylum.

The variety of strategies put into play within the text indicates that what is at issue for Packard is who wields power over writing itself, who has the right to tell whose story. She writes that upon arriving at the asylum she is allowed substantial privileges, probably because she begins as a paying patient with an educated background. She soon becomes aware of the abuses exercised against the other patients and resolves to take up their cause, writing a letter of complaint to the superintendent that "depicted their wrongs, oppression and received cruelties, in the most expressive terms I could command" (p. 87). This is the first time she puts pen to paper in the asylum for the purpose of expressing wrongs, and she soon discovers that her words really have no power at all to elicit changes by the establishment.

Throughout, Packard expresses her fear that McFarland's silencing does more than leave a blank void where her words might have been; it also allows the blank to be filled by others' assumptions or his own words. Her indignation at being deprived of her "post-office rights" is always tied to her indictment of the doctor's "dictation." After a long exposition on McFarland's injustice in not allowing her to write freely, Packard says she knows "that all my favors, rights and privileges, were suspended entirely upon the will of the Superintendent, and therefore entirely subject to his dictation" (pp. 86–87). She associates the censorship of her writing with dictation in both meanings of the word:

the "dictator," the despot, is one who tells her what to write. Packard feels that McFarland's dictatorship gives him the power to write history. She is continually frustrated by the fact that those who look at the asylum from the outside never see it informed by her insider's perception. She makes the plea, "O, Illinois! State of my adoption, when, when will you look intelligently, with your own eyes, into the practical operation of your Insane Asylum system, as it is now being practiced in your State Institution at Jacksonville? Never, never, will you see it as it is, until you can look at it through some other medium than Dr. McFarland or his Reports" (p. 159). McFarland's reports were published regularly in the *American Journal of Insanity*, while the letters of Packard and other inmates rarely reached the outside world. Given that McFarland was an established alienist who was both a respected landowner in the town of Jacksonville, where he was superintendent of the state asylum from 1854 to 1870, and president for a time of the Association of Medical Superintendents of American Institutions of the Insane, his accounts of asylum life held authority in both the public and professional eye. As a result, a single version of asylum reality was transmitted to the world; McFarland's asylum was considered to be the only one that existed.[3]

According to her narrative, from the first time she tries to write within the asylum about her experiences, she suffers the consequences of speaking out against such asylum abuses as the prohibition of writing materials, interception of letters to the outside, use of physical restraint and beatings, punishments by dunking in cold water, threats of violence or removal to the worst wards, transfer of patients from ward to ward without warning, denial of patients' simplest requests: "This document cast the die for my future destiny. The transition time had fully come, when comfort, attention, respect, privilege, all, all, were in the dead past, and discomfort, inattention, disrespect, contempt, wrong and deprivation are to mark the future of my prison life" (p. 87).

Here, as throughout the work, she emphasizes her own subjectivity by claiming the authority of the historian. By so doing, she violates the nature of women's sphere not so much in asserting her subjectivity, which has a place within that sphere, but by asserting it within the context of philosophical and psychological discourse. In the nineteenth-century world of separate male and female spheres, writing that created a personal world was gendered as feminine, while writing that presented itself as impersonal discussion of ideas related to the political realm was gendered as masculine. Packard's writing challenges this separation by blending personal narrative with psychological and political theory.

Yet Packard's text never abandons the feminized forms that would be expected of her. Woven into the fragments of political treatises, stories, letters, and journal entries in Packard's autobiography is a progression of events that in many ways repeats that of most nineteenth-century domestic fiction, which dominated literary sales from the 1820s until after 1870. However, Packard ultimately deviates from the standard formula in a way that reminds her reader that she is writing autobiography, not fiction, and that popular literary forms cannot contain her experience. Where domestic novels usually end with marriage and the reform of cruel men, Packard's story ends with a call for reforms in laws related to marriage and institutionalization of women.

Nina Baym has pointed out that most women's novels of this period follow a standard plot line: a poor lonely orphan or disinherited heiress is thrown out into the world alone, where she learns to make her own way and develop an independent identity before she inevitably settles down and marries a good man (p. 35). The primary message of these novels for the largely female reading public was that a woman should escape from those who abused their power over her (usually fathers, uncles, or guardians), establish her own sense of self, take responsibility for her life, and use her then well-founded moral strength to educate those around her. If she fell in love and was swept away by a man before she established her independence, she was destined to learn her lesson the hard way and be forced to begin anew (Baym, pp. 40–41). In E. D. E. N. Southworth's *The Curse of Clifton*, for example, when young Zuleime clandestinely marries Frank Fairfax while still under her father's thumb, she is destined to suffer as a consequence through widowhood, extreme poverty, and the humiliation of becoming an actress to support herself. Only after the heroine has established a strong sense of self, can she then marry a good man and settle down.

Just as these novels begin when a young woman is thrown from an oppressive domestic situation out into the cruel world, Packard's history of her asylum life opens when she is being removed from a home characterized by conflict with her husband to an asylum where she, "his constant companion of twenty-one years, was entrusted to the hands of my prison keeper to be led by him to find my bed and lodging, he knew not where, and to be subject to insults, he knew not what"

(p. 59). Her husband, with his "brute force claims upon my personal liberty" (p. 44), denies her ability and desire to act independently, just as the cruel father of the domestic novel allows his daughter little control over her life. This battle for power continues in the asylum. Like the fictional heroine, Packard draws on her moral strength to fight for independence. She makes mistakes along the way, such as trusting the superintendent to protect her, but, like the heroine, she begins again, relying more and more on her own resources. Just as most domestic fiction centers on the heroine's involvement with a tyrannical male character, Packard's autobiography focuses on her struggle with the asylum superintendent, Andrew McFarland, and the power he represents, a struggle that revolves primarily around her attempts—as well as those of other women—to speak and write their thoughts and experiences. Her story recalls the epistolary sentimental novel, precursor to the American domestic novel. In Richardson's *Clarissa*, Lovelace controls the letters of the kidnapped heroine. He writes them, signs them, and sends them, just as he controls and violates her body. Like Harriet Jacobs, who, in *Incidents in the Life of a Slave Girl*, engineers her escape from slavery by writing and sending letters, Packard revises Richardson's form to give women control over writing.

Ultimately, the book itself becomes the most powerful character in its own story, the chronicle of her attempts, finally successful, to gain access to writing. The narrative describes her transfer to one of the worst wards, where she is denied writing implements, and forbidden to obtain paper on her own. She claims that because McFarland knows she holds influence among both the staff and the inmates, he tells her at various times that she must not speak with anyone, nor may the other inmates speak to her. At one point she is instructed "to hold no more prayer-meetings, lend no more books, and those she has lent must be immediately returned" (pp. 74–75). Much of her narrative describes her attempts to avoid these mandates by obtaining paper clandestinely, hiding copies of everything she writes, communicating with the other inmates, or turning to the staff for help denied her by the superintendent.

Packard finally appeals to the asylum's board of trustees and obtains her release. The board forces her back into her husband's custody, however, denying her request to stay on at the asylum voluntarily, with freedom to come and go, so that she can finish her book and begin to support herself financially. She ends her story by describing her successful efforts to gain her freedom from her husband and have her sanity legally revindicated, concluding that she has established herself as an independent, financially solvent writer who is now willing and able to take responsibility for her family "in order that society and their friends be relieved of the burden of their support and education" (p. 315).

Thus while in the fictional conventions of domestic fiction the heroine's marriage ends her tale, Packard's story ends with her separation not only from the asylum but from her husband and children. She writes, "At about fifty years of age I have been compelled, in consequence of the unreasonable position the law assigns me as a married woman, to begin life's struggle alone, and unaided, having no other capital to depend upon, but my good health and education. With the aid of this capital alone, I have paid the entire expense of printing and selling eighteen thousand books, by my own efforts entirely" (p. 344). The fact that her book ends differently from most domestic fiction suggests that Packard has worked to develop a concept of female subjectivity quite different from that of the dominant culture and of contemporary women novelists. For, as Baym points out, while nineteenth-century popular women novelists espoused a kind of domestic feminism based in a woman's strong sense of her self and her ability to influence the world around her through her moral purity and sacrifice, in the end these novelists usually portrayed the married heroine as reconciled to the social order, performing a difficult balancing act in marriage between submission and "suicidal defiance" (Baym, p. 37). In the real-life experience after the storybook ending, perhaps, these middle-class women would tend to fulfill Tocqueville's characterization of American women as independent young ladies and submissive wives. The novels may well end at marriage precisely because it would be difficult for the writers to carry the self-dependence established by their characters into a portrait of married life.

Packard counterposes her own ending to the expected marriage and anticipated life of happiness. In order to maintain her belief in her status as creative subject she must remain apart from the familial hierarchy or at least redefine her relation to it. Unlike the fictional heroine, who supposedly holds her own once she comes to know herself, Packard feels she can never be certain that the independence and respect she has worked so hard to establish and maintain is a permanent state. Moreover, she comes to believe that if she wishes to be regarded as a creative, rational person, she must reject the identity of wife.

Packard turns away from marriage largely because, given her asylum experiences, she sees it as linked to the powerlessness she felt when incarcerated. She writes that McFarland kept women in the asylum "until they begged to be sent home. This led me to suspect that there was a secret understanding between the husband and the Doctor; that the subjection of the wife was the cure the husband was seeking to effect under the specious plea of insanity; and when they began to express a wish to go home, the Doctor would encourage these tyrannical husbands that they were 'improving' " (p. 81). She claims McFarland deliberately exercises power over her in order to keep her in her place: forbids her to meet with the other inmates, confiscates her personal belongings, and, most importantly, restricts what she calls her "post-office rights," which guarantee she can send and receive letters.

As Packard challenges McFarland's claims to authority she draws parallels between what she sees as her minister husband's unreasonable authoritarianism and that of the doctor. The domestic novel genre enables her to portray both men as part of a family drama in which, in addition to proving themselves to be weak debating partners, they inappropriately seek to exert power over her. That Packard sees an intimate connection between the authority of husband and doctor corresponds with the historian Nancy Tomes's assertion that asylum superintendents tended to adapt themselves to the definitions of insanity understood by a patient's family. Packard's case reinforces Tomes's contention that "the only party likely to challenge the doctor-family consensus, that is, the patient, had little power to dispute the decision" (pp. 121, 127–28). The link Packard sees between doctor and husband is their shared belief in men's mental superiority and naturally endowed authority over women. When she asks McFarland for "liberty to support myself, as other wives do who cannot live with their husband," he replies, " 'The only right course for you is to return to your husband, and do as a true woman should do; be to him a true and loving wife, as you promised to be by your marriage vow, unto death, and until you do consent to do so, there is no prospect of your getting out of this place! For until you will give up this insane unreasonable notion of your duty forbidding it, I consider this institution the proper place for you to spend your days in' " (p. 134). In chapter after chapter, she reports similar confrontations with the doctor, emphasizing the hopelessness of her appeals to him and stressing that she is doubly bound by the authority of doctor over patient and man over woman.[4]

It is this sense of a double oppression that leads Packard to link reform of insanity laws to advocacy of laws reforming and protecting the rights of married women. She points out in her later work *Modern Persecution* that the law under which she was incarcerated, passed February 15, 1851, held that married women and children judged insane by the medical superintendent of the state hospital could be committed at the request of the husband without further evidence. Writes Packard, "Thus I learned my first lesson in that chapter of woman law, which denies to married women a legal right to her own identity or individuality" (*Modern Persecution*, p. 55).

Packard's insistence that a link existed between the unreasonable authority of physician and husband is telling in the light of Elaine Showalter's finding that asylum life simply exaggerated the home lives of many nineteenth-century women.[5] Indeed, the interrelationships between family and other societal institutions often become startingly clear in the language of superintendents themselves. In the same 1869 article in the *American Journal of Insanity* that describes McFarland's persecution before the Illinois State Legislature by "a handsome and talkative crazy woman" ("Illinois Legislature," p. 204)—namely, Elizabeth Packard—the writer explicitly compares the asylum director to a father:

> No father of a household allows of interference with his private and domestic arrangements or discipline; and he is not responsible to the community except for some criminal abuse or neglect. His domestic affairs are his own, and are not properly liable to any general inquisition; and he may defy any impertinent intrusion simply to gratify curiosity or for obtruding advice as to management and discipline. So of the great households committed by the State to the charge of such as are intrusted with them, and who stand to them *in loco parentis.* ("Illinois Legislation," pp. 214–15)

The asylum becomes the place where the contradictions inherent in the separation of spheres and the rhetoric of democracy are made explicit. If the "private," "domestic" sphere belongs to women, it is also the place where male law is sovereign and the democratic rule of the public realm has no place. The asylum represents that point at which women, while they may hold a certain amount of moral power within the home, are reminded of where the power really lies. Both the name and the use of the notorious and controversial restraining device, the

Utica crib, a box in which the patient was locked beneath wooden slats, reinforce the infantilization of women in these surrogate, often motherless homes in which father-superintendents seek to exert absolute control.[6]

If the "household" metaphor is not a strong enough reminder, the *American Journal of Insanity* narrative reinforces it with another metaphor—that of a military ship. After one writer warns, "not more assuredly can the small worm that riots in the massive timbers of the ship becalmed in the tropics, send her with all her rich freight to the bottom, than can a troop of ill selected and ill disciplined hospital attendants wreck the reputation of any institution in which they find lodgment," he admonishes, "certainly, the stern necessities of military service do not require any more prompt compliances than our own" ("Annual Meeting," pp. 54–55). The conflation of family metaphors with military ones exposes the intersection of these two institutions in which white male dominance is supposed to reign supreme. Such a conflation makes it virtually impossible for Packard's narrative to end with a return to marriage and family.

■

Unlike the domestic novel, Packard's narrative is meant to persuade her audience to take political action. Her efforts to persuade are both subject matter and form in her autobiography. The reader, like McFarland, must be convinced that she is sane. Packard must show that she *can* reason as much as she must persuade her readers with the content of her arguments. For a woman, let alone an "insane" one, this effort to persuade is itself suspect. Packard holds that "even [a married woman's] right of self-defense on the plane of argument is denied her, for when she *reasons*, then she is insane! and if her reasons are wielded potently, and with irresistible logic, she is then exposed to hopeless imprisonment, as the response of her opponent" (p. 126). First as a wife and then as an asylum inmate, she is deprived of her ability to be accepted as a reasoning being. The fact that her husband committed her already cast such doubt on her sanity that everything she says in her own defense is seen merely as a symptom to be analyzed and examined.

Packard's focus on persuading her reader both to believe her story and to take action for legal reform invokes the slave narrative alongside her domestic romance tale.[7] Packard's narrative clearly borrows from slave narratives the use of legitimating documentation to support her tale of personal experience. *Insane Asylums Unveiled* is structured much like what critic Robert Burns Stepto refers to as a "first phase" slave narrative. In this early version of slave narrative the writer creates an *"eclectic narrative* form," in which authenticating documents are appended to the central tale, so that "the documents collectively create something close to a dialogue—of forms as well as voices" (p. 225). By appropriating a form that would help give her credence in the eyes of white antislavery readers, Packard obscures significant differences between her own position and that of most slave narrative writers (her white middle-class upbringing, her preasylum access to literacy, her connections, however tenuous, to white middle-class legislators outside the asylum). Still, Packard connects her story to an autobiographical tradition in which personal experience and the documents used to verify it provide grounds for argument against injustice directed at an oppressed group.

Like many slave narratives, Packard's text uses Christian rhetoric to establish her right to speak and be considered a legitimate subject. Her views on Christianity are consistent with the movement in the nineteenth-century United States away from Calvinism toward forms of Christianity that rejected the concept of natural depravity. She knew that in her struggle against Theophilus Packard's religion, she would have supporters among her readers, as she did among the jurors who eventually declared her sane after her release. Many would agree with the words she reports speaking to her Bible class, " 'the religion of authority has had its day—a reasonable religion, such as will bear the infallible tests of truth, based on arguments drawn from God's word and works is the religion for us" (p. 19). Many of her contemporaries had long since adopted a Christianity that allowed each of them to analyze the Bible and argue theology without fear of being thought heretics.

She knew that she would find less sympathy, however, when she went beyond discussing "a reasonable religion" to advocating a reasonable legal system that would recognize a married woman's separate identity and reasonable belief system that would grant women's ability to decide their own fate. She realizes that she may have been imprisoned and declared insane by an outdated Calvinism but what keeps her in the asylum is less her husband's religion than the strength of his legally-sanctioned authority over her. It is for this reason that she opens her book with a plea not against Calvinism but against "the legalized usurpation of human rights" as manifested in the absence of laws protecting married women from their husbands' authority (iii).

Still, once institutionalized, Packard feels she must assert and support her own right to religious choice. She describes a confrontation with McFarland in which she argues that her anti-Calvinist religious opinions cannot be used as evidence of her insanity. Comparing herself to a sighted woman declared blind by the superintendent of a "Blind Institution," Packard first asks, "Must not the individual herself be tested, in order to settle this controverted question?" (pp. 292–93). She then asks the doctor,

> "But supposing he should admit that the lady can see, but she don't see *right;* for instance, she contends that the moon looks to her as large as a cart wheel, while he says it should look only as large as a saucer. Now the common people, or the public tribunal, more than ever, see their Superintendent's folly; for the very fact that it looks to her as large as a cart wheel, demonstrates that she is not blind, and that her organ of vision, too, is not peculiar, for there is just this difference in the size of the same object, as seen through different organizations. Now, Dr. McFarland, tell me, is reason, which is the eye of the Soul, extinct, while the individual gives every evidence that it is in full and healthy exercise?"
>
> He replied, "There is a certain kind of disease of the eye which can not be detected by common people; it takes great learning and the highest kind of professional skill to detect it; and besides, this kind of optical disease is hopeless—there is no cure for this kind of blindness." (p. 293)

Here, as she blends personal narrative with rhetorical skill, Packard denies that there can be an external measure of whether someone is rational or not. The symbols that Packard uses tie this discussion of rationality to her insistence that women are equal to men in their credibility. As both the "blind" woman and the doctor look at the moon, traditional symbol of female power, the woman compares it to a cart wheel, symbol of locomotion, travel, freedom. The doctor, on the other hand, compares it to a saucer, an object from a woman's domestic life. Packard implies here that the doctor and his patient see differently depending upon the subject position of each. The doctor insists that what she sees should remind her of the domestic sphere; the "blind" woman wishes for power to decide the course of her own life. By using this example of the moon "as seen through different organizations," Packard implies that the interpretation of the image depends upon the position and desires of the observer rather than upon an absolute external reality identifiable only by an expert.

By the time Packard was writing, scientists in the United States both claimed that they could describe a solid external reality and expressed a profound distrust of the "reality" perceived by the senses, a distrust that went back on the one hand to Locke's ambivalence about the verifiability of external reality and on the other to Calvinist doubts about signs of sainthood. In addition, white middle-class Americans in the 1860s were in search of categories, hierarchies, ways of ordering their unstable and all-too-democratic post–Civil War world. As medicine and psychology became more professionalized, experts encouraged the average citizen to depend more and more on their ability to interpret the "facts" of human behavior and the human mind. Experience itself—the individual interpretation of perception, essential to the constitution of the Lockean self—was increasingly seen as untrustworthy, unless it was accompanied by expert training and knowledge. A decade or so after Packard was writing, prominent neurologist George Beard expressed this growing suspicion of uninformed observation. According to Beard,

> On the principles of evidence as drawn from the testimony of human beings, it has thus far been undenied that the senses are worthy of trust, that the first quality of an observer and reporter is not expertness but honesty, and that what is good evidence for one class of claims is equally good for any class. These three assumptions—the common basis of law and logic—the neurology of the future must push utterly aside; and in their place it will be established that in science or organized knowledge only the testimony of experts can be of value, and that the quality and amount of evidence needful to establish any claim must vary with, and be relative to the nature of that claim (p. 70).

The growing specialization of the age is evident here in Beard's insistence that claims be divided into classes, each of which requires a separate body of evidence identifiable only by a certain category of experts. The "testimony of human beings" based on information gathered through the senses, the kind of testimony Packard wishes to give, must be replaced in both the classroom and the courtroom by the "testimony of experts" (here differentiated from "human beings"), who, like McFarland, have a special kind of vision.

Beard's words reverberate with the claim to authority of medical superintendents who battled throughout the century with state legislatures intent on monitoring their institutions. After Packard brought superintendent Andrew McFarland to the attention of the State under suspicion of mismanagement and abuse of power in late 1867, the editors of the *American Journal of Insanity* defended his autonomy and attacked the state investigating committee by claiming, "It is this exposure to open general observation and criticism which, with all its obvious security to the public, is the most apt to lead to suspicions and distrust, and to annoying and idle examinations. Many details of management and discipline cannot be accurately judged of by an undiscriminating populace, and undue publicity would also destroy their purpose and effect" ("Illinois Legislation," p. 214).

Packard continually shows that within the asylum the doctor's authority, his ability to decide whether the vision is diseased or not, takes precedence over her own. Yet while she challenges this authority, she does not reject science altogether. Since she advocates a science redefined to admit the reasoning power of every individual, she supports the primacy of evidence, of fact, but what she calls fact or evidence is different from McFarland's concept of the same terms. "Fact" in her view is inseparable from subjective experience. For her, personal narrative is itself a kind of science, in which the voice of the narrator is a necessary correlate of the "data" collected and reported.

In the preface of her book, she defines her personal experiences as "data": "In disclosing to the blinded public the real character of their Insane Asylums, the author has relied mainly upon her own personal observation, and three years experience, as data from which to draw her own conclusions; and if from this data her conclusions are not legitimate, she asks the reader to be the judge" (v). She does not draw the classic Baconian distinction here between herself as observer and that which she studies.[8] Even as she provides her reader with legitimating documents, she ignores the question of how objective she is or is not. She claims the right to report her own experience in her own words and have it be accepted as legitimate evidence.

When Packard reports her own experience as acceptable data, she both gives her narrative the legitimacy of the researcher's perspective and maintains that a human mind cannot be observed as an object of science. There will always be subjectivity and context to take into account, both that of alienist and that of patient. This belief naturally undermines what she sees as a major premise of McFarland's authority—that he may observe and pass judgment on the asylum inmates without actually interacting with them.

In one of her arguments with McFarland, Packard asks him,

> "Now if you, Doctor, or any other individual, will bring forward one act of my own, showing lack of reason in it, I will own you have a right to call me insane."
>
> After waiting a long time, he said, "was it not an insane act for you to fall down stairs, and then to be carried back to you ward?"
>
> "That was not *my act* in being carried back to my ward. It was your own act, and my falling down stairs, was an accident, caused too, by *your* ungentlemanly interference; and the object I had in view by asserting my rights, was a rational one, for I had good reasons for doing so."
>
> "O, no, no, the *reasons* are nothing."
>
> "Yes they are; for unless you know the reasons which influence the actions of others, many acts would appear insane, that would not, if we knew the reasons which prompted the act." (pp. 251–52)

Packard is interested in going beyond the observed behavior that serves as evidence in the doctor's eyes. As Foucault has shown, "under observation madness is constantly required, at the surface of itself, to deny its dissimulation. It is judged only by its acts, it is not accused of intentions, nor are its secrets to be fathomed. Madness is responsible only for that part of itself which is visible. All the rest is reduced to silence. Madness no longer exists except as *seen*" (p. 250). Inherent in the nineteenth-century definition of madness is the idea that it exists beyond dialogue, beyond interaction. Observed and interpreted by the expert's inner eye, madness is an object of study, doubly so for women, who are already regarded as objects of study by the medical profession.[9]

Foucault's statement finds resonance in McFarland's own idea that mental illness assumes a deceptive surface that must be read by the psychiatrist. In an article warning physicians untrained in mental illness about how easily they may be deceived by a patient's physical ailments, McFarland writes, "The history of cases of insanity presented for treatment often reminds us how frequently the disease has commenced with some delusion upon the subject of health; and the time spent in the treatment of a disease wholly imaginary, and the number of practitioners who will be successively deceived by the same case, is a matter of continual surprise. The forms which such imaginary diseases assume are truly Protean, and practitioners are much to blame for their readiness to give a name for the thousand shifting and transient sensations to which all persons of ill-regulated sensibilities are more or less subject" ("Minor Maladies," pp. 14–15). The patient's language, like his or her behavior, is also liable to be deceptive, so that "the terms applied by different individuals to the same degree of personal suffering vary to the widest extremes; and the physician should be carefully on his guard against those whose minds conceive such a state only in the superlative degree" ("Minor Maladies," p. 13). The patient's description of his or her own condition should fall under the physician's discerning gaze as do body and behavior. If the diagnosis is indeed mental illness, the patient's mind comes even more readily under the microscope.

Packard is concerned throughout the narrative with showing that if someone's self-expression is treated only as symptom or ignored altogether it becomes impossible for that person to behave in ways considered normal. She claims that McFarland not only stops communication between inmates, but rebuffs her attempts—and those of many others also—to speak to him personally. In one case, after he has transferred her to the Eighth Ward, the "maniacs' ward," she appeals to him to separate her from the more violent inmates. She remarks: "I have sometimes thought the Doctor put me there for the very purpose of getting me killed by these maniacs. I have been nearly killed several times, and I have appealed most earnestly to Dr. McFarland to save my life, but he would simply turn speechless away from me!" (p. 91). She tells us that this is not the only time he "turns speechless away" from her or from another inmate appealing to him for help or criticizing his actions and policies. For Packard, his refusal to respond is a refusal to acknowledge that she has even spoken, has the ability to speak. It is a way of denying her stance as subject and using his authoritative position to define her language itself as an object to be observed or ignored, not as the medium of communication of a rational mind. Packard becomes frustrated again and again as she musters her thoughts, puts them into reasonable words, then speaks into a void.

In reaction against the contemporary idea that madness is to be observed and interpreted by an expert, Packard struggles to develop a kind of evidence based on sympathy and the assumption that each patient has a story to tell. Here Packard uses a supposedly innate quality of nineteenth-century middle-class femininity—sympathy— to cross over into the masculine discourses of medicine and psychology, in which "data," "evidence," and "conclusions" are integral to legitimate science. Packard's stories become a litany of her fellow inmates' experiences as she presents the "data" necessary for an indictment of the asylum. All these stories provide evidence the superintendent has neglected to mention in his reports, which chronicle supposed cure rates and detail physical improvements to the asylum buildings.

Thus after speaking with a man who says he is Jesus Christ, Packard finds that by his own logic the claim makes sense. In her chapter on Mrs. Bridgman—one of many sections describing other patients— she tells how asylum attendants fail to understand her friend's disease and consequently can only make it worse. According to Packard, Mrs. Bridgman's

> appearance of restless uneasiness, would seek vent from the ends of her fingers by nervous twitches upon something tangible, which effort seemed to be an almost instinctive act of self-defense from the overflowings of her pent up mental agonies. I could not blame her any more than I could blame a drowning man for catching at a straw as a reliance of self-defense. Although the drowning man's act is in itself an unreasonable act of self dependence, yet we do not call it an insane act under his surrounding. (pp. 242–43)

Packard attaches as much importance to the internal reasons for a patient's behavior as she does to the appearance of that behavior itself. Like the drowning man, the so-called insane person may have logical reasons for his or her seemingly nonsensical behavior. Even as Packard occasionally distinguishes herself from the "maniacs" in the asylum, she calls into question the distinction between sanity and insanity that is integral to nineteenth-century American discourse on the human mind.

■

As Packard herself points out, for her to engage in debate on the subject of madness is to risk being seen as inappropriately outside a

middle-class woman's proper sphere. The challenge with which Elizabeth Packard struggles in her narrative is to present herself finally
as rational and independent while still maintaining enough "femininity" to qualify as sane. She must overcome the fact that, within
the dominant culture, to identify as sane she must be rational, but
to identify too vehemently as rational can also place her outside her
proper sphere. Female rationality, by definition, was applicable only to
domestic concerns. The institution of middle-class motherhood provides her with a discourse with which she can expand what counts as
"domestic." Motherhood is one area of women's sphere where middle-
class women were expected to exercise reason and strength of mind,
despite the conflicting ideology that described them as incapable of
these qualities.[10] The autobiography is in a sense the chronicle of her
changing relationship to the ideology of motherhood as she comes to
see it as connected to her incarceration.

The issue of personal liberty comes to inform her definition of true
maternal duty, "How can a mother defend her children, unless she
can defend herself? I must defend myself not only for their sake, but
also for the sake of society where I belong" (p. 141). Using strategically the discourse of pious maternity, she claims it is God's will that
she not give into her husband's demands only so that she may return to her children. By claiming that she is making a mother's best
possible decision, she gives legitimacy to her choice to become a reformer over returning to her husband and children: "If I could only
feel as some undeveloped women do, that it is right to give up the responsibility of their own actions to their husbands, I could then say 'I
will do and think as he pleases, since I am a nonentity after marriage!'
If God regarded me as the law does, in this respect, I could willingly
yield my conscience to get my children. But he does not. He holds
me as an entity, subject to his own laws equally with my husband"
(*Insane Asylums*, pp. 192–93). Christian attention to conscience here
becomes the only avenue to proper maternal action, which in this
case means the abdication of her children's care.[11] Self-dependence becomes a woman's first priority and the necessary prerequisite to true
motherhood. In a key incident in which McFarland and two other men
allow Packard to fall unaided, she comes to see that she can depend
on no one but herself: "The fall had so stunned me, that for a few mo-
ments I hardly knew whether I could rise or not, but when I saw the
three men who ought to be my protectors, and helpers, under such cir-

cumstances forsake me, I began to try my powers of self-dependence, and found I could not only rise myself, but could also stand alone too, without a man to lean upon!" (p. 212).

At one point Packard berates herself for trusting McFarland to help publish her manuscript of *The Great Drama*, the first version of her autobiography, which she wrote while in the asylum. She learns through this experience and the reactions of the other women inmates that she has been naive to count on connections of class and education that tend to dissolve within the institution. She relates that after the superintendent took her book away, "from every part of this spacious house I could hear that the wail of pity for me was being expressed in language as various as the sources whence it came—I received many of the most tender messages of sympathy suited to the emergency. But in one particular all agreed that I would never see my book again" (p. 323).[12] According to Packard, every woman in the asylum expresses pity in her own way because she has in her own way experienced this sense of trust betrayed. The very fact that these women are in the asylum means that they have lost their children, if they had any, as well as their ability to express themselves and be heard. In a way their "wail of pity" is a maternal wail that would have evoked the sympathy of Packard's readers, themselves well-versed in an ideology that revered the connections of middle-class women to their children.

The significance of Packard's stolen book is made clear when she explains that, "like Abraham, I felt that my darling book would in some way be saved, as was his darling Isaac" (p. 323). The child, who to a large extent reflected and thus defined the identity of a nineteenth-century women, has here become a metaphor for writing. The metaphor is especially interesting in Packard's case, since one of her sons is actually named Isaac; like Abraham, she must offer him up to a higher cause. The figure of mothering allows her to present herself as a legitimate author, extending the sphere of women, as did many women writers of her period.[13]

Yet ultimately, in the context of the asylum, the metaphor undermines the ideology of motherhood that brought it into being. The grieving voices of the other inmates reveal to Packard that her trust of the superintendent has been based on illusions about the power of her class-based connections to him. Even as it draws her readers into the scene, the ideology of motherhood dissolves before the image of women locked up "for their own good," mourning for their literal and metaphorical children.

By the end of Packard's book, the bond with her writing and her political work has clearly taken precedence over that with her children. Significantly, in the dedication of a later edition of her autobiography (*Modern Persecution*), she tells her children, "Every earthly love has died within me—but oh! the death agonies of the *maternal love* well nigh rent soul and body asunder. Yes, the mother has died! But she has risen again—the mother of her country—and her sons and daughters are *The American Republic*" (*Modern Persecution*, dedication). Here Packard transforms the concept of the "republican mother"— the mother who educates her children according to the ideals of the republic—to mean a mother who educates not the children within her own family but everyone—adult and child alike—within the country defined now as her larger community.[14]

In the chapter called "My Journey," she describes her passage from her home and family to the Jacksonville Asylum. On the train ride she contemplates her fate and the choices before her, deciding that she must accept the separation from her children, since she can do nothing about it, and redefine her duty as the restoration of her own liberty. Immediately on deciding this, she writes,

> After exchanging a few remarks respecting the beauty of the country through which we were passing, and the delightfully calm and clear atmosphere, so tranquilizing in its influence over one's disturbed feelings, I looked about to see who were my companions, when I met the eye of a young lady, a stranger to me, whose eyes seemed to fasten upon me with such a penetrating look, that I could hardly withdraw my own without bestowing upon her a smile of recognition. Upon this she bent forward and spoke to me, and extended to me her hand, saying,
> "I am very sorry for you. I see they are carrying you to the Insane Asylum, and you do not wish to go." (p. 54)

The "penetrating look" of her companion and her own "smile of recognition" suggest that her plight is one potentially shared by other middle-class women. Packard's companion here acts as a figure for the middle-class reader who sees in Packard's predicament the tenuousness of her own class privilege. Through the smile, Packard also suggests that she will gain a new sense of identity—throughout her struggle, and especially within the asylum itself—that will upset any complacency she may have had with her middle-class existence, a complacency revealed in her enjoyment of the scenery as if she were out for a Sunday carriage ride. "The Journey" is a spiritual and emotional one, in which Packard relinquishes, however partially and reluctantly, a traditional middle-class sense of entitlement to material comfort and privacy.

Toward the end of her experience in the asylum, then, she comes to define herself less in relation to the family she has left behind and more in relation to her emotional and intellectual interactions with the others in the asylum and with those who either hinder or help efforts to reform the asylum and improve the rights of married women. In the course of the autobiography, she relates having learned to distrust the legal and medical systems that she previously believed to be on her side. Her privileged place in relation to state and familial power has been exposed as an illusion. She has learned to communicate with the outside world not by handing her manuscript to the asylum superintendent but by sending clandestine letters, written on anything available and secreted out of the asylum: "As all communication with my children was cut off by the authority of Dr. McFarland, I was led to resort to strategy to secure this end. Therefore I procured some nicely dressed bleached cotton, and embroidered my daughter some double underwaists, on which I could easily and legibly pencil a long communication, such as my feelings prompted, hoping thus to bring myself to their recollection, so that I might not become an object of indifference to them" (p. 116).

As she tells how she secretly communicates with her daughter, Packard reveals her discovery that the sacred status of the maternal and of familial relations that she might have experienced as real in her preasylum life disappears once she has been deprived of her property and civil rights. In this "journey," the narrative rewrites the captivity version of American spiritual autobiography. Where Mary Rowlandson tells that she was captured by Indians, removed to increasingly remote locations, and redeemed by God back into her Puritan community, Packard relates that she was delivered into captivity by those she trusted in her own community, removed to increasingly remote asylum wards, and then redeemed into a new life through her own efforts and those of asylum reform activists. In her new world, the private sphere she was supposed to inhabit as a middle-class woman has slipped into the male public sphere of institutions, revealing that it was there all along. Her survival strategies must shift accordingly.

As she develops new ways of writing—penciling her messages in

cloth, inserting her writing behind her mirror, and keeping her journal "all rolled up in small separate portions in the different articles
of my wardrobe" (p. 321)—she grounds her creativity and her sense of
self in her female world. As she sews messages into her daughter's
underclothing, she passes on to her not only her own secrets but the
idea of female secrecy itself, hidden away beneath the outer clothing seen by men's eyes. Indeed, it is by keeping her writing linked
to women's things—clothing, embroidery, mirrors—that she outwits
McFarland, watching him pass unsuspectingly over her hiding places
again and again.

By always keeping some of her writing beyond his grasp, Packard
makes clear that she ultimately has overcome his power to dictate.
She thinks about her hidden journal after McFarland confiscates the
diary he had allowed her to keep openly: "I begged that he would return [the diary] without tearing it. But he heeded nothing I said, either
in defence of its truth, or of my claim to it, as by his consent I had obtained it. But instead, put it into his vest pocket, and walked off with it.
This is the last I ever saw of this part of my Asylum diary. My journal
covering this period is complete" (p. 121). By following her statement
that the diary has been lost with her assertion that the journal is complete, she reaffirms her ascendancy over the superintendent. Whatever
he tries to destroy of her writing and thus of her sense of identity—
here especially represented in her personal diary—there will always
be more writing, more self-creation that she has kept hidden beyond
his grasp. Packard's hidden writing comes to represent, then, a part of
herself that is beyond his power to destroy or co-opt.

Even while Packard reconstructs class distinctions in her narrative
of her asylum experience, she has learned new strategies within the
asylum and has learned to distrust the privilege upon which she used
to depend. Throughout her autobiography, she struggles to appropriate
the terms of the dominant discourses available to her—motherhood,
paternal authority, Christianity, sanity/insanity—and to reveal those
terms as parts of the carriage that bore her to the asylum.

# 2

## Elizabeth Packard and Sophie Olsen

### Violence, Spiritualism, and Writing in the Asylum

■   As she asserts her own coherence and autonomy, Elizabeth Packard challenges the othering of the insane that makes sanity a viable concept. She wishes her work to expose not only her own experience but that of the other asylum inmates. Her stories of other inmates work against the perception that those labeled insane are undifferentiated in their lack of subjectivity. Foucault describes the ways in which nineteenth-century asylum inmates were forced to accept their madness by recognizing themselves mirrored in the madness around them. According to Foucault, eventually the madman is "pitilessly observed by himself. And in the silence of those who represent reason, and who have done nothing but hold up the perilous mirror, he recognizes himself as objectively mad" (p. 264). The implication here is that what allows the mad to recognize themselves in the mirror is the insistence of the authorities that madness does away with difference. The superintendent holds up a mirror that shows only one picture— madness—that the insane person recognizes because the category of insanity subsumes all other distinctions.

By questioning asylum superintendent McFarland's reading of herself and others as insane objects of study, Packard resists the growing insistence of mid-nineteenth-century American scientists of the mind that they alone had authority to interpret what they called madness. Packard emphasizes instead the voice of lived experience, which for her is at the root of all perception. She both challenges traditional male scientific authority and claims that authority herself.

From this position, however, she often risks recreating as "other" the women in the asylum she speaks for and describes. This ambivalence within the text is brought home by Packard's inclusion of a first-person narrative by Sophie Olsen, another middle-class inmate, who entered the asylum as a voluntary patient in 1862, but soon became convinced of the need to reveal her experiences of the institution to the public.[1] Read beside Packard's call for "reasonable" reforms of the asylum, Olsen's narrative tells a story of revolution in the making within the walls of the institution. While Packard appeals to asylum authorities to respect her vision as that of a rational observer seeking to help the "truly insane," Olsen describes the violent resistance of those who have little hope of asserting their subjectivity in any other way.

■

While Packard resists the extreme version of the self-other split within the asylum, which denies the patient her own subjectivity and rationality, she often tends, nevertheless, to distance herself as a writer from the world she describes. Her narrative voice often occupies the position of observing subject who, like the scientist, collects evidence by observing the world around her, becoming a kind of anthropologist of the insane asylum. In her struggle to claim authority as legitimate investigator, she often comes close to identifying with the administrators, taking the stance of sane individual observing and judging other women, however generously. The chapter titles themselves—"Old Mrs. Timmons Deserted by her Children," "Mrs. Cheneworth's Suicide—Medical Abuse," "Abusing Mrs. Stanley," "Mrs. Emeline Bridgman—or Nature's Laws Broken"—convey images of women who are powerless, abused, defeated. According to Packard, these women cannot tell their own stories; she must tell them herself, from her position as the stronger woman who has managed to preserve her selfhood. In portraying them only as victims, she in a sense denies them any strength they may have even in their misery. What keeps her from resolving her conflict over locating herself as an empathetic observer is largely her own fear of the "otherness" of insanity coupled with an unwillingness to relinquish her superior position as a middle-class woman incarcerated in a predominantly lower-class institution.[2] This ambivalence in relation to both dominant concepts of insanity and the class divisions reproduced within the asylum will show itself even more intensely in the later autobiographies of Lydia Smith and Clarissa Lathrop, who write from asylums that have virtually become cities reproducing in microcosm the class conflicts of the larger society.

While she expresses sympathy for other inmates, Packard often writes as if she is superior to most of them. She points out that she was treated comparatively well when she first arrived at the asylum. Her privileged reception is not surprising given that she was a middle-class, educated minister's wife. This treatment accorded with the fact that patients from different backgrounds were treated quite differently within most nineteenth-century American asylums, with native-born paying patients receiving the best treatment and indigent immigrants and African Americans the worst (Grob, pp. 222–23). In addition, though Packard struggles to understand the insane and questions their classification as mad, she nevertheless is so insistent on her own sanity that she often looks upon them as "other," even as she seeks to help them. In the early part of her internment, she records that

> by the omnipotent power of God's grace I was inspired with moral courage sufficient to espouse the cause of the oppressed and the defenceless, even at the risk of becoming one of their number by so doing. I plainly saw and felt that on the part of their oppressors there was power, but that they had no comforter. I felt conscious that I held an influence and power over Dr. McFarland, and I deliberately determined this influence should be felt in their behalf. And, like Queen Esther, I felt willing to cast in my lot with these despised captives, if necessary, to be their deliverer. (p. 87)

Like Queen Esther of the Old Testament, who can save the Jews because she is the favored wife of King Ahasuerus, Packard sees herself as able to aid the insane largely because she has not relinquished her association with McFarland. She continues to hold herself superior in her class background, in her relation to God, and in her sanity.

Packard's need to separate herself from the other inmates shows itself most strongly in an incident that Packard herself barely mentions but that Sophie Olsen, whose narrative is appended to *The Prisoner's Hidden Life*, describes in vivid detail: a "Reign of Terror" implemented by the patients against the administration. Olsen narrates with great energy that, after all the inmates decided that something must be done in reaction to the administration's repressive measures, "at every opportunity, we banded together in little secret societies, in earnest, agonizing consultation." Decisions were made by vote, with everyone's opinion taken into consideration, so that a plan to kidnap the superintendent and threaten his life "was eloquently presented by one of the speakers, and the final fate of this bill was to be unanimously voted down." It was finally decided "that we should make a general onslaught or campaign against the State's property, and in various ways, destroy all we possibly could, without discovery" (Olsen, pp. 81–82).

Olsen self-consciously describes their actions in military terms, insisting that "it was the complete desperation of our circumstances which evolved this 'military necessity!' " Using the rhetoric of the Civil War, Olsen claims "our liberty, even the liberty of speech and writing had all been taken away, and we wished for emancipation from this inexorable thraldom with an agony of desire that none but the victims of such a bondage can even appreciate" (Olsen, p. 82).

The power of the rebellion lies largely in the fact that its perpetrators are anonymous, each individual self lost in the communal urge to revolt. Olsen takes obvious delight in relating that

> windows, looking glasses, goblets, and crockery, were dashed upon the floor, at different times, on all possible safe occasions. Tea-spoons, knives and forks, were stealthily taken from the table, and thrown out of the window; clothing and curtains torn and mutilated, doors were smashed, cushions opened, the walls were scratched and strange literature in conspicuous places written there! It was astonishing how many opportunities they had in which to effect their plans, in triumphant defiance of all our vigilant guardians. (Olsen, p. 85)

Because any blatant show of rebellion would be met with reprisals, these women resist with a kind of communal anonymity based in an absence of individuality. The distinctions of the domestic world are leveled as chaos overtakes woman's sphere. Windows and looking glasses both become glass to be shattered. The differences in function between goblets and crockery, between knives and forks, between clothing and curtains are made meaningless in this distinctly feminine revolution.

Their rebellion is successful largely because of the collective anonymity and the inability of those in charge to account for the destruction in any rational manner. When questioned, the inmates take refuge in the very madness by which the institution defines them: "Respecting the fact of the nice new blankets, on Lizzy's earnest inquiry of the very person who destroyed them, the latter very gravely informed her that the devil appeared to her in the night and carried them away! Skeins of expensive sewing silk, and spools of thread next vanished mysteriously from the work-room, and were found tangled up in inextricable confusion. 'Spirits,' were accused of abducting them away" (p. 84).

The questioned inmate is in a sense telling the truth here. The "insane" rebels are themselves devils and spirits, mysterious beings whose actions are defined as having no reason behind them. By assuming the roles the institution has assigned them, they are in a sense beating psychiatry at its own game, refusing to take responsibility for acts that they would supposedly be unable to formulate in rational response to an oppressive situation. They are saying, in effect, "You claim we are not responsible beings, so we could not possibly have invented and perpetrated these acts of destruction."

This conception of their rebellion points to the intersection of madness and Spiritualism. Spiritualism was a subject of acute interest among the inmates, many of whom had been committed as "religious monomaniacs," a diagnosis that alienists tended to see as necessarily a result of Spiritualist belief.

The medical profession's aversion to Spiritualism is not surprising given that as a movement it undermined the authority of medical and religious "experts." From its beginnings with the mysterious rappings heard in 1848 by the adolescent Fox sisters of Rochester, New York, Spiritualism as a nineteenth-century movement was characterized by an absence of central authority and organization, a privileging of young girls as the most likely spiritual mediums, and a preference for seance, planchette (a heart-shaped board used for spirit communications), and trance over medical explanation and diagnosis.[3]

No training or expert knowledge was necessary for someone to become a spiritual medium; anyone could be visited by voices from the other side. For women this had particular significance, since even though women played important roles in church life, they were usually not leaders or ministers (Hogeland, p. 140). As a spiritual medium, a woman could speak with a certain authority and have her voice heeded.[4] That Spiritualist mediums posed a threat to traditional authority is clear in the fact that more and more laws were passed to prevent them from practicing (Moore, pp. 126–27). Mediums were not only a threat to traditional church hierarchies, however; they represented a movement—largely composed of women—away from a male professionalism based on exclusive knowledge and training. Often mediums either became healers or experienced cures themselves of illnesses beyond the reach of the medical profession. Many female mediums further undermined established authorities by giving voice to spirits who supported divorce and espoused women's rights (Moore, pp. 111–25).[5]

In attaching themselves to Spiritualism as a movement, the asylum rebels place themselves at the center of conflicting social forces of their time. On the one hand, the medical world, including psychiatry, was moving to expand its sphere of control by becoming more specialized and professionalized, while on the other, the more traditional Protestant churches were trying to maintain control over their congregations. Meanwhile, Spiritualists threatened the authority of both these male-dominated areas by claiming that anyone—including women—could have access to the world of the unseen, a world that concerned both psychiatry and religion. It is no coincidence that psychiatrists published articles condemning Spiritualism in the second half of the nineteenth century. Psychiatry attacked Spiritualism's positivistic claims, reasserting the authority of experts to assess evidence objectively. Writing about the dangers of Spiritualism, Dr. George Beard held that "the rejection of nonexpert human testimony is, and has ever been, the first step in the development of a science; it is only by rejecting or ignoring all testimony save that of experts that any science is possible" (Beard, p. 70).

Neurologists strove to debunk Spiritualism by explaining so-called spiritual visions in organic terms. In an article entitled "The Physics and Physiology of Spiritualism," Dr. William Hammond holds that "as regards purely imaginary images,—that is, images not based on any sensorial impression—that difficulty is in the brain. An excess or deficiency of blood circulating through this organ, or a morbid alteration of its quality, such as is induced by alcohol, opium, belladonna, and other similar substances, will often lead to hallucinations" (p. 235). Hammond gives examples of so-called Spiritualist experiences that can be explained "scientifically." It is interesting that almost all of his examples focus on women, considering that only about half of the mediums in the movement were female (Moore, pp. 126–27). Clearly, Hammond is concerned above all with women gaining spiritual power. In his examples, the women enter trance-like states and become impervious to outside influences, including the doctor's attempts to command their attention.

Often Hammond claims that a physician must go to great lengths to "experiment" with his patient's responses: "Thus an hysterical woman will suddenly take to her bed and declare that she has no feeling and no power of motion in her leg or arm. The most careful examination shows that she is speaking the truth. Pins may be thrust into the affected limb, it may be scorched *ad libitum*, and yet the possesor does not wince" (p. 251). Violent passages such as these show that more is involved than simply a desire for scientific truth. The ignored physician is frustrated by the female medium's passive withdrawal from his control. The only way he can once again gain power over her is to circumscribe her trance within the limits of his medical definitions, claiming he "does not now believe that the bodies of lunatics, epileptics, and hysterical women are inhabited by devils and demons, for he has ascertained by observation that the abnormal conditions present in such persons can be accounted for by material derangements of the organs or functions of the system" (p. 233). In fact, while physicians such as Hammond claim to have progressed beyond the witch-hunters of the sixteenth and seventeenth centuries, they still take the stance of judges seeking to control a threatening force. In either case, a woman's withdrawal from the sphere of male control is seen as dangerous and in need of treatment. In the seventeenth century a woman who fell into this category would be executed as a witch; in the mid-nineteenth century she was often declared insane.

Spiritualism permitted female mediums to assume an authority previously inaccessible to them by allowing them to exchange the less respected mental abilities of women for the more mysterious and authoritative capacities of spirits (Moore, p. 103). In a sense, the rebellious asylum women do the same thing in the form of dramatic enactment. When they claim their actions are the work of spirits, they imply that the destruction has a higher authority, a higher reason behind it than the attendants and superintendent may even conceive. Especially when they point to the devil, they imply that these acts are the result of a rational force that, while evil, is at least responsible.

Olsen's story reverberates with Packard's insistence that, unlike asylum inmates, "a criminal is regarded as a moral being. He is not locked up to be deprived of the godhead within him. His capacity to become a wicked, guilty person is allowed him; and this capacity, even with guilt attending it, is less to be dreaded, than a feeling of annihilation, an extinction of human capacities and being" (p. 273).

The women inmates play with the levels of meaning in their responses when they are asked to explain the destruction. Both the superintendent and the questioned inmates know their answers are a screen, but in this case the women are in the more powerful position since they possess and withhold the information the authorities want. Defended by their collective anonymity and power to cause further violence, the inmates relish their ability—as Olsen enjoys the telling of it—to communicate to the authorities that they are indeed behind the destruction and capable of deciding to pursue it, even though this particular incident has seemed to have little effect on asylum policies. In this way, they are finally able to speak and be heard.

Against this background of collective anonymous resistance, Packard describes her own repeated attempts to change asylum conditions without relinquishing her claim to personal identity, class identity, and authorship. While she exercises various forms of passive resistance—such as continually refusing to reenter her ward of her own free will—she primarily struggles to effect change and assert her identity through writing. Like the middle-class northern abolitionist she is—she is originally from Massachusetts and openly espouses the pacifist abolitionist cause—Packard withholds her approval from the violent rebellion that Olsen so gleefully describes. She maintains that for her such rebellion, while largely justifiable, represents a plunge into chaos. The anonymity of the rebels and their bestowal of responsibility on spirits deprive them of the individuality and order Packard seeks to maintain. In Packard's view, the inmates in a sense become the insane creatures psychiatrists describe.

Early in the book Packard states that a talk she gave on "spiritual gifts" was censured at her husband's church because the deacons feared it advocated Spiritualism. Later she comments that some of the women on the seventh ward "were Spiritualists, and they taught me many new ideas, and set me on to a new track of exploration. They told me their visions, and trances and prophecies, many of which have been already fulfilled, in the events of war" (p. 83). She relates that many women were committed for their beliefs and in her appendix she includes the testimony of some of them. Packard's own version of Spiritualism keeps her voice connected to scientific method and theory as well as to the ideology of individualism. Her claim that individual human testimony is valid evidence coincides with a belief in an individualized Christianity that tends towards what might be called mainstream Spiritualism. Many Spiritualists of her era claimed to ground their belief in a scientific concept of an unseen world.

Though Packard does not explicitly identify herself as a Spiritualist, her redefinition of science is based largely on ideas shared by Spiritualists. Like most of them, she believes that spirit rappings and voices could be explained scientifically if we knew the principles behind them:

> The law by which these supernatural events takes place, is unknown to us, and may be beyond our present ability to comprehend. For example, had we never seen or known that a caterpillar could be changed into a butterfly, we should call it a miracle. The facts occurring daily on the telegraphic wires would have been considered miracles to past generations . . . I believe these spiritual gifts are all controlled by established laws of our spiritual existence, of which we are at present comparatively ignorant. (30)

Packard's belief in an invisible spiritual realm governed by secret laws parallels her interest in the reasons behind the behavior of the insane. In both cases she assumes that laws exist that determine a surface reality, and in both cases she claims we must listen to human voices—those of mediums or those of the insane—in order to understand this reality. Those voices, like her own, are the mirrors that lead, as does Alice's looking-glass, into another world. In her science, everyone's observation is valid, so that if a woman says she sees spirits from the past we must accept her word as evidence of a possible truth.

Packard holds that she herself is the medium of a truth whose higher authority gives her voice validity. She makes herself into a medium, however, who is more than the vehicle of another voice. Her voice itself—and the intellect it represents—become crucial to the communication of that higher authority. Unlike the asylum rebels or other "mediums" who claim to have been taken over completely by another being, thus largely relinquishing a claim to authorship, she in a sense has it both ways: she writes with the authority of a God-given truth and with the sane voice she calls her own. Thus she can call her writing a "mental vision," saying, "I commenced writing out this mental vision, and in six weeks time I penciled the substance of 'The Great Drama,' which, when written out for the press, covers two thousand five hundred pages of note paper. Can I not truly say my train of thought was engineered by the 'Lightning Express?' I had no books to aid me but Webster's large Dictionary, and the Bible" (p. 311). Not unlike Harriet Beecher Stowe, Packard implies here that the book was written so quickly and voluminously because it was inspired by some higher force, but she leaves no doubt that it was she who actually wrote it, claiming, "It came wholly through my own reason and intellect, quickened into unusual activity by the perfect state of my health" (p. 310). The Bible and Webster's dictionary lay side by side as she wrote the work with her own mind, her own reasoning abilities, using both books as references. If she was inspired by God-given truth through the Bible, it was still her intellect that scanned the dictionary and put that truth into words, and she wants her reader to make no mistake about that. Where the typical nineteenth-century female medium attempts to gain credibility from her link to a voice other than her own, Packard wishes to be believed for herself, for her own rational ability to describe her experience.

Packard claims to choose writing over violence, saying that, in avoiding violence, "I could look down upon the [management] on their lower plane of passion, policy, deception and brutality, and, from this standpoint, I could command the moral courage to be their reprover, and their reporter to the world" (p. 285).

Rather than destroy the state's property, Packard claims she wants to work within the system, to inform the state of asylum abuses and thus influence the legislature. She considers it her duty to record the events she sees around her. On the level of civic responsibility, she holds that "instead of going to the wash-room to serve the State of my adoption by my labor, I am trying to serve it by writing facts and impressions respecting this Institution, hoping thus to promote the interests of the State more directly, than in any other manner" (p. 125). While in her relations with authority within the asylum she often repudiates control from above, she rarely challenges the state itself as the other inmates do when they destroy asylum property. Despite her move toward self-sufficiency, Packard never abandons the idea that she should be protected by the system of laws that govern the state. She insists that both her husband, who has become "my persecuter, instead of my protector" (p. 44), and the state, which she has willfully adopted as her "parent" state, owe her a paternal protectiveness. While she learns from her experience with McFarland that she should not turn to another man for protection, she uses for her purposes the ideal image of a larger protective power. Thus she vacillates between one vision in which human society is an association of independent though interrelated beings and another in which it is a hierarchy in which paternal figures provide protection.

She holds that because of her continuing loyalty to societal laws she feels ambivalence about using even nonviolent, but secretive and forbidden, methods of resistance, such as writing. Discussing her establishment of an "underground express" to send inmates' letters to the outside world, she reflects, "I have already tried by force of argument, reason, and entreaty, to induce Dr. McFarland to allow me some chance at self-defence, but all in vain. I cannot get his consent in this matter, therefore, the act being right in itself, and a duty also, I must act not only without this consent, but without his knowledge. Therefore, under the circumstances, a clandestine act of self-defence is not a sinful act because of its secresy" (p. 141). She justifies her secret acts of resistance by claiming that religious duty impels her to act in her own self-defense. This strategy of appeal to duty—the primary value for middle-class women in the nineteenth-century United States—enables Packard to maintain the attention and sympathy of a middle-class audience.

The only way Packard can undermine, under the circumstances, the hierarchy of which McFarland is a part is to appeal to a larger paternal authority—God—whose rules are stricter. Because she cannot completely renounce her position as middle-class dutiful wife defined by her social relations, she turns to God as ultimate husband, father, protector, claiming, "it is enough for me to know and keep my proper place, as an employee under the Master workman's control. I believe I have a body-guard of invincible power to defend me in the discharge of every duty, and until my work is entirely done I am immortal. Although I am called to pursue a comet-like orbit, yet I have my path to revolve in, and no other planet can affect it, beyond its appointed limits" (p. 168).

It is likely that Packard's insistence on her own importance in

God's eyes is proportional to the possibility of her psychic disintegration in the face of both the asylum authorities' denial of her sanity and the chaos she sees in the violent rebellion of the other inmates. Refraining from becoming part of violent collective action, she seeks salvation from madness in a definition of self that must take on grandiose significance to be effective. While this grandiosity threatens to win her the diagnosis of monomania, it also invokes the claims of dissident Puritan Anne Hutchinson, whose belief that the Holy Ghost resided within her and superseded the authority of the magistrates was considered seriously even if it was ultimately denounced. Packard also writes here in the tradition of American spiritual autobiographers, such as William Bradford, John Winthrop, and Jonathan Edwards, whose belief in their divine mission to set an example and reform a backsliding people held a respected place within their particular Christian context. At any rate, Packard's grand role in God's "Great Drama" allows her to remain aloof from the other inmates even as she champions their cause. Despite her sympathy with her fellow inmates, she negotiates the danger of becoming too much like them, bereft of both her sanity and her middle-class distinctiveness. For a middle-class woman, these two aspects of her existence would necessarily be linked, given that the logic of sanity/insanity assigned rationality to the economically and educationally privileged.[6]

At the same time, the fact that Packard includes within her book statements made by other women implies that she feels a connection with other women's lives, as does the fact that the different women's stories are sufficiently complementary to form a whole text. But while she shows a sense of identification and relation with the other women in the asylum, Packard's sense of community is not without ambivalence. The collection of individual, signed testimonials that she has brought together in her text emerges out of a wider background of threatened sameness, silence and violence, of selflessness and consequent insanity.

Even though Sophie Olsen does not emphasize the importance of writing in maintaining her sanity as much as Packard does, she nevertheless fights as does Packard against the loss of self she sees in the other inmates. While she relates the story of the rebellion, she remains outside the action, occupying a middle ground between Packard and the rebels. Olsen shows that it is important for her to fight the fear of insanity when she tells of being kept awake by two women—one old and one young—who scream curses throughout the night. One begins by condemning her "tormentors" to an eternity of "fire and brimstone," and the other answers, " 'Yes, I mean to send McFarland's soul to hell; there it shall be roasted and burned for thousands, millions, millions, trillions, trillion years!' " Olsen is struck by the repetition of words, remarking that the older woman "emphasized and prolonged the first syllable, m-i-l-lions m-i-l-lions" (Olsen, p. 65). She is terrified by these women's voices repeating over and over again seemingly infinite expanses of time; she is afraid of a world without time, without individuality, a world filled only with the impotence and hatred of insane women whose only identity lies in that insanity. Above all, she is afraid of losing her distinction from those around her and turning suddenly to see herself mirrored in their faces.

She does not blame these women for subjecting her to their screams, but she names the threat they represent for her; she thinks they are tools of "Dr. McFarland's seeming decree that my sanity should become annihilated!" (p. 65). She fears that McFarland is purposely placing her sanity in danger by showing her what she can become herself, holding up to her the "perilous mirror" of insanity. It is not only that she hears them evoking time without measure that makes her afraid; it is that she understands the extremity of their hatred, of their alienation from the world. She sees how they have reached a point where they can only speak to each other through their hatred of the power that oppresses them, shouting curses as their only intercommunication. Their power to define themselves through each other as separate beings has been reduced to a shared hatred. Through his silence, McFarland has held up to each of them the "perilous mirror" that is the other, a mirror in which each one sees herself reflected. The two women have in a sense become one, screaming out into the night.

Olsen tells of her need to fight for her own sanity against the strength of these women's voices: "Sitting up, erect in my bed, with as loud a voice as I could possibly command, to help drown these opposite voices, I repeated passages of the most beautiful and attractive poetry I had ever learned in former years" (p. 65). Olsen resists the anarchy implied in their curses by repeating to herself the poetic voices of her culture, of the ordered world outside the asylum. To maintain her sanity, she must hold on to something she loves in the world, so that she has reason—literally—to communicate with it. To do this, she in a sense becomes culture itself shouting against an anarchy that tempts her to join it. To have a voice at all that connects her to others she must invoke her subjectivity as it has been shaped by her culture. She turns her eyes away from the insane and, like Packard, looks into the mirror she brought with her from outside the asylum, a mirror that allows her to preserve the difference between self and other. She asserts her culturally defined subjectivity against the danger of the annihilation that could accompany the complete rejection of a coherent social world that she hears in the curses of the insane. At the same time, however, her fear is largely a reaction to the temptations of that rejection, since, as she presents them, these "opposite voices" are not "pure" anarchy; their imprecations form a dialogue in which they clearly implicate the "tormentors" who control their lives.

Where Olsen counters insanity with the poetry of her youth, Packard defies insanity with her own writing, the journals and letters hidden about her room. In the end, both Packard and Olsen struggle to remain sane, often othering the "truly insane" in the only gesture toward subjectivity the dominant culture has made available to them.

Yet Packard's apparent fear of disintegration must be understood in the context of her larger resistance to the definitions imposed on her. In her autobiography she often uses the chaos that she herself fears as a threat against the powers that be, a warning as to what can happen. She urges her readers to support progressive legislative change rather than allow despotism to bring on revolution. After reporting a conversation with McFarland in which he claims, "the government of the family is vested entirely in the husband," she holds that "every family established on such a basis ought to be overthrown, as well as all other despotisms; and it is this principle which is at the present day sending devastation throughout the whole social fabric of society" (p. 163). She equates the husband's authoritarianism with that of the slaveowner often described in contemporaneous literature as a despot who must be overthrown. She threatens her readers that the kind of devastation and disunion seen in the practice of slavery, in the South's secession, and in the Civil War could result also from inequitable relations in the family and the asylum.

At the same time, she voices tacit understanding of the inmates' rebellion, commenting on "the extravagant, unnecessary, and unreasonable amount of property destroyed here, merely as the legitimate result of this insane management" (p. 158). With an ambivalence that may be read as strategic, she both criticizes the violent action and places responsibility for it on the administration. Despite her disapproval and fear, after all, she does include Olsen's account of the rebellion, which contains description of Packard's own role as a leader of the inmates. Olsen tells us that before the rebellion itself, Packard had in a sense mobilized her allies in response to a series of inordinate restrictions. Even at this point Olsen describes the situation as

> a regular civil war with the Institution. All the seventy patients in the Eighth Ward who took the least interest in anything, sympathised with Mrs. Packard; and, so far as I could learn every attendant, both male and female, in the Asylum, defended, and very highly respected Mrs. Packard. This state of affairs created increased apprehensions in the camp of the enemy. Something must be done. Our potent commander, after holding a war-council with several of his allies, the chief of whom was Bonner, the Prime Minister, now issued officially from his "sanctum," a new and startling proclamation. It was this:
>
> "All intercourse between Mrs. Packard and the inmates of the west division of the Eighth Ward, must be prohibited except under strict guard of an attendant! Mrs. Packard must not be allowed to go into the hall, except when accompanied by an attendant. She is to hold no more prayer-meetings, lend no more books, and those she has lent must be immediately returned."
> (p. 74–75)

By including Olsen's description of her role in defining the lines of battle, Packard implies that she has a certain power over the forces of revolution, even though she expresses fear and disapproval of those forces at other points in the work.

Maintaining a delicate balance, Packard both plays upon and denies the tendencies of alienists to associate revolution not only with women they called insane but with women's anger in general. Protesting the fact that Superintendent Andrew McFarland resigned in response to a legislative investigation that Packard initiated after her release, the editors of the *Journal of Insanity* claimed that the investigation "seems to have been aimed towards sacrificing a victim to a popular clamor, rather than vindicating the truth. If truth were its purpose, it pursued arbitrary and unaccustomed modes of reaching it. Instead of examining a hospital, it sought rather, apparently, to criminate its officers and subordinates, on most suspicious evidence, to gratify a woman's spleen, a partisan purpose, or a popular frenzy, and perhaps all three" ("Illinois Legislation," p. 216). This passage shows how alienists' concept of insanity was highly colored by ideology that connected insanity, "frenzy," with popular movements, political subversion, and physically rooted female anger. In a clear reference to Packard's reforming activities, the editors expressed anxiety over losing control of both knowledge and institutions.

In a sense, their fears were founded. After her release from the asylum, Packard did work furiously in several states to pass laws guaranteeing maternal rights, married women's rights, and the rights of those called insane. Many of her efforts were successful. Whereas at the time of her own incarceration Illinois law allowed a husband to commit his wife without further evidence, in 1865, largely as a result of Packard's sale of her books describing her own experiences, the legislature repealed this law, which specifically discriminated against both women and children (Himelhoch and Shaffer, p. 360). By 1884, when British alienist Daniel Tuke visited ten asylums in the United States, Illinois commitment laws had become "the most stringent of all," requiring trial by jury before a patient could be committed. Tuke quotes McFarland as writing to another physician that " 'the Illinois law of which you inquire is injurious, odious, barbarous, damnable, and you may add as many more expletives to it as you please and still not say the truth in regard to its evils' " (Tuke, p. 69). It was just such a trial, taking place on January 12, 1864, that had finally won Packard her freedom not only from the asylum but from imprisonment at home by her husband after her release.[7]

Packard's success as a reformer is powerful in the light of psychiatrists' fears. Writing in the *American Journal of Insanity* in 1860 about the superintendent's need to exact absolute obedience from the asylum attendants, McFarland remarks, "I doubt if there be any man whose conduct toward others is regulated by the ordinary dictates of probity, that can look back on a few years of experience in such a duty as ours, and feel that his errors towards this class of subordinates have ever been a too severe exaction in the performance of duty; and the position of that man (if any such there be) whose orders must be executed by those over whom he has not entire control, must be unhappy indeed" ("Annual Meeting," p. 56). By claiming in her autobiography not only that the inmates could rebel but that the attendants could take her side, Packard plays on the asylum authorities' fear of losing control. Olsen's violent rebellion becomes the backdrop against which Packard's voice and writing can appear as the more rational alternative, the sources of a clearer vision.

Elizabeth Packard's text, with its inclusion of the words of Sophie Olsen, offers us a way of thinking about writings by other nineteenth-century middle-class women reformers, such as Harriet Beecher Stowe, Jane Addams, Elizabeth Cady Stanton, who were torn between a fear of and desire for social upheaval. Packard's autobiography is built of layers of different kinds of visions and voices, each of which both obscures and opens space for the emergence of the one below it: Packard, who has the most prominent voice, expresses the most faith in rational individualism and the possibility of changing the system from within; within Packard's text, Sophie Olsen gives a glimpse of the revolutionary forces in the asylum, as she struggles to maintain her separateness; and, within Olsen's text, women who do not have access to or who have given up socially acceptable forms of communication practice a language of anonymous resistance. Thus, while Packard does rely on hierarchy to define her own place in the world, she also suggests that the women around her are, like her, seeing subjects whose testimony—in its various forms—expresses their lived experience. In the otherness of female madness, where she sees her capacity to be a thinking subject utterly denied, Packard maintains— if ambivalently—that every life story must be heard.

# Part 2

## The Secrets of Madness
### Asylum Autobiography
### as Exposé and Popular Novel

# 3

## *Lydia Smith and Clarissa Lathrop*

### Whose Paranoia Is It Anyway?

■ Elizabeth Packard felt that God had endowed everyone with an ability to reason that would not desert him or her and that faith in God and Spiritualism placed her beyond the reach of the doctors' probings. She claims she was able to hold her ground within the asylum and has faith that her writing can provide "the mystic key" to unlock the secrets of the asylum. This sense of her own spiritual importance may explain why Packard interrupts her chronological tale of capture and escape with various fragments of different kinds of writing— letters, philosophical and religious meditations, poems. Throughout her shifts in narrative voice and form, she maintains the idea that all forms of writing contribute toward God's project of reforming the asylum and saving its inmates through Elizabeth Packard.

Lydia Smith, who published *Behind the Scenes* in 1879, and Clarissa Lathrop, who published *A Secret Institution* in 1890, are not interested in demonstrating that all asylum inmates, equal before God, speak from an internal rationality. Unlike Packard, who struggles to identify ontologically with the other inmates, Smith and Lathrop for the most part maintain distinctions between economic classes, ethnic groups, and even types of insanity. Like Packard, they do speak out against asylum abuses, and become spokeswomen for the other inmates, but they do so less out of a sense of spiritual mission than out of a growing consciousness that they belong to a larger socially defined group—those incarcerated as insane. Lacking Packard's spiritually based conviction in her own sanity, these two autobiographers register self-doubt, wondering why they are in the asylum and how the incarceration is affecting them.

As they unfold their narratives, Smith and Lathrop struggle with both their own anxieties and societal perceptions of their mental stability. Unlike Elizabeth Packard, who throughout her narrative expresses certainty that she is sane and that she is doing God's work, Lathrop and Smith question both their own sanity and their importance in God's eyes. The reader sees doubt and fear in much of their writing, especially in their seemingly limitless suspicions of those around them.

Given the depth of their fear and suspicion, both writers adopt strategies of dissimulation that contrast sharply with Packard's frankness and refusal to battle with McFarland through deceptive means other than clandestine writing. This difference exists not necessarily because Packard is braver but because the avenues she uses are no longer available to Smith or Lathrop. Even though McFarland was less than receptive to her ideas, Packard was able to speak with him fairly often. In the "cities" of the Utica and Kalamazoo asylums, however, the two later writers were treated by several doctors, none of whom saw them very often.[1] They were also under the constant threat of medication and other forms of restraint. They wrote from and about asylums that were overcrowded and understaffed at a time when cure rates were becoming abysmal, the press and investigating agencies were demanding reform, and both neurologists and asylum superintendents were trying to consolidate their professional legitimacy. Ellen Dwyer points out that in New York State not only did the absolute number of women sent to asylums rise (as did the number of men) during the second half of the nineteenth century, but "the probability of a female's being committed by a public official more than doubled over the course of the century" ("Historical Perspective," pp. 40–41). At the same time that asylums were coming under criticism from press, legislature, and reform associations, families and public officials were becoming, according to Dwyer, more willing to send women to asylums who displayed less clear-cut or obviously threatening "symptoms" ("Historical Perspective," p. 40).

Largely as a result of these conditions, Smith and Lathrop do not trust their own ability to counter the doctors who probe them with questions. Packard describes her relationship with McFarland as ambivalent in that while he often turns silently away from her, he also frequently engages her in debate. In contrast, the doctors only question Smith and Lathrop when they are testing their sanity, looking for signs of melancholia, monomania, or deluded thinking. Professional alienists had a large stake at this time and in these asylums in asserting their status as scientists studying their subjects. The women's language itself is even more objectified than Packard's; the doctors turn to it to substantiate the idea that the women are "really" insane.

In their interaction with and divergence from popular fiction, the two autobiographies enact the writers' reconceptualization of their social positions and identities. These two texts are particularly interesting taken together because, unlike Packard's work, which continually interrupts the narrative line with other forms of writing, the autobiographies of Smith and Lathrop subordinate any divergences to the development of a central story: the tale of their confinement, experiences in the asylum, and eventual release. While this central narrative maintains links to the early captivity narratives, in which all action and thought had spiritual resonances, it is much more closely allied to the sensation novel, with its dramatic tales of women battling confinement. As she expresses her fears of the world around her, each narrator constructs a subject position that would have been familiar to a late nineteenth-century American novel-reader—that of the potentially paranoid but in the end justifiably suspicious narrator.

By elaborating sensational details and focussing on a personal story, these texts identify themselves as "women's" narratives. Where Packard's autobiography slips in and out of masculine and feminine forms and discourses, the narratives of Smith and Lathrop maintain the focus on personal lives found in the "feminine" sensation novel.[2] At the same time, these two autobiographies differ from popular fiction in important ways. Contemporaneous fictional texts tended to reinforce cultural stereotypes of middle-class women as either submissive and gentle or powerful and dangerous. These two autobiographies, like Packard's, upset narrative conventions by confronting stereotypes of women—especially of "insane" women—and creating new identities that reveal themselves largely in the narrative form itself. In these two autobiographies, two standard tropes of English and American nineteenth-century sensation fiction—the insane woman and the family secret—take on new meaning as the writers make their readers all too aware that these autobiographical narrators fail to reconstitute the social order that is shattered and rebuilt in the standard tale.

More important, the use by Smith and Lathrop of these popular-ized conventions and strategies reveals connections and gaps between the supposedly insane woman's paranoia—a new diagnostic category in the late nineteenth-century—and the class and gender paranoia being enacted in the larger culture through both psychological theo-ries and popular genres. Where psychological discourse and sensation novel alike rebuild social hierarchies by defining and excluding "the insane," the two autobiographies both gesture toward that rebuilding and redefine that exclusion as itself paranoid and delusory.

■

While Packard expresses, often unconsciously, a fear that all hier-archies and differences will be abolished, she does claim that God granted every individual a rational sense that can not be judged from the outside, a sense that leads her to approach other inmates with self-confidence and understanding. Smith has Packard's religious sense, believing that God can show her sympathy with another "creature" and grant her power to help that person, but her sense of power easily flips over into helplessness, as she feels persecuted and afraid. Lathrop exhibits both a more limited sense of her own power and a stronger need to maintain distinctions within the asylum. Both Lathrop and Smith express a profound distrust of their families and of the tra-ditional feminine qualities with which they are supposed to meet the world. In their distrust they both blame oppressed groups within American society—the insane, immigrants, the lower classes—and find themselves to be the targets of such blame as well.

Born in 1835, Lydia Smith was, like Packard, incarcerated by her husband, who abducted her from their home and placed her in two asy-lums from 1866 to 1872. Before her institutionalization, Lydia Smith lived in Jonesville, a small town in Michigan, with her husband, step-daughter and son. Also part of her household were a female boarder—the daughter of family friends—and occasionally her husband's sis-ter. Smith, who was often ill and unable to take care of her children, suffered, like many middle-class women of the period, from an un-specified neurasthenic complaint.[3] She was dedicated to her role as wife and mother, and, like Packard, she espouses in the narrative the standard contemporary rhetoric on the importance of a mother's love. She remarks that before her commitment she "fervently and devoutly prayed for grace and strength to enable me to discharge my duty faithfully as wife and mother" (p. 185). The situation she describes typified the white middle-class American woman's plight: feeling the double-pull of the ideal female image, she was torn between being a strong, devout, competent mother and household organizer and a dependent and submissive supplicant to husband and Creator.[4]

Throughout the narrative, she bases her sense of identity largely in "her piety and zeal in the church and in the cause of Christ," letting us know in the preface that "her husband not being a professor of religion, she conducted the family worship herself, and educated her children in the love and fear of God." Like Packard, she remarks that from the beginning her faith separated her from her husband, giving her a certain independent sense of self that she could turn to later in the asylum. However, while her autobiography registers that her faith enabled her to connect with the other inmates, it also tells a story of fear and powerlessness, a story more submerged in Packard's text, that undermines her spiritual security.

According to Smith, her husband was interested in another woman and wanted her out of the way. She opens her narrative, "I was taken from my residence in Jonesville, Michigan, August 16, 1865, to Canadaigua, New York, where I remained one year and seven months, when I was removed to the State Asylum at Kalamazoo, Michigan. Here I was 'imprisoned' four years" (p. 1). Like Packard, she tried to secure her own release while she was there by sending letters written secretly with materials obtained through clandestine means. She finally escapes with the help of an attendant, who looks the other way when she climbs aboard a carriage that a Quaker friend drives by the asylum grounds at a prearranged time.

Smith's sense of identity and relation to the world evolves throughout her stay in the asylum. At first, she is struck by her own sense of difference from the other inmates; she is reluctant to relinquish the distinction between sanity and insanity and the sense of wholeness she derives from it. In her preface, she states,

> It is the author's design to call attention to this subject for the benefit of the really insane who are not capable of self defence, and who have none of the privileges granted to a free and enlightened people, but are cruelly and inhumanely treated under the ordinary asylum usages.
>
> It is the author's design also to call attention to another class

who are more unfavorably situated, if possible, than the really insane. It is those who are not insane, and who are kept confined in an asylum either from a false belief in regard to their condition, on the part of their friends, or from a desire on their part to keep them thus confined. It is high time the public was awake to the uses and abuses of an asylum management. (preface)

Smith divides asylum inmates into two distinct classes—the "really insane" and the "not insane." Thus, while she need not identify with the insane *as* insane, she brings both classes into the scope of her larger "design."

Smith's narrative shows that her attitude toward the "really insane" changes from fear to sympathy as she became more familiar with the asylum. At one point, locked into a room with another woman, she asks:

> Patient reader, did you ever imagine yourself shut in alone with a maniac? If not, give it a moment's thought before reading any further. Yes, she came directly toward my bed, until within about two feet of it, and there she stood with her large unearthly eyes, staring at me. She remained there so long—not speaking nor moving from her position—that it seemed terrible to me. If she would only speak; or move, or take her eyes off from me, it would be a relief. Her appearance was so unearthly and strange that great beaded drops of perspiration stood upon every part of my body. It seemed as if I could not endure the silence much longer, and I offered a prayer for guidance and protection; after which a feeling of sympathy took possession of my heart for that poor, unfortunate creature. No telling how much she had suffered, and still was suffering, both in mind and body. (p. 77)

While Smith is similar to Packard here in that she appeals to God's guidance, she emerges not as Queen Esther, the deliverer of her people, but as an unrelated person caught in a common plight with a woman she doesn't quite understand. Like Packard, she feels around in her cultural handbag for a way to exist in this situation, taking the reader along with her. She is "shut in alone with a maniac," forced to confront her own fear of the image of madness that she must have known the word "maniac" itself would evoke for her nineteenth-century reader. Through the course of the passage, her understanding of what a maniac is changes. At first she sees the woman as insane—a "poor, unfortunate creature" rather than a human being.

What makes the woman most inhuman to Smith is her failure to speak. As the woman stares at her in silence, Smith begins to lose a sense of her own difference from her. Smith too is standing still and staring in silence. When she relates that "her appearance was so unearthly and strange that great beaded drops of perspiration stood upon every part of my body," it almost seems as if she is looking in a mirror; the two women are locked in a mutual gaze in which the physical appearance of one provokes a bodily response in the other. It is only when Smith offers a prayer that she is able to separate herself enough from the woman to feel sympathy for her. For Smith, language thus allows her both to separate from the "really insane" and to reconnect through piety and sympathy—the ideal traits of the nineteenth-century American woman. The masculine discourse of mental science, which creates this woman as insane and therefore "other," gives way before the power of the woman's silence. Smith invokes instead the more feminized discourse of piety and sympathy, which give her a way to be locked in the same room with a "madwoman" without becoming her.

Yet the fear invoked by the initial confrontation dominates the scene. Where Packard's mirror is the hiding-place for her writing, her re-creation of self and sanity, Smith's mirror here is the madwoman, who threatens to reflect Smith's own image throughout the autobiography.

Like Packard, Smith is anxious to establish her sanity after her release. She relates,

> Immediately after my safe arrival among friends I wrote to Judge Dickenson, of Hillsdale, informing him of my escape from the asylum, and demanding an investigation, telling him I would appoint two physicians, and he could appoint two or more as he desired, and we would have it settled about my sanity or insanity. I appointed a day and an hour when I would be there. I was there at the appointed time, my brother being my escort. The judge needed no further proof of my sanity, and in due course of time I sued for and obtained a bill of divorce, with a certain portion of the property which belonged to me before I was taken to the asylum. (p. 166)

She publishes her autobiography in order both to prove her sanity and to promote investigation of asylum abuses. As her impulse to write to the judge immediately after her escape reveals, her ability to establish her sanity depends on her capacity to become the narrator of her own story.

Smith may have been encouraged to couch her own predicament in legal terms by the case of Nancy Newcomer, who brought charges against VanDeusen (of the Kalamazoo asylum) for false imprisonment, assault, and battery in 1878, a year before Smith's autobiography was published. While the judge in the case ultimately ordered the jury to find no cause of action in the appeal, Newcomer initially won the case, which granted her damages of six thousand dollars. This was a notorious case in which public opinion was largely on Newcomer's side.[5]

In the courtroom, the stakes of narrative authority become clear. If Smith can tell her story and it is believed, she will go free. Yet it is a story in which her sanity is constantly on the verge of dissolving. Whether this impending dissolution is a strategy used to solicit the reader's interest or a chronicle of her experience as she remembers it or both, it shapes the narrative with a kind of wave motion, a vacillation between the narrator's power and her psychic destruction.

Clarissa Lathrop, like Smith, suffered from the unexplained chronic illnesses that seemed to plague many middle-class women of the era. Her family and religious situations as she describes them, however, were quite different from those of Smith. Before her incarceration, she lived in Rochester, New York, where she worked as a schoolteacher to help support her mother and sisters. Because economic survival was a struggle, her family took in boarders to supplement their income. Like many middle-class families, they also employed a domestic servant, who lived with the family and helped with the boarders. As an unmarried woman approaching thirty, Lathrop was outside of the traditional pious wife/mother role that Smith tried to fill. Her autobiography and analysis of insanity are marked by this difference.

Whereas Lydia Smith was incarcerated by her husband, Clarissa Lathrop was committed by her mother and sister—on the affidavit of a physician largely unknown to her—because she feared that Miss Hamlo, a boarder in the house and another unmarried woman, was poisoning her. Lathrop believes that Miss Hamlo has invented a false lover who will come and marry her. Lathrop herself is obsessed with a Mr. Zell, a former lover who married someone else after she rejected him. Repenting her decision about him, Lathrop becomes convinced that Miss Hamlo is somehow in league with his wife. Lathrop begins to see Mr. Zell everywhere, to think about him constantly, and to believe that he has divorced his wife and will now marry her if Miss Hamlo fails to kill her first. These beliefs convince her family that Lathrop is insane and precipitate her incarceration.

For a contemporary reader, it is tempting to dismiss Lathrop's suspicions as paranoia and to conclude that she was understandably sent off to the asylum. Such conclusions can lead us to miss the most compelling aspect of this narrative. Whether or not her suspicions about Miss Hamlo are justified, once she enters the asylum, Lathrop begins to live her worst fears of powerlessness. She is forced to take medication, forbidden to communicate with the outside world, abandoned by her family, and threatened with physical restraint, such as the "Utica crib," which both infantilized patients with its name and appearance and terrorized them with its threat of cramped, humiliating confinement. The asylum "cure" enacts the very fears that led her to be incarcerated. Her telling of this story connects her initial suspicions to actual beliefs and acts of oppression within the larger society, especially regarding the treatment of women. She fears being poisoned, an act in which those people she is supposed to trust would take control of her body and harm her against her will. This is exactly what ends up happening to her. The discourse on mental illness and its treatments would advocate that she be locked up, force-fed medication, and forbidden decisions about her own body and own life. According to this discourse, women knew little about what was good for them and needed to submit to the advice of experts.

Lathrop was an indigent patient at the New York State Asylum at Utica from October of 1880 to December of 1882. Unlike Smith, who obtained her release clandestinely, Lathrop secured hers with the help of a reformer, James B. Silkman, who was working with the state legislature to investigate asylum abuses. Silkman managed to release Lathrop and another inmate by obtaining writs of habeus corpus. The difference here between Smith's release and Lathrop's highlights the increasing public interest in reforming asylum abuses in the 1880s and 1890s, an interest that would continue into the next century. Because she was an inmate during this particular period in the Utica asylum, which was the target of several investigations by both press and legislature, Lathrop illuminates in her writing the crosscurrents of thought about insanity in the 1880s and 1890s and the role of professional experts in treating it.

Like Smith, Lathrop relates that her perception of the other inmates shifts radically during the course of her imprisonment. When she first arrives, an attendant tells her to get ready for a walk with the other inmates:

> "No, indeed," I replied, as I looked from the door and saw the motley group arraying themselves in nondescript garments, old hats, hoods, bonnets, and shawls, a rare collection of old-fashioned clothing, which looked as if it had been "through the wars." Thus arrayed, they crowded out of the hall, presenting an odd and grotesque appearance. After they had gone, I again went to Miss Sterling's room, and had a little talk with her, as I felt I must have some one to speak to, and I also hoped that I might be able to understand the situation, in order to know what I could do in order to leave that place. I asked if she would kindly loan me a pen, ink and paper, as I had none with me, for I wished to write a letter. (p. 111)

It soon becomes clear that her efforts to communicate and ally herself with Miss Sterling, an asylum worker, are naive and fruitless. Her first impulse when brought to the asylum is to speak and to write, but she soon discovers that she will not be allowed pen and paper, nor will she be able to converse with anyone considered sane. Eventually she realizes she must walk with the others, though "I felt that by so doing, I was in one sense classing myself with lunatics" (p. 131). Despite her initial feelings, she begins to express more sympathy for those around her, remarking that "I was not at first inclined to talk with my strange companions, and shrunk away from them in undisguised horror and alarm. As I was brought daily in contact with them, and saw their utter harmlessness, I began to divert myself by observing their different peculiarities, even though they were repulsive to me, for I could not remain in this contact with them without having my deepest sympathies aroused for their misfortunes" (p. 129).

Rather than turning to God for help here, Lathrop finds sympathy to be a result of her own daily contact with the other inmates, a contact that she mediates with the distance of an observer who "diverts" herself by watching them "even though they were repulsive to me." Lathrop's asylum experience strains her religious feeling, leading her to ask herself, " 'where is the just God who watches over the unprotected one?' " (p. 132). Packard would claim she found the answer to this question in her writing itself. This approach finds its historical roots in the Puritan captivity narrative in a writer such as Mary Rowlandson. In the captivity narrative, the question would mark the necessary moment of doubt that would inevitably be followed by a revelation of God's greatness. In the sentimental novel, on the other hand, the question would increase the reader's sympathy for the victimized woman whose virtue was necessarily guaranteed by her martyrdom. Lathrop leaves the question of God's role in her experience unanswered. The question stands as an accusation against God and the piety she herself is supposed to express. All three women were writing at a time when repeated financial crashes had shown that middle-class people could no longer be sure of their economic position. Widespread secularization during this period also reflected a greater spiritual insecurity, or at least a search for new outlets. Packard responded by turning to Spiritualism and to a beneficent Christianity. Lydia Smith relied on the Episcopalianism of her upbringing. For a single woman such as Lathrop, who worked as a schoolteacher before her incarceration in order to support her family and who in any case had no desire to "stay quietly at home, a useless and inane member of the household" (p. 10), the pressures to survive both economically and psychically were especially acute. As a working woman, she also had little attraction to the qualities of feminine piety and sympathy that accompanied the picture of woman as wife and mother keeping the hearth.

Lathrop's marginality as a single woman in a sense made her more "modern" than Smith; Lathrop fit into the fin de siècle trend of middle-class women who were moving out of the private home circle and defining themselves more within the "public sphere" of work and activism. This world, which had a place for single women such as Lathrop (Ryan, p. 108), would not be so foreign to her when she later became a working woman and reformer after her release from the asylum.

Not only was Lathrop less interested than Smith in the traditional wife-mother role, but she also maintained a more explicitly secular worldview. Her narrative reveals that once committed to the asylum, as she searched for ways to define herself in what she perceived as an oppressive setting, she looked for a community not as a Christian woman but as a secular political organizer.[6] Like Charlotte Perkins Gilman—who emerged from madness and its destructive treatments to become a radical feminist and social critic—Lathrop did not adhere to the model of domesticity and piety; like Gilman, she came to advocate women's activism based not on the separation of spheres but on a political equality she saw as superceding gender.

By presenting a much more detailed picture than does Packard of their home lives, these two writers illuminate the fact that the nineteenth-century middle-class American family found itself beset by contradictions as the spheres of work and home became increasingly separated in the dominant nineteenth-century American imagination. Dominant ideology held that the male world of work outside the home was rough, unstable, and competitive, while the female world of home was untainted, loving, and cooperative.[7] One problem with this picture was that in reality the domestic scene had never been as separate from the "public sphere" as middle-class Victorians wanted to think. Given that many middle-class families accepted boarders to supplement their income or employed domestic servants, the line between work and home was in reality often difficult to define. Middle-class women especially found their roles confusing because— as in Lydia Smith's case—while on the one hand they were supposed to be submissive, gentle, and pure, on the other they were supposed to be strong and assertive enough to order a household that often included servants, boarders, relatives, and children.

Lathrop shows an intense awareness of the class distinctions intersecting the middle-class home both before and after her commitment to the asylum. She begins her first chapter by identifying and validating herself by her heritage, claiming, "my father and mother belonged to what is sometimes called 'the good old New England stock,'— my father's people were of the old Yorkshire Lothrop-Lathrop family, whose descendants are among the prominent citizens of the United States, conspicuous in pulpit, bar, army and literature" (pp. 93–94). By identifying herself in this way in 1890, when Yankee anxiety about immigrants was paramount and when popular and scientific journals alike constantly debated the nature of heredity, Lathrop was stating her claim to being recognized as above suspicion. This legitimation of her own social position is particularly striking in Lathrop's self-presentation considering that she was admitted as an indigent patient and, despite her middle-class background, would thus most likely be seen within the asylum as lower in the hierarchy than the paying patients.[8]

When Lathrop begins to fear she is being poisoned by Miss Hamlo, the family's boarder, her anxiety is based largely in the fact that she has seen Miss Hamlo interacting with one of the family servants. Writes Lathrop, "What seemed oddest of all was her apparent enjoyment of the society of Lizzie Conlin, the servant girl, for she would often sit with her in the kitchen, usually before and after meals" (p. 38). Her suspicion of Lizzie apparently extends to others of her class, since Lathrop remarks that on one occasion, "I found a party of three or four people, gathered around the kitchen table, who, from their manner and attitude, seemed to be in some secret conclave with Lizzie" (p. 27).

While Lathrop's fear may at first seem dismissible as individual paranoia, it reflects a larger class tension that was often expressed in quite physical terms. As Charles Rosenberg has pointed out, servants often presented an "intrusive emotional reality" in middle-class households, reminding family members of the tenuousness of their class status ("Sexuality," p. 143). The historian Hasia R. Diner has shown that anger and fear of their dependency on Irish servants affected middle-class employers' discussions of Irish immigrants (p. 88). Servants in general were commonly suspected of corrupting middle-class youth. The physician Sydney Elliot wrote of domestic servants, "It seems as if this class took special delight in poisoning the minds of the young and innocent and initiating them into habits of vice" (Rosenberg, "Sexuality," p. 173). It is no coincidence that Elliot chooses poison as his metaphor: it connotes a real physical invasion of the boundaries of the individual physical body as a metaphor for the autonomous middle-class self. Lathrop herself would adopt the same metaphor in her perceptions of how she was being threatened.

Lathrop's anxiety about the lower classes continues into the asylum, where she discovers that "the principle studied was to reduce the whole ward to the same level,—the sane as well as the insane, the refined and cultured, the vulgar and ignorant" (p. 114). She not only mistrusts such leveling but also fears the power that both lower-class attendants and favored patients have over her. She describes one woman who

> seemed perfectly sane, worked in the ironing-room, and was a coarse vulgar Irish woman of the lower stamp. On inquiry I learned that she was placed in the asylum as an insane woman on account of having roasted her two children to death over a

red hot stove. I also learned that she had still an opportunity to exercise her fiendish propensities. She was allowed the privilege of carrying the medicine trays, which were heavily loaded with cups usually filled with drugs, through the ward for the attendants. (p. 115)

Whether or not the story about the Irishwoman is true, it echoes a common stereotype of the Irish servant woman, who was often characterized not only as lazy and incompetent but also as violent. Diner cites one middle-class woman who, in describing her servant Mary McGuire in 1907, claimed that "her mistakes seemed almost diabolical" (pp. 86–88). Lathrop has clearly brought her middle-class prejudices with her into the asylum, prejudices that had to confront the reality that, as a state hospital expected to accommodate indigent and low-income populations, the Utica asylum held a majority of immigrant and working-class inmates in the late nineteenth century (Rothman, *Conscience,* p. 24). She also expresses bitterness about the fact that the superintendent has hired Welsh attendants "on whom he could rely to guard any secrets which he desired concealed, and who would carry out his behests without question, 'might making right' in the eyes of those employees, whose interests he had taken pains to bind so closely to his own by means of mortgaged homes and other interests of a pecuniary nature" (pp. 138–39). She sees an alliance here between immigrant female attendants, all of whom were poorly paid, poor immigrant female patients and the powerful male doctor. These are all forces that she sees as threatening her physical and emotional security.

■

The need of Lathrop and to a lesser extent Smith to maintain distinctions—especially between the sane and the insane—illustrates an intensifying of insecurity and confusion in late nineteenth-century middle-class American culture over whether the individual middle-class self could really maintain its coherence and autonomy. At the same time that they express that insecurity, they experience having it projected upon them as "insane" women. Their very real powerlessness is the lived fear of a middle class struggling to hold onto its distinctiveness and its belief in natural hierarchies. Their lack of control over their lives represents the fear of middle- and upper-class men that they will lose hegemony within American society.

The specialization and professionalization of medicine and accompanying objectification of the body reinforced the idea, fostered under the rapid industrialization of late nineteenth-century America, that the individual was a separate figure operating competitively in the economic and social realms. This competitiveness was further complicated by the fact that as the bureaucracy and corporate structure became more complex, individuals were actually more dependent on each other for survival. In the ideology of individualism, the body no longer expressed the spiritual being to the "outside" world, as it had two centuries earlier, but marked the limits of the individual self and served to defend that self against the violation of its autonomy.[9] The development of germ theory, in which illness was seen as an enemy that attacked from without, usually from the body of another person—just as in the economic realm the financial and job security of the individual could be attacked from without—represented this fear of destructive outside agents. The body became a metaphor for the self, even as it was separated from it; the invading germ represented the threat of dissolution of autonomous identity. Fear of "contagion" referred to both disease invading the body and immigrants invading the cities.

The contradictions inherent in this worldview are apparent in Oliver Wendell Holmes's assertion, as he distinguishes between doctor and minister, that "the habit of dealing with things seen generates another kind of knowledge, and another way of thought, from that of dealing with things unseen" ("Medical Profession," p. 364). The division of spirit from body, of unseen from seen, breaks down within medicine as physical symptoms lead the way to supposed physical causes, which themselves are unseen. When Holmes writes on "The Contagiousness of Puerperal Fever" in 1843, he is unable to name the cause of the contagion (p. 132); in 1891, he claims, "the whole matter has been looked at in a new point of view since the *microbe* as a vehicle of contagion has been brought into light, and explained the mechanism of that which was plain enough fact to all who were not blind or who did not shut their eyes" (*Essays*, xvii). The number of references here to light and vision alone reveals a preoccupation with seeing root causes. In this case the unseen, the microbe, had become visible, explainable, at least to the expert eye. Holmes expresses the medical profession's obsession with making the unseen visible, an obsession that revealed to the middle class that an invisible attacking agent could threaten the personal integrity of the individual.

Even more threatening than the microbe, which invaded the body from the outside, was the unseen hereditary element that resided in the body and appeared seemingly without warning. The hereditary disease was an invisible enemy already lodged within the body.

One of the most widely discussed nineteenth-century hereditary diseases was hereditary insanity. In 1883, prominent neurologist William Hammond quoted Esquirol that "hereditary influence is the most ordinary predisposing cause of insanity" (p. 82). The idea of a "predisposing cause" made insanity even more dangerous because it implied that an unseen element lay latent in the body ready to manifest itself, to reveal the possibly disastrous hidden truths of the self.

Anxiety over the invisibility of the true causative agent was apparent in neurologists' frustration over their inability to locate insanity in physical manifestations in the brain. Writing in 1887, well-known neurologist Edward Spitzka unwittingly showed his confusion in his definition of insanity. At one point, he claims that "Insanity is a term applied to certain results of brain disease and brain defect which invalidate mental integrity. It is inaccurate to state that insanity is itself a disease. It is, strictly speaking, merely a symptom which may be due to many different morbid conditions, having this one feature in common: that they involve the organ of the mind" (p. 17). Conflating the distinction of earlier alienists between brain and mind, he refers to "the organ of the mind," implying that aberrant behavior relates directly to the physical brain. Spitzka's reference to brain "defect," a word that was becoming more and more common in discussions of insanity, further implies that insanity may be due primarily to a congenital structural problem.

At another point, contradicting the assertion that insanity has its roots in brain disease or defect, he writes later that "the views of sound authorities are unanimously to the effect that the connection between the symptoms and lesions of insanity is obscure, and that the cerebral disease underlying insanity is in many cases undiscoverable" (p. 96). Here he asserts his inability and that of other "authorities" to locate the true causes of insanity in the brain, despite the fact that he was confident those causes existed.

Fellow neurologist Hammond similarly contradicts himself, stating in one place that

> a disordered mind is just as surely the result of a disordered brain as dyspepsia is of a deranged stomach; . . . a scarcely appreciable increase or dimunition of the blood-supply to the brain will lead as surely to mental derangement of some kind as an apparently insignificant change of the muscular tissue of the heart to fat will lead to a derangement of the circulation; . . . in the one case there may be a hallucination, a delusion, a morbid impulse, or a paralysis of the will, just as in the other there may be an intermittent pulse, a vertigo, or a fainting-fit. (vii)

Later, he admits tersely that "in the present state of the patho-anatomy of insanity, a classification, based, as it should be, on the essential morbid conditions giving rise to the symptoms, cannot be made" (viii).

Historians of psychiatry discuss the differences among nineteenth-century alienists, but they look less closely at the contradictions that often unite them, contradictions that can give us insights into the ideologies of the period.[10] Like Holmes, both of the aforementioned neurologists expressed a desire to see the physical reality behind the symptoms, in this case to explain what they defined as insanity by referring to visible causes and manifestations. The rising interest of neurologists in the pathology of insanity supports this idea that they sought to identify changes in the brain that would correspond to "defects" in behavior.

However, neurologists' doubts about insanity's primary causes also suggest they were unsure whether they could even draw a distinction between sanity and insanity.[11] Smith voices a common doubt about the etiology of madness when she writes, "impaired health and physical weakness can not alone produce insanity. Persons supposed to enjoy perfect health are very suddenly taken violently insane" (pp. 199–200). In his sensation novel of protest against asylum abuses, *Hard Cash*, Charles Reade—whom Lathrop often quotes in her autobiography— warns his readers, "think of it for your own sakes: Alfred's turn to-day, it may be yours tomorrow" (p. 346). Hammond himself expresses ambivalence about his own definitions, his own ability to recognize insanity, when he remarks, escalating into panic, "There is a large proportion of the population of every civilized community composed of individuals whose insanity is known only to themselves, and perhaps to some of those who are in intimate social relations with them, who have lost none of their rights, privileges, or responsibilities as citizens, who transact their business with fidelity and accuracy, and yet who are as truly insane, though in a less degree, as the most furious maniac who dashes his head against the stone-walls of his cell" (vi).

Given that, as Elaine Showalter has pointed out, to be called insane during this period was to be feminized (*Female Malady*, pp. 3–5), medical explanations of insanity more often than not depended on references to women's bodies and behavior. Insecurity about the predictability of insanity also showed itself in the commonly held scientific belief in "the potency of maternal impressions to affect the shape of the foetal body and its organs" (Spitzka, *Maladay*, p. 84). In this "connate" as opposed to "purely hereditary" insanity, neurologists held that a shock to the mother while she was pregnant could make the child insane in later life (Hammond, p. 77).

Discussions of puerperal insanity, a form of insanity affecting women after childbirth, reinforce the idea that women can be dangerous to the family. In puerperal insanity "unreasonable prejudices against relatives and intimate friends are especially apt to be engendered, and the husband is not infrequently singled out for particular aversion and hatred" (Spitzka, p. 640). In its "acute maniacal form," there occurs "a change in the natural instincts of the mother as to cause her to acquire a feeling of the most determined aversion to the child of which she has just been delivered" (Spitzka, p. 642). Here the woman is a dangerous element; her "natural" feelings as wife and mother become deranged and the family is in danger of dissolving. Interestingly enough, the fears of the afflicted women themselves take the shape of distrust and suspicion, mirroring the larger anxiety over the childbearing woman's propensity to madness. In other words, while it is the woman who is labeled "insane," distrust and suspicion seem to pervade every relationship within the family.

This suspicion marks the extent to which gender and class distinctions within the family troubled middle-class hegemony during this period. As Foucault has pointed out, the nineteenth-century middle-class perpetuated itself through "the interplay of powers and pleasures" in both the family and institutions such as school and asylum (*History of Sexuality*, p. 46).[12] At the same time, this interplay kept the family always in an unbalanced state, on the verge of recognizing the power distinctions operating within it. Such a recognition could be effectively purged through the exclusion of the paranoid individual, such as Smith or Lathrop, who carried the weight of the family's connection to larger systems of power relations, systems in which the white upper and middle classes held privileged positions.

By emphasizing more and more the the biological nature of insanity and its basis in heredity, professionals in the growing field of mental science did their best to appease fear of race, class, and gender equality. Class structure could be maintained in an open economic and political environment by the limitations imposed by biology. Similarly, distinctions between sanity and insanity based in heredity could ensure middle-class families of their privilege and security. Just as middle-class fathers could dissuade their daughters from marrying into poverty, now they could check the groom-to-be's family tree for signs of insanity to make sure his descendants would remain untainted.

As is often the case, however, the very solution unconsciously devised to provide security held a new threat within it. Heredity itself became the secret of which one could never be sure. A preoccupation with the personal or familial "secret"—represented as and representative of heredity—pervaded not only the literature of the period but also professional and popular discussions of madness. "Secrecy" captured the late nineteenth-century popular imagination, as did the idea of unveiling secrets for the public good. The rise of detective fiction, the continuing popularity of the sensation novel in America, and the increase in sensationalistic journalism and investigative reporting all suggest a preoccupation with the hidden story that had to be revealed.

In late nineteenth-century America, insanity came to represent that secret unseen source of destruction that could come from within and against which people had few defenses. Madness threatened both the destruction of the family and of the individual. The conception of "the individual" is predicated on a split between self and other, mind and body, outer and inner, divisions in which the first term is gendered as male, the second as female. Because this split is a construction, a product of social and ideological forces, when those forces destabilize, the self is in constant danger of dissolving. The more the individual tries to assert an autonomous existence, the more he or she is in danger of collapsing.

The mysteries of heredity are so threatening because even as they allow the supposedly untainted individual to create an other—the other race, other mind, other class—that other can suddenly attack from within. The hereditary "predisposition" can always emerge unexpectedly. In popular and scientific writings on madness in the second half of the nineteenth century, we thus find those two contradictory assertions—that heredity can help assure us of our potential to remain sane and that insanity can strike anyone at any time. In popular fiction, that potential for insanity is represented by the character of the madwoman or of the madman whose insanity feminizes him.

This threat to individuality and autonomy had different meanings in the last third of the century, depending on the sex, class, and ethnic background of the individual.[13] White middle- and upper-class men found themselves caught between the ideal traits of autonomy, willpower, and aggressiveness necessary in the business world on the one side and the seemingly deterministic nature of economic forces and the growing hereditarian worldview on the other. It is not unlikely that they then displaced onto white middle- and upper-class women not only the purity and selflessness they lacked in their own lives—as Carol Christ has pointed out (p. 147)—but the destructiveness that lay just beyond their always inadequate willpower.[14]

As a threatening force, insanity was projected onto various identified "others" in American society, most notably African Americans, poor people, immigrants, and, of course, women. Hammond expressed the widely held conception that African Americans were becoming insane in larger numbers since emancipation (p. 121). The historian David Rothman writes that middle-class Americans saw immigrants in asylums as untreatable aliens who were not worthy of improved conditions (*Conscience*, pp. 24–25). An 1886 *New York Times* article entitled "A Burden from Abroad" attributed the recent increase of insane people in asylums to "the shipment of insane men and women to this country from Europe." The writer claimed, "the insane and the paupers stop here. They fill our asylums, and the people must pay for their support. Moreover, a majority of the vicious and the lazy stop here. The additional tax which must be paid for the support of the imported insane and the imported paupers is more than doubled by the other tax imposed by the evil work of the vicious and the lazy" (*NYT*, Mar. 21, 1886, pp. 1–3). In conflating paupers, insane, vicious, and lazy, and seeing them as a drain on the "American" taxpayer, the writer betrays his fear of difference, which he identifies with invasion from without. In language that describes these "others" as if they were goods, the writer also make them objects of one-way exchange in an economy of scarcity, an economy in which imports threaten the well-being of native producers. A late nineteenth-century paranoia behind the writer's words shows itself when he describes the immigrants as "imported," a word which requires an actor, a villain who is perpetrating this destructive importation of goods, or at least allowing it to continue.

I have discussed in the previous section how women were identified with insanity in nineteenth-century America. Where the middle-class male self was perceived as autonomous and individualized in the increasingly competitive economic sphere, the female self was defined in relation to the family (Ryan, 113–19; Barker-Benfield, pp. 336–37). Women represented both the source of connectedness unavailable to men and the cause of male loss of connectedness. In the discourse on the decline of the native middle-class white American family, women were cast as the responsible parties both biologically and morally. Middle-class women were supposedly upsetting the natural order by entering the paid work force, promoting divorce, and going to college—all activities that were seen to damage their reproductive capabilities and lead to insanity.[15]

William Hammond supported the idea that women were especially prone to insanity when in a chapter on sex and its relationship to insanity, he devoted fifteen pages to discussing women and one paragraph to discussing men. This is especially interesting in the light of the way he begins this one paragraph: "Notwithstanding all these [aforementioned] factors, which are only effective in the female sex, there are others acting with so much greater force on males as to cause insanity to be much more common in them than in females" (p. 117). He then enumerates the causes of male insanity, including "the cares incident to providing for a family, the anxieties and wear and tear of mind connected with business and other affairs of the world, and, above all, excessive indulgence in the use of alcoholic liquors and of the sexual organs" (p. 117). In contrast, he ties the causes of female insanity not to outside influences, but to the very physical realities of female constitution, especially to what he describes as the dangerous influences of menstruation and menopause. His perception that more men become insane because of their activities and responsibilities, while women, who are less often affected, go insane because they are women, implies that women represent the threat, the embodiment of insanity.

∎

Not surprisingly, in nineteenth-century sensation fiction the representative holder of the "secret" whose discovery usually ends the novel —whether madness or something equally destructive—is almost always female. This is especially ironic given that it is the often male author who holds the power to disclose or guard the secrets of the narrative. As classic other, however, the woman is the one who invades and brings destruction to the family or the self. As I discussed earlier, madness itself is usually represented as feminine in nineteenth-century literature, so that even if the insane character is male, he is usually a feminized man. Thus Richard Hardie, whose mental stability is questioned in Reade's *Hard Cash*, gets headaches "like a girl" (p. 19) and Mr. Fairlie in Wilkie Collins' *Woman in White* preens himself as a woman would (pp. 38–39). In any case, it is usually a woman whose surface is suspect—to men, to other women, and often to herself.[16]

In nineteenth-century popular and medical literature, the female body became the essential seen that could not be trusted; it hid the unseen, destructive element, the microbe, the hereditary, degenerative "taint" (p. 89). Spitzka supported a widely held idea when he claimed that "the chances of the transmission of insanity are greater if the mother is mentally affected than if the father is insane" (p. 82). This reasoning led men to displace their fear of self-dissolution onto women, while women often feared both themselves and the women around them. It also meant that—especially as American society became more competitive and financially unstable—the middle-class family might fear the foreign element within itself, the individual member who could destroy the unit.

Oliver Wendell Holmes's novel *Elsie Venner*, whose title character is a dangerous young woman whose mother was bitten by a rattlesnake while pregnant with her, connects women to poison in ways that reverberate in Lathrop's story. Holmes is ambivalent about whether Elsie's will is "poisoned at its very source, so that it shall flow dark and deadly through its whole course" (p. 435), or whether it conceals "folded up in the depths of her being, a true womanly nature" (p. 432). Yet a "true womanly nature" seems itself to be basically poisonous, according to Holmes. He relates that Elsie once tried to poison a governess, using "unlawful means, such as young girls have been known to employ in their straits, and to which the sex at all ages has a certain instinctive tendency, in preference to more palpable instruments for the righting of its wrongs" (p. 193). Young girls' desire to poison those who displease them is here seen as "instinctive" rather than alien to their "true womanly natures."

It seems likely that the "something not human looking out of Elsie's eyes," the "something" that both is and is not a part of her womanhood, represents a displacement of a wider split in late nineteenth-century dominant American consciousness between what Holmes called "a longing for sympathy" and "the impossibility of passing beyond the cold circle of isolation" surrounding the individual self (*Elsie Venner*, pp. 434–35). That "something" emerges not just in one fictional woman character but in a wider discourse that holds that what seems to fulfill that need for sympathy—most often, woman—can also threaten destruction and death. The most threatening women are the mother—who can pass on her poison—and marginal figures such as the spinster—who, like Elsie, is untempered by love for a man; her poison in a sense feeds upon itself.

Not surprisingly, both Smith and Lathrop pinpoint other women within the family circle as the true culprits in their incarceration, showing that women themselves internalized distrust of other women as bodies harboring unseen purposes. Smith relates that she was originally committed by her husband with the help of a young female boarder, "the demon of the household," with whom he was in love, and "the cloven-footed sister-in-law" (p. 182), who "was the cause of all the trouble of my married life" (p. 185). She describes the boarder as deceptive:

> It was astonishing with what ease and grace she would glide from one degree of iniquity to another without being suspected. She was so angelic she would deceive the very elect. She was so childlike, so innocent, and dependent. She would get your sympathy only to wound you. Her manner was very affectionate toward me for a time, and never having heard anything derogatory to her private character, she won upon my regard and affec-

tions for a while, until I began to see through the mask she wore: but it was then too late to remedy the evil. (p. 183)

While Smith may here be telling the truth of her perceptions, she is also describing a type of woman well-known at that time in popular literature—the "angelic" woman who seemed "so childlike, so innocent, and dependent," but who in reality was cunning and deceitful. The clearest example of this type is Lucy Graham in Mary Elizabeth Braddon's 1862 English novel *Lady Audley's Secret*, which went through numerous editions and was widely read in America throughout the last third of the nineteenth century (Hart, p. 122). In this novel, Lucy explains her attempts to murder her husband as the result of an inherited insanity. Braddon's description of Lucy is strikingly similar to Smith's words about the boarder, even though one comes from fiction and one from autobiography. Braddon writes:

> Lucy was better loved and more admired than the baronet's daughter. That very childishness had a charm which few could resist. The innocence and candor of an infant beamed in Lady Audley's fair face, and shone out of her large and liquid blue eyes. The rosy lips, the delicate nose, the profusion of fair ringlets all contributed to preserve to her beauty the character of extreme youth and freshness. She owned to twenty years of age, but it was hard to believe her more than seventeen. Her fragile figure, which she loved to dress in heavy velvets, and stiff, rustling silks, till she looked like a child tricked out for a masquerade, was as girlish as if she had just left the nursery. (p. 35)

We find out soon that Lucy Graham—Lady Audley—is not at all what she appears; beneath her surface childishness is a murderess interested only in maintaining her place as a lord's wife.

For Lathrop, the female culprit is not a seemingly innocent young woman, but the spinster Miss Hamlo, also a boarder in the home she shares with her mother and sister. Lathrop describes her first impression of Miss Hamlo after the boarder moves into the house:

> Miss Hamlo was, I now saw, a woman of about thirty or thirty-five years of age, of angular figure, rather over medium height, with a coarse sandy complexion, light blue expressionless eyes, and most peculiar hair,—what I should call "Judas color"—not sandy, hardly red, but a something approaching an unnatural yel-

lowish red, which she wore in false waves and puffs on the top of her head. Her voice was peculiar and exceeding disagreeable, having a kind of rasping, nasal or cracked sound suggesting the idea of catarrh, or the tone one sometimes detects in one when saying something which they know is not true, which gives a peculiar insincere intonation to the voice, easily detected by a student of human nature. She was dressed in an old-fashioned black silk, and immediately proceeded to make herself entirely at home. (pp. 33–34)

While her surface is certainly different from that of Smith's boarder, Miss Hamlo here appears full of insincerity and falseness. Her eyes are "expressionless" giving no clue to her true interior self, her hair is "Judas color" and "unnatural"—worn in "false waves"—and her voice has a "peculiar insincere intonation." Most important, she "[makes] herself entirely at home," becoming that foreign element that takes up residence within the family. Lathrop suspects Miss Hamlo of pretending she is engaged when she is not and of trying to poison her.

The truth of her suspicion, which is impossible to determine, is less important here than the fact that Lathrop perceives Miss Hamlo as a certain type that held sway in the nineteenth-century popular imagination—the spinster, who was either devout, modest, and pure, or bitter, scheming, and unnatural. The spinster was common fare in the nineteenth-century sensation novel. Wilkie Collins' popular novel *Woman in White* features two such characters, both described as unnatural. Marian Halcombe's "expression—bright, frank, and intelligent—appeared, while she was silent, to be altogether wanting in those feminine attractions of gentleness and pliability" (pp. 29–30). Where Marian is frank and respectable, if strange, Anne Catherick is a madwoman who shrieks without warning and claims to hold the key to a mysterious, dangerous secret. Her power is connected to her mystery, just as in Coleridge's "Christabel" the witch-like Geraldine's power is connected with hers. Where Marian is ultimately circumscribed by the patriarchal world, Anne in her madness exists on the margins of that world, controlled only by incarceration in the madhouse.

For Lathrop, Miss Hamlo's dangerousness is clearly tied to her status as spinster. Both autobiographers support what Helen Waite Papashvily has said about American domestic novels—that as the century progresses, plots focus less on the struggle between man and woman than on the conflicts between woman and woman (p. 150).

Like many middle-class women, Lathrop responds to male displacement of fears onto women by shunning the marginalized women around her. When she fears being poisoned by Miss Hamlo, she reacts to an image of spinsterhood made clear in the dominant cultural vision—an image that could all too easily become herself. Similarly, it is no coincidence that among Lathrop's first impressions of the asylum is an Irishwoman who supposedly roasted her children over a hot stove and now carries the trays of medicine of which Lathrop is so suspicious. In Lathrop's eyes, this immigrant woman whose female nature should lead her to nourish others instead threatens to poison them.

Ironically, by embodying a more general fear of poisoning, the insane woman became the victim of poisoning. Asylum inmates were routinely given drugs against their will. Both women describe the widespread terror in the asylum that if inmates do not take drugs voluntarily they will be forced to take them (Lathrop, p. 217, 192; Smith, p. 189). Hammond acknowledges that chloral hydrate "is used extensively in lunatic asylums" (p. 749) in the late nineteenth century; historians of psychiatry verify that drugs were used as a matter of course in most asylums (Rothman, *Conscience*, p. 37).

The increasing use of drugs as opposed to "moral treatment," which was based in environment, suggests that Americans dealt with their sense that they were not in control of their physical bodies by controlling the bodies of the insane, especially of insane women. After all, the physical body could contain "special influences which work in the blood like ferments" (Holmes, *Elsie*, p. 228). Smith and Lathrop express how it feels to be the targets of this control. They often feel powerlessness within the asylum, where they are vulnerable to intrusion in the form of drugging, beating, and rape. Both writers describe incidents where doctors or male attendants raped young female patients, and Lathrop claims that she herself was drugged and raped repeatedly. She also tells about several other cases in which young women became pregnant while in the asylum (p. 210–14). Aware that her reader may be skeptical, she acknowledges that "horror-stricken with the disclosure, and perhaps convinced of the truth of her statements, the fond relative goes to the doctors with her tale of wrong, only to be assured by them in a careless and contemptuous manner, (as

Dr. Grey stated before the Legislative committee of 1884) that 'such a belief is the most common delusion of insane patients' " (p. 215).

Lathrop's accusation echoes the concerns of other reformers. For example, in the euphemistic understatement typical of the period, law professor Emily Kempin urged in an 1891 meeting of the Woman's Legal Education Society, attended by Dr. Mary Putnam Jacobi and Dr. Emily Blackwell, that female asylum patients should be attended by female physicians (*NYT*, Dec. 10, 1880, p. 3).

By assuming positions of narrative authority in their autobiographies, Smith and Lathrop enact in their narratives the fear and enjoyment of both their own power and the power of other women. We see the fear as they vacillate between feeling omnipotent and powerless— the two sides of the popular image of women in general and insane women in particular. Smith claims that she was manipulated and deceived into entering the asylum by the two women in her household, women who held power over her life. Once she is in the asylum, where her sense of powerlessness is intensified by her inability to exert control over her own situation, she begins to move back and forth between feeling that the asylum doctors are conspiring to kill her and that— with the help of God—she has superhuman power to save her own life. One night when she hears the furnace explode, she asks herself, "Did they intend to burn the whole asylum to get me out of their way: Could it be they would sacrifice the whole building with its inmates just to get rid of one troublesome patient?" (p. 66). She is terrified that the asylum doctors are intent on killing her. At times, however, she expresses confidence that she is unkillable. When she hears the doctor plotting outside her door, she speaks to him through the keyhole: " 'No, Sir, you can't kill me; do your worst. God is mightier than thou art, and He will defend me. He is able to strike you dead this instant. He will not let you kill me. Your evil deeds will certainly fall upon your own head; and if you send me poison to drink it shall not harm me. If you prepare any sharp instrument it shall not hurt me, for the Lord has promised to defend me and espouse my cause, because I have trusted in Him and believe in His name' " (p. 64).

With this biblical invocation of divine power, Smith places herself in the position of God's chosen one. Now it is the asylum officials who have cause to fear, given that her text casts them in the role of evil-doers.

This sense of potency is important in the narratives of Smith and Lathrop; it also differentiates them from the sensation novel, in which the madwoman, while powerful, is ultimately removed from the social world recreated in the narrative. Mary Elizabeth Braddon ultimately relegates Lady Audley to an asylum, describing her as a "wretched woman" (p. 279) and her actions as "my lady's wickedness" (p. 286). She is not one of "the good people" whom Braddon leaves "all happy and at peace" (p. 286). She is rather a foreign element that disrupted family peace and that now has been removed for the good of all. The fear of family and individual dissolution has been displaced onto her, so that now the story may have a happy ending as the family is constituted anew.

In contrast Smith's and Lathrop's narratives do not provide us with the sense of closure we find in the popular sensation novel, which always leads the reader to expect resolution of conflict and the reconstitution of the family. Lathrop especially was aware of this popular novel tradition, a fact which she makes clear by her continual references to Charles Reade's *Hard Cash*. In this widely read attack on the private English insane asylum, young Alfred Hardie is committed to an asylum by his father, who wishes to gain control of his money. In the end, he vindicates himself in a trial, marries his sweetheart, and lives his life happily ever after with his new family. The specter of "hard cash," which seems to be at the root of moral evil, ultimately fades before the power of justice, family loyalty, and the manipulative hand of the author.

Both *Behind the Scenes* and *A Secret Institution*, on the other hand, all too obviously lack explanations and fail to bring families back together. Lathrop never reveals the true motivations and desires of Miss Hamlo and Mr. Zell. Lathrop's autobiography ends with her in the role of a woman alone in the world who must fend for herself. She makes explicit to the reader her inability to wield authorial power to make the longed for narrative connections:

> I pondered continually upon the discrepancy of statements in regard to Mr. Zell, some of which must be true, and those which my knowledge of the truth taught me must be false, and I puzzled my brain to harmonize the discordant elements which still existed, and which possibly through legal advice he felt obliged to sustain. How easy I thought these enigmatical ques-

tions could be answered while shut away in my cruel prison! Now upon my release after so much time had elapsed, I found that I could not establish facts without great expense and legal complications. I had no money to pay a detective, and after all my bitter experiences, I could not be positive that if I employed one, the party in possession of the greatest amount of money, might be benefitted, not myself;—and to gather up the loose threads and weave them into a continuous and unbroken chain unaided, seemed a task which I was powerless, under existing circumstances, to perform, as they were broken off so suddenly by my hurried incarceration, with the apparent object of thwarting any idea I might have of convicting the guilty, or tracing their identity or whereabouts. However, I resolved to discover what I could. (pp. 328–29)

As she "[puzzles her] brain to harmonize the discordant elements," she seems like a disappointed reader of her own narrative. Unlike Reade, who produces a detective to unravel the story, Lathrop is unable "to gather up the loose threads and weave them into a continuous and unbroken chain." Not only does she feel powerless to accomplish such a feat but she also fears that the reality of "hard cash" is insurmountable. As a woman marginalized by both her poverty and her categorization as insane, she is forced to confront the limits of her authorial control.

This difference between the two autobiographies and the popular novel highlights the question of how paranoid the writers really are. Both Smith and Lathrop demonstrate a kind of paranoia in their suspicions of those around them, but a passage such as the one above leads the reader to look rather at the paranoia inherent in the very act of creating a narrative fiction. D. A. Miller has pointed out that the novel is perfect for the paranoid modern reader because it provides a place of safety from which to watch the conspiracy plot unfold (p. 116). Reade, Braddon, Collins, and other novelists create characters whose suspicions are virtually identical to those expressed by Smith and Lathrop—fears about poisoning, conspiracy, deception— and nineteenth-century readers in England and America bought their books by the thousands. Lathrop's failure to resolve her suspicions points to a nineteenth-century middle-class paranoia that expressed both a desire to see connections and patterns in a fragmented society and an anxiety that none existed. The resolved novel writes fragmentation into wholeness by justifying the narrator's suspicions of a deviant "other," excising that "other" from a now known and comfortable world. Lathrop and Smith each challenge this narrative gesture by being both narrator and "other."

Writing in the 1880s, Edward Spitzka introduced "paranoia" as the new rubric for "monomania," which had formerly been broadly defined as the obsession with one subject, often religion. What Spitzka was describing was really a new disease in which "the occurences in the outer world are anxiously examined by the patient with a view of tracing their connection with himself" (p. 314). In their failure to resolve the fears and suspicions they introduce, Lathrop's and Smith's texts reveal that societal hierarchies reasserted by the sensation novel are really constructs. The autobiographers' paranoia thus shows itself as not so different from that of the reader, who has been seduced by reading expectations into a promised confirmation of his or her own place in a world sanely and naturally ordered according to gender, class, race, and other categories. Neither Smith nor Lathrop provides this confirmation.

In both autobiographies, the narrators themselves express a fear that the structures they were raised to trust—familial, legal, medical—may be rotten to the core. Both Smith's and Lathrop's feeling that family members are plotting against them continues when they are in the asylum, an institution which, as I mentioned in the previous chapter, was seen in the first half of the nineteenth century as structured on a family model. In Smith and Lathrop, that sense that the asylum should be like a trusted family is clearly changing. Where Packard expected Dr. McFarland to be her protector as if he were her husband, Smith and Lathrop see asylum officials as family-*like* people who should be trustworthy and helpful in their expertise, but who in reality violate ideals of family trust. Smith conceives the asylum as being somewhere between a family and a city. Listing all of the workers employed there, she writes, "You see, it was quite a city of itself. If Vandusen had been a shah he would have had quite a harem" (pp. 206–7). In its connection to the asylum-city, this family has become what by nineteenth-century American standards would have been seen as exotic and deviant—a harem. Given that the analogies of asylum to family and doctor to husband/father were still in circulation at this time, with the "harem" image Smith appropriates a stereotype of a foreign and supposedly immoral family structure to reflect back upon both American family and American asylum. The image collapses male political, sexual, and familial power in a way not available in the dominant discourses on both family and asylum, which mask the intersections of power and sexuality in those two institutions.

Smith rebels against this control when she warns her readers of the dangers of trusting the asylum superintendent:

> He has the appearance of being a gentleman in every sense of the word. He has the appearance of being deeply interested in the welfare of your daughter, and you have no reason to doubt his word. Has he not been employed by the wise and good men of our State? Then why should you doubt him? It is a hard thing to think a person who appears so courteous and gentlemanly, so sincere and sympathizing, a man who has the semblance of goodness itself—can be evil disposed, can be anything and everything except what he has the appearance of being. (p. 115)

As in Robert Audley's case in *Lady Audley's Secret,* it is up to her to take the reader "behind the scenes" of this world, to destroy the idealized image of asylum as family. When she urges her reader to think about the daughter entrusted to the superintendent, she invokes the specter of the smooth-talking man with nefarious designs on the young, innocent, middle-class girl.

Smith's description of the "night of terror," in which, she claims, the superintendent and his accomplice try to kill her, shows that although she is afraid that any security she has will be penetrated, she will continue to strategize in her own defense. When she hears someone outside her room, she

> hastily took the stand, and as quietly as possible put it against the door. I took out the bureau drawers and put them on the stand; then, putting my hands through the space where I took the top drawer from, I lifted the bureau back against the stand, then taking my water-proof cloak and an old dress and flannel skirt, I rolled them tight together and wedged them in the ventilator. I then got down and carefully lifted the head of the bed against the bureau, being careful not to make a noise. (p. 43)

Her room here becomes the outer shell of her physical self; she adjusts the furniture just as she strategizes mentally to protect her bodily self. She fears that the authorities will enter the room or release poisons into it through the ventilator to harm her, just as she fears they will inject her with deadly drugs, confine her to the "Utica crib," or beat her. More important, however, her blow-by-blow suspenseful description of the confrontation reveals her desire not only to show that she resisted but also to gain narrative control over the events she recounts.

Like Smith, Clarissa Lathrop continues to distrust appearances after she has been committed, fearing conspiracy in the asylum as she feared it at home. While she is with her family, she distrusts the "outward harmony" that "reigned in the household," just as Braddon has us distrust the surface calm of Lord Audley's estate. Lathrop constantly reads the surface to try to discover hidden meanings. She watches Miss Hamlo closely, asking herself, "Could it be that any one was trying to poison me, or to make me sick? If so,—whom? What object could any one have in so doing? Could it be Miss Hamlo? Did she desire to keep me home for company for her, or had she a sinister motive? Suddenly like links in a chain, every circumstance of her sojourn with us came up before me" (p. 50). Like a detective in popular fiction, Lathrop tries to piece together the circumstances around her. At this point, however, she feels powerless to discern the secrets around her. She questions whether this other woman wants to keep her company or destroy her.

Once in the asylum, Lathrop, like Smith, distrusts the doctors. When she first meets Dr. Blumer she describes him as having "dark blue eyes which were concealed by glasses, and an open-mouthed expression, half wondering and half sinister" (p. 109). Like Smith, she complains that abuses occur within the asylum that go unnoticed by investigators. She claims superintendents "prevent any action that would interfere with their supreme power in the control of the asylums, thus rendering each asylum a *secret institution*, where all the crimes and abuses which we imagine existed only in the dark ages can be repeated without fear of detection, and which are almost invariably concealed behind asylum bars, as the bold exposer can be easily denounced as 'deluded' or 'insane' " (p. 182). Secrets are hidden in the asylum, she claims, as powerful as the family secrets that are so difficult to uncover.

Both Smith and Lathrop express a consciousness that those who control the secrets are those with "supreme power," the authors, as it were, of the institution. Both narrators are in the position of being characters in someone else's novel—a Marian Halcombe or Robert

Audley—who are caught in a conspiracy. Both Smith and Lathrop are characters, however, who seek to gain narrative power, to become the authors of their own stories.

The cost—or perhaps the benefit—for Smith and Lathrop of rewriting the conventional ending so that social and familial order remain in disarray is that they leave us with a sense of discomfort, an inability to locate them or see them as having well-defined identities. Where Braddon casts Lady Audley as evil and reconstitutes the family solidly without her, Lathrop and Smith leave us with their undiscovered secrets and divided families. Their texts occupy that place where social order and identity can fall apart. In this respect, these autobiographers contrast explicitly with the mainstream American literary tradition, in which the deviant woman dies—Hester Prynne in *The Scarlet Letter*; Zenobia in *The Blithedale Romance*; Isabel in *Pierre*; Elsie Venner. Lathrop and Smith end with their own voices, alive and very difficult to categorize.

The only resolution provided in each autobiography is the narrative itself, which, despite its incongruities, becomes an act of connection that tells the story of each writer's particular asylum experience. In its effort to connect writer to reader, the autobiography both enacts and replaces each writer's paranoia. In its incompleteness, the narrative points to each writer's limitations as narrator and thus makes explicit the traditional fictional narrator's impulse to control events and insist on closure, an impulse that thrives on an illusion of omnipotence and omniscience. Thus even as they at times construct an omniscient narrator who can provide the reader with an objective reality, they end with the impossibility, and danger, of such a project. When Smith's and Lathrop's texts make us see the limits of their narrative power, they suggest that the omnipotence of the traditional narrator reenacts that of the asylum superintendent or any other force that tries to create and control a world.

# 4

## *"The Hidden Things of Darkness Shall Be Brought to Light"*

■ Lathrop's feeling that she was left "with no one to appeal to for help or redress, with no escape, no refuge,—powerless to protect myself" (p. 212) led her to make "the solemn vow, 'that if the Lord would spare my life to leave that horrible prison, I would devote the rest of my life, if necessary, to the cause of the insane, particularly those of my own sex" (p. 213). Her feeling of powerlessness leads her to identify with insane women as a class, giving her a more public sense of identity than that with which she entered the asylum.

Despite the fact that their confinement made Lydia Smith and Clarissa Lathrop more isolated from the world, their position in a public institution, the "city" of the late nineteenth-century asylum, gave them a greater awareness of the competitive public realm and ultimately a stronger sense of their own ability to act in the world and to shape a reality through narration than they had had previously. Their writing itself, as well as their action to reform insanity laws and policies, supports this point.

At the same time, the techniques of a rapidly developing mass culture provide them with strategies for crafting their experiences for consumption by a nonexpert reading audience. On the one hand, as I discussed in the previous chapter, the sensation novel served as one model for exciting stories of madness and captivity, stories likely to appeal to a reading audience hungry for romances and adventure tales. On the other hand, the methods of new journalism and realist fiction enabled them to counter the expert knowledge of neurologists and asylum superintendents with their own empirical observation, attention to detail, and insistence that with these techniques they could construct an indisputable reality. To the extent that they assume the position of objective journalists recording reality, Smith and Lathrop adopt a "masculine" stance, one in which the personal, marked as feminine, can simply be set aside or denied. As Smith and Lathrop move in and out of the realist mode, they risk mimicking the voice of male neurologist or asylum superintendent, a voice that can objectify "the truly insane" and posit its own reality as the only one. The autobiographical strain in each work tends to disturb this masculine stance with its feminine assertion of personal subjectivity, as does the implicit reference to the sensation novel with its emphasis on emotion, crisis, and internal conflict.[1] The realist voice balances delicately as it both legitimates the reality it creates and then retreats before a personal voice describing the narrator's own reactions and emotions.

■

As with Elizabeth Packard, their experiences in the asylum lead Smith and Lathrop to develop a sense of a social and political world surrounding and intersecting the domestic one. For both women, the asylum experience transformed and expanded their vision of societal and familial relations, giving them a sense that they were part of a complex web of interactions going beyond their private lives. Smith does express nostalgia for a past family life she may never have had, a life of unity and domestic happiness. She asks, "would it not be the desire of my heart above all things else to unite the hearts so long severed, that our family might again be united in one?" (p. 218) The image of a united family continued to hold sway for her, occupying a dominant place in her writing and providing the most conspicuous metaphor for her vision of a just world. Her autobiography ends with poems about family life, one of which laments, "Oh, how lone and sad my heart, / Far from home and kindred dear" (p. 244). Here, she places herself partly within the genre of advice manuals that instructed men and women about how to live healthy, moral lives, manuals that were the product of what Jackson Lears has described as an increasingly secularized therapeutic culture (pp. 47–58).[2] When she concludes her narrative with advice to husbands, wives, young women, and young men—telling them to respect each other and "let your first consideration be the good of your own household" (p. 196)—she echoes the writing of such women as Eliza B. Duffey, who claimed in 1873 that "the one institution most sacred in all the world is the family; and the abiding place, the retreat, the altar of the family is the home" (p. 109).

However, Smith acknowledges that in the reality of her life after her release, the family unity she longs for is impossible. Both her daughter and her brother, who would have supported her financially and emotionally, die unexpectedly, so that "aid was cut off from every quarter where I might expect it, and there was no other alternative but to rent, and seek employment in order to sustain myself" (p. 181). Smith does remarry, but she devotes only two brief sentences to this occurrence (p. 181), placing much greater emphasis on her status as "a working woman" (p. 219) speaking "to secure the greatest possible amount of good to this unfortunate class of people" (pp. 225–26)—the insane. She acknowledges she is not alone in this effort, remarking that "a committee visited me after my return home, and told me if I would commence suit against that institution they would sustain me; that their farms and every dollar they had was at my command, and should go before such an outrage should go unpunished" (p. 225). She further includes a "letter from a lady patient of the Kalamazoo Asylum," who addresses her as "my dear sister in affliction" and tells her, "with your assistance I intend to bring them up standing; for if a premium were to be awarded to the two greatest villains in the United States, VanDeusen and Palmer would carry it off for their villainy" (p. 232). By including this letter, she shows that while in the beginning she distrusted the women in her family life, now she has appropriated the idea of "sisterhood" (as did many nineteenth-century feminists) to create a sense of common cause with other women in the asylum.

While Lathrop never completely abandoned a romantic fantasy that a man would transform her life, she ultimately embraced more fully than Smith an involvement in the larger asylum reform movement, which became a source of identity for her. She writes, "I had resolved from the time of my release, that I would never borrow a cent from one of my relatives, and I am happy to say that I was not obliged to break this resolution. The miles I walked in order to avoid doing so, and the efforts I made in different directions, I will not recount" (p. 314). Discovering that "the inexperienced laborer has a hard and bitter struggle to sustain life" (p. 315), she lives in poverty for several years as she works as a "lady artist in oil" (p. 315), a self-taught stenographer, a typist, and a social welfare worker in a settlement house.

Once she has left the asylum, Lathrop is again forced to confront the limits of her narrative power. When she decides to conceal her asylum experience in order to gain employment and a place in the community, she becomes a frustrated author unable to tell her story:

> Oh, the long, weary years, filled with patient toil and study! Work, work was my motto, and above all,—*no time to think!* Thought pursuing me must be fought away. I must banish the past and all its associations, crush back the cruel memories that brought with them so much anguish, sorrow and despair! . . . How often I have longed for some Lethe to still this anguished heart, to destroy this blighting memory which overpowered me with its crushing weight. To wear a smile and work with feverish avidity to drive away the pursuing recollection and the knowledge of the baffled purpose, the isolation and loneliness in the crowd of a great city. (pp. 324–25)

Here she must deny the story to herself; memory, which is a source of identity and connection with the past, is only a blight if it cannot be acknowledged as part of her present life. While her decision to keep silent is itself an act of narrative control, it only represents the lesser of evils. Ultimately this decision only leads to "isolation and loneliness."

Eventually, through working and especially through supporting the cause of the insane, she begins to redefine herself from being a daughter, sister, and teacher, who works to support her family, to being an independent woman who lives alone and works for a larger cause. By speaking publicly for the cause of the insane and by writing her autobiography, she begins to create a new set of connections within herself and with those around her. She describes this transition when she relates her appearance before the 1883 investigating committee of the state legislature: "It was a trying position to me, who had never before appeared in a strictly public position; still, my heart was so full of sympathy for the poor sufferers and enthusiasm for what I hoped would be an effective attack upon the asylum, which would result in securing aid and relief to the poor patients, that I forgot about my own feelings or personality, and was surprised to learn that I had spoken an hour before the committee and a large number of auditors" (p. 303).

When she forgets her "personality," she both transforms her former sense of identity as someone who could not speak in public and loses her feeling of isolated individuality. She establishes a two-way connection here: on the one side she resurrects her asylum story and the links with the asylum community that it enacts; on the other side she creates a connection between herself and her listening audience. By speaking and being heard she acquires a sense of authorial power.

Her words reverberate with the experience of many late nineteenth-century women reformers who were entering the "public sphere" on the tide of their feminine "sympathy" for suffering (Ryan, pp. 198–205). She speaks at a time when many middle-class women were redefining themselves as actors or potential actors in the public realm (O'Neill, p. 252; Ryan, p. 108).[3]

For Smith and Lathrop, their experience in the asylum politicizes their view of the world. While in the asylum, both writers—in different degrees—become highly conscious of the relationships between the superintendents and legislative agencies; they become aware of how much money is spent and on what, how and when the asylum is visited, how the inmates' labor is used, and how the doctors are perceived in the outside world.

For example, Smith proposes that the Michigan public has misplaced its trust in superintendent VanDeusen. Applying her own sense of domestic economy to the administration of this public "home," she claims that "with proper management this institution would be self-supporting. Three hundred and ninety acres of land belongs to the asylum grounds, which, if properly cultivated, would furnish no small item. Then there are all the county patients, which each county has to support, say nothing about the private patients who pay from five to ten dollars a week" (pp. 132–33). She goes on to refer her readers "to the appropriation laws of Michigan—1869–70, page 170, No. 63" (p. 133), laws with which she herself is clearly familiar. She itemizes and criticizes the appropriation of large sums four years in a row for the addition of a north wing. In "a more trifling circumstance," she points out, VanDeusen sold damaged cotton prints to the patients "at 12½ cents per yard, when good prints could be bought retail for 10 cents a yard" (p. 134). The mis-management of public funds becomes the focus of her effort "to show the character of this man" (p. 134).

The two writers' consciousness of the public realm expands during and because of their stay in the asylum. Most important, they educate themselves about the legal details of their commitment and connect themselves to the lay movement to gain control of and investigate insane asylums. They thereby retain a strong faith in the popular will and the power of democracy. Smith begins chapter 14: "To the People of the State of Michigan: come, let us reason together. Let us look at this asylum question in its true light. Let us who pay our money for the support of this institution demand that it be conducted on the same principle the law makes provision for" (p. 212). Smith claims that Dr. VanDeusen "would like to become a great personage, where he could control the will of the masses. But he can't do that in America" (p. 207). She contrasts what she sees as his despotism to the popular will that she sees as a basic American principle. Like Packard, she uses the rhetoric of the American Revolution as it was used by abolitionists and, more recently, women's rightists, to argue against the power of the expert.[4]

Her belief in individual rights and popular will emerges again when she discusses VanDeusen's mismanagement of the asylum and misuse of public funds. She asks, "to whom does this institution belong? To the people who are taxed, who pay their hard-earned money to support it. Have you any idea how much it costs us yearly to support this institution? The Lansing Reports will show the appropriations granted; but there are other considerations separate from these. I think you would be not a little astonished to know the amount it costs yearly" (pp. 132–33).

Smith has gone from being a frightened, physically ill wife and mother "unable to attend to my domestic duties" (p. 185) to a public reformer who has informed herself about current appropriations laws and who, like many middle-class women reformers entering the public realm in late nineteenth-century America, now applies her "housekeeping" skills to management of public institutions (Ryan, pp. 202–3; Smith-Rosenberg, p. 264).

Speaking from her experience of imprisonment, however, Smith goes beyond the typical woman reformer in her overt criticism of the expert and her appeal for lay management of asylums: "And I am convinced that these institutions will never be what they should be until the people take it in hand and make them such. These sinks of impurity will never be made what they should be until the people get awake to the fact of just how they are conducted. They need an overhauling and thorough investigation; they need ventilating" (p. 112). Through "ventilation," the very means that Smith feared was being used to poison her, she hopes to open up the asylum to public scrutiny, airing the secrets that it holds, secrets that the public wishes to know.

While Lathrop has always considered herself as more of a public figure than Smith has, identifying herself from the beginning as a teacher wanting to act in the public realm, her sense of her role in the world of organizations and reform movements increases dramatically in the asylum. She becomes an avid reader of the newspapers, and it is through reading the *New York Times* and other papers while in the asylum that she becomes aware of the asylum reform movement and currently debated ideas about the insane. She writes, "Previous to my leaving the second ward, I had borrowed of Miss Sterling a *New York Times*, and, on looking it over, to my joy I saw a long article descriptive of a new society that had just been organized, which was denominated 'A Society for the Protection of the Insane and the Prevention of Insanity.' I could not cut out this paragraph, but I read it over carefully and copied the names of the officers which I had put away for future emergencies" (p. 141). Because of this article, she clandestinely initiates correspondence with the society and after later articles becomes aware of the actions of a New York State Senate investigating committee in asylum reform (pp. 176–77).[5] In order to take these steps, she has necessarily come to identify herself as part of a class—those imprisoned as insane—an identification that gives her strength to act.

Like Smith, Lathrop initially trusts that the popular will acts in her benefit, and she advocates public control of the asylums, berating what she calls the "one man power" (p. 181) of the superintendent who "knows he is accountable to no one for his abuse or neglect of duty, his conscious supremacy having a tendency to create indifference on his part, even in regard to revelations by the public press" (p. 181).

Much more than Smith, Lathrop shows an acute awareness of the press and the power of publicity. She refers throughout her narrative to newspaper accounts of asylum investigations and of her own case. For example, she remarks that Dr. Brush, one of the asylum physicians, "was severely criticized by the press for his unwarranted opposition to my release" (p. 287). She also reacts strongly when she feels the press is being used against her:

> in order to place me in a false and unpleasant position with the public at the time of my release, Dr. Grey caused his answer to the writ of habeus corpus to be published in full in the Utica paper with a view to impress the public with the idea that I was legally committed to his asylum, as he swore in his answer that I had been, and still was as insane as when admitted to the asy-

lum, (which was true in point of fact). Not satisfied by forcing my
private affairs into court, and finding their laudable efforts to fix
any scandal upon me futile, Dr. Brush caused his own report of
the trial to be published in the Utica papers, containing as much
as possible of what he thought might reflect unpleasantly upon
me in my unfortunate but innocent complication with Mr. Zell.
(p. 306)

It is not insignificant that her preoccupation with publicity is tied to
her sense of propriety and her "complication" with Mr. Zell. As she is
writing, the question of the appropriateness of women's acting in the
public sphere was still being hotly debated (Smith-Rosenberg, pp. 258–
63; Haller and Haller, pp. 33–38). By connecting herself to the issue of
publicity, Lathrop in a sense tries on the public realm, experimenting
with public identity. She recognizes here that when she allows someone else to construct her public identity by narrating her story, she
further loses power over her own life.

She clearly ties the issue of publicity to the question of propriety
in her autobiography. After James Silkman has served Dr. Gray with a
writ of habeas corpus to obtain her release and then gone public with
the story, Lathrop spars with Dr. Gray:

"You have kept me all this time. I am sorry you have forced
me into this publicity, but I must have my liberty, and if I cannot have it without, then I must meet it."

"Do you wish to have it said that you wished to marry a married man?" asked Dr. Grey, catching at the idea of perhaps sham-
ing me into a withdrawal of my efforts for release.

"If you chose to betray to the public my private affairs which
you have learned from my letters, and twist them to suit your-
self, I am ready to meet you, and if you oppose me on the charges
I was placed here on, I will meet you there." (p. 269)

Later Gray chides, "It is better to say you are insane than bad"
(p. 269). The public becomes a third actor in this drama, an actor
who was present in Packard's work primarily in the form of the
reader. While McFarland and Packard discuss morality itself, Gray
here claims it is not necessarily worse to *be* bad, but to *say* you are
bad. For a nineteenth-century woman, the threat of publicity, let alone
of negative publicity, could well be used to dissuade her from action.

The nineteenth-century woman reformer, however, was often as entranced by publicity and its call both to act and to identify with a larger popular will as she was frightened by the threat of exposure. Always in danger of threatening middle-class women's "sensibilities," Lathrop walked a thin line between offending and attracting her female readers with shocking material.[6]

Besides, in an era when sensationalism of all sorts was becoming increasingly popular, Lathrop could count on the newspaper-reading audience at least being interested in her "private affairs" in a way that could ultimately work to her advantage.

Lathrop's awareness and use of the press reflects the fact that by the end of the nineteenth century the press had become a crucial part of American life. From 1870 to 1900, daily newspapers increased six times over, from 387 to 2,326. Circulation rose from 3.5 to 15 million. In addition, newspaper machinery became more sophisticated and the extension of the railroad and telegraph speeded up production. Journalism also became more of a force because after the Civil War the population as a whole became more educated; from 1870 to 1900, the number of public school pupils increased from 6.9 to 15 million, and colleges and universities expanded as well (Kobre, pp. 350–56).

Many of the independent newspaper publishers, editors, and writers that emerged in this post–Civil War era of "new journalism" dedicated themselves to exposing corruption and promoting what they described as the good of the common people in the face of monolithic corporate and political structures (Budd, 30). With increasing sensationalism, they sought to expose everything that needed exposing, whether it was political corruption—as in the Tweed ring brought to light by the *New York Times* in the early 1870s—or crime, or abuses in prisons and asylums. The exposé became the piece of the period, as reporters became detectives searching out the "real story" (Kobre, pp. 401, 357, 383; Mott, pp. 414, 436). The importance of revelation is clear in Charles A. Dana's 1866 claim that the new *New York Sun* "will study condensation, clearness, point and will endeavor to present its daily photograph of the whole world's doings in the most luminous and lively manner" (quoted in Kobre, p. 368). In line with the "realistic" trend of the age, Dana was interested not in telling stories in beautiful, eloquent language, but in condensing the language in order to convey a clear "photograph" of what "really" happened, to shed light on what was previously covered up.

The issue of the public's right to know, even through deceptive means, became foregrounded in the papers' discussion of what had been discovered. This was especially true in the case of asylum abuses, such as beatings and even murders, which were discussed constantly in the newspapers in the last third of the century.[7]

For example, in 1887, Elizabeth Cochrane, who was popularly known as Nelly Bly, one of the first American women reporters, feigned insanity in order to be admitted to Blackwell's Island Asylum, where she spent ten days doing research for the *New York World*. Cochrane discovered firsthand not only that the patients were poorly treated, but that, once imprisoned, a sane person such as herself had little hope of release. She wrote, "From the moment I entered the insane ward of the Island, I made no attempt to keep up the role of insanity. I talked and acted just as I do in ordinary life. . . . The Insane Asylum on Blackwell's Island is a human rat-trap. It is easy to get in, but, once there it is impossible to get out. I had been shut off from all visitors, and so, when a lawyer came and told me I was finally leaving, I was overjoyed" (quoted in Rittenhouse, p. 105).

While other papers may have cringed at Cochrane's success in pulling off her investigation, they nevertheless used it to support the idea of investigative reporting and to further question the judgment of asylum experts. For example, the Norristown, Pennsylvania, *Times* commented, "the investigation was not only a neat piece of journalistic enterprise, but it may lead to reforms which will be for the decided advantage of the insane" (quoted in Rittenhouse, p. 108).

The role of newspapers in exposing asylum abuses emerges clearly in Charles Reade's novel *Hard Cash*, in which supporters of the wrongly incarcerated Alfred Hardie finally go to the newspapers, claiming, "Justice is the daughter of Publicity . . . cast the full light of publicity on this dark villainy; and behold it will wither, and your oppressed and injured fellow-citizen be safe from that very hour" (p. 528). In her preoccupation with newspapers, then, Lathrop tied her own writing into a larger movement that on one level exposed asylum abuses and on another gave precedence to the public eye—represented by the journalist—over expert knowledge. In the publications of a mass culture, both Smith and Lathrop saw possibilities for telling their stories and finding an audience that would be all too willing to doubt the official descriptions of the insane put forth in professional journals. They were able to tap into the market not only for sensation fiction but for new journalism and realist fiction that found its subject matter in class tensions and other forms of oppression.[8] When Lathrop refers to her own methods of empirical observations, she adopts the perspective of the realist novelist recording the facts of the world. Amy Kaplan has pointed out that realism came into being at a time when middle-class Americans were experiencing a deep sense of unreality due to "intense and often violent class conflicts which produced fragmented and conflicting social realities, and the simultaneous development of a mass culture which dictated an equally threatening homogenous reality" (p. 9). For Smith and Lathrop, themselves categorized as unreal, the position of realist recorder and observer enables them to legitimately construct the details of stories that will then be read as reflecting reality. From the nonbeing to which they have been assigned, they appropriate the omniscient and thus transparent (invisible) perspective of the realist narrator.

■

The techniques of realist fiction and journalism—empirical observation, the distant narrative voice, recording of detail—allowed the nonscientist to take the position of scientist. Asylum autobiographers like Smith and Lathrop could use these techniques to add their voices to the late nineteenth-century debate over who should really be controlling asylums and the treatment of the insane.

As the historians Barbara Sicherman, Bonnie Ellen Blustein, and others have pointed out, American neurologists headed the crusade to abolish asylum abuses in an effort to prove that specialists in neuroscience understood more about the pathology and treatment of mental disease than did asylum superintendents, who rarely had any specialized knowledge or training. Neurologists such as Hammond, Spitzka, Edward Seguin, and other members of the New York Neurological Society used the press to put forward the idea that asylum superintendents were often backward in their medical thinking. In fact, in 1878, Hammond charged John P. Gray, asylum superintendent at Utica, where Lathrop was interned, with allowing abuses such as physical restraints and beatings within the asylum. The debate between the Neurological Society and the Association of Asylum Superintendents —begun around this time—was one of the first medical controversies to play itself out in the public press (Blustein in Scull, p. 256). When Lathrop questioned Gray's mismanagement, she was echoing the skepticism of the Neurological Society and of the National Association for the Protection of the Insane and the Prevention of Insanity (NAPIPI), which neurologists founded with lay reformers, the same association that Lathrop turned to for help after she read about it in the newspapers. Spitzka wrote in 1878 about a New York State asylum that "the work there done is not only without value, but absolutely misleading; that the claims advanced are founded on that happy combination of effrontery and ignorance, which currently passes under the designation of, and is certainly kin to, charlatanism; in short, that the State has paid $50,000 for what is little better than the private advertisements of one medical superintendent" (quoted in Blustein, p. 246).

In fact, it is likely, given Lathrop's own theories about the causes of insanity, that she was familiar with the neurologists' belief in organic causes and their conviction that insanity should be treated as any other disease. Writes Lathrop, "In an acute form of typhoid fever when the patient is called delirious, the disease is understood and the cause located and no one calls such a patient insane, because it is known that on the disappearance of the fever the mind will resume its former vigor; so it is with insanity, which the most prominent alienists attribute to disease alone" (pp. 184–85). But while she claims that "a consciencious and able physician" (p. 185) might be able to cure the patient, one sentence later she denies the need for expert knowledge, maintaining that asylum superintendents "[debar] regular practitioners from knowledge which is quite as necessary to the people at large as the treatment of a broken limb, resuscitation from drowning, etc., knowledge which concerns the well-being of every human being living, it is time these barriers that obstruct public scientific knowledge of insanity were torn away!" (p. 185). Her language here seems ambivalent. Does she want "regular practitioners to take care of the insane" or does she think everyone should know about the cause and treatment of insanity? What is "public scientific knowledge"?

Her words here suggest that the neurology-asylum superintendent debate went well beyond an argument over professional territory. The voices of the lay public, which was often ambivalent about what it wanted from experts, engaged both groups of professionals, often siding with neither. At the time Lathrop was writing, the public's desire to know was beginning to make itself felt in the mental hygiene movement, which, while depending still on the advice of experts, sought to give nonexperts power over their own health. Lathrop's words point to the often neglected debate within the public press between neurologists and superintendents on one side and the non-expert voice on the other.[9] For example, on August 18, 1884, the *New York Times* published an editorial describing the case of Mrs. Weldon, an Englishwoman who had recently conducted a "lawsuit for damages because of a false charge of insanity."[10] The writer claims that this English case should warn Americans about how "the law may be at once obeyed and broken, and the consequent danger to innocent individuals who may have 'fads,' but who do not deserve to be treated worse than common thieves" (*NYT*, Aug. 18, 1884, p.4).

On August 21 of the same year, Edward Spitzka wrote a letter to the *New York Times* expressing distress about "the ridicule to which the opinions of the medical men in the Weldon case are treated." Citing the editorialist's dismissal of Mrs. Weldon's belief that her dog had a soul as a reason for her commitment, Spitzka counters, "Permit me to say that if a patient were brought to me tomorrow who imagined she heard voices which had no real existence, and for which there was no basis, and who believed that she exhaled a 'halo' or any other mysterious, luminous, or magnetic influence, and I found the general mental complexion usually coinciding with such beliefs, I should strenuously urge the commitment of such a patient to an asylum" (*NYT*, Aug. 21, 1884, p.4).

Here Spitzka, who usually uses the press to criticize asylum superintendents and their lack of scientific knowledge, reacts against the suggestion that "the opinions of medical men," no matter who they are, are questionable. Spitzka's letter is doubly revealing because it points to a theme underlying the split between expert and lay claims to knowledge—the split between religion (marked as feminine) and science (marked as masculine) in an increasingly secular age.

In Packard's writing, we saw that while her belief in Spiritualism was questioned, "religious monomania" was to some extent still an accepted category whose boundaries were open to debate; in her report on the trial to determine her sanity, her religious beliefs were taken seriously and even shown to be progressive compared to the Calvinism of her husband and some of the asylum directors. By its very existence as a category, "religious monomania" suggested a line between sanity and insanity that was not so easily definable. By the last third of the century, however, neurologists such as Spitzka were relabeling "monomania" as "paranoia" and engaging in an all-out war on religious groups, such as Spiritualists, that tried to unite science and religious faith (Shortt, p. 345). As James Turner has pointed out, while in the early nineteenth century many people saw in science support for their religious faith, in the 1870s and 1880s the scientifically minded increasingly claimed that science and religion should be kept separate and that, more important, material proof of God's existence was an impossible dream (pp. 171–79). According to Spitzka, Hammond, Beard, and other neurologists, anyone, such as Mrs. Weldon, who saw material manifestations of the spiritual realm, was probably insane and best locked up in an asylum.

Of course the nonexpert public was also becoming more secular during this period, so that even some religious groups were adopting a language of science, as both Spiritualism and rapidly growing Christian Science demonstrate. Perhaps more important, many people became interested in a different, more secular kind of revelation—the revelation not of inner faith but of outer truth in the material world. Where Smith still believes in God's truth Lathrop writes less of inner faith than of the "revelations by the public press" (p. 181). It is no coincidence that when Spitzka referred to the "luminous" influence that deluded Mrs. Weldon might feel, he was echoing the words of Charles Dana, who sought to promote the "luminous" character of journalism. Spitzka may have suspected both kinds of luminosity—the first for being evangelical, the second for being spiritual in the name of objective observation.

The discourse of journalism combines references to revelation with a scientific preoccupation with evidence and objective truth. Both Smith and Lathrop appropriate this combination of qualities in their language. For Smith, the religious element is explicit: "God has promised that the hidden things of darkness shall be brought to light. A woman who had been a patient there, told me she had prayed for years that the inequity practiced in that institution might be brought to light. I could tell you many things which I have heard—said to have transpired within those walls; but I shall tell the reader nothing but what actually transpired under my own observation, and to which I will testify any time I am called upon to do so" (29–30). Here, Smith brings together spiritual revelation, exposure of the institution, and use of evidence based on careful observation.

■

By connecting discourses of objective observation and religious truth, the writings of Smith and Lathrop unmask the preoccupation with morality that informs the diagnostic categories and explanations of mental science.[11] As they separated themselves from religious concerns, late nineteenth-century neurologists actually became increasingly interested in defining the causes and symptoms of socially inappropriate thinking and behavior.

By identifying mental illness as a hereditary disease with organic causes and manifestations, neurologists threw into question the relationship between mind and brain, suggesting that an insane patient had no more responsibility for his or her actions than a physically ill person had for his or her sickness. The anxiety over the nature of moral responsibility and the spiritual self played itself out in the courts as expert witnesses testified against each other to help juries determine whether criminals were insane or not and, if so, whether they were responsible for their actions. The debate exploded particularly over the trial of Charles J. Guiteau, who assassinated President Garfield on July 2, 1881. Lathrop read about the assassination and trial in the papers and threw her own voice into the debate, giving us a sense again of another perspective besides those of the conflicting doctors who examined the defendant.

As Charles Rosenberg has described, Guiteau's trial, which resulted finally in his conviction and condemnation to death, largely played itself out through the conflicting opinions of John Gray and Edward Spitzka (Rosenberg, p. 74). In the debate over Guiteau's "moral insanity," a condition in which the moral sense supposedly became deranged but the intellect remained intact, Gray maintained that no individual could relinquish God-granted moral responsibility, while Spitzka held that no one could be called responsible for actions committed because of a hereditary, biological condition (Rosenberg, pp. 68–74).

Lathrop's account of the trial is enlightening in that it suggests that the asylum community responded with interest and often indignation to the news of the assassination and Gray's role in the trial, demonstrating that the women on Lathrop's ward had a sense both of their relation to political events and of Gray's power to tell the story of insanity. She writes,

> The news spread rapidly on the ward, and we were allowed the daily papers to read the particulars of the tragedy, and the details attendant upon his death. Later the account of the investigation as to the sanity of Guiteau, which I selected from the old

papers sent to the asylum from the newspaper offices, especially the expert testimony given in that famous trial, was read by me with unceasing interest, particularly that of Dr. Grey, the supposed wonderful insanity expert, who was called upon to testify in this celebrated case. With what bitterness I read his carefully expressed opinions of the sanity of the prisoner and his definitions of insanity, and how I hated and despised him more and more as I read the elaborate and detailed reports! I felt, however, that this trial was a great source of education to me, situated as I was and having the objects of study before me daily, in fact brought into constant contact with them. (pp. 244–45)

Here, Lathrop places herself on the same level as Gray, claiming that as an observer of and participant with the asylum inmates, she knows more about them than Gray himself, who "confines her indefinitely in his own institution which he never visits, and where he knows nothing whatever of what takes place within its walls, unless he visits it in the night, when we are unconscious of his presence" (p. 245). Unlike the unincarcerated observers of the case, Lathrop is less concerned with Gray's definitions themselves than with what she sees as his double standard in applying them. She tells herself,

Dr. Grey can go to Washington to see a man like Guiteau, and can testify to his belief in the sanity of an unfortunate man who commits a murder without any particular provocation, a man evidently of impaired perceptions, because he receives a large sum from the Government for so doing; but a helpless patient who was kidnapped and trapped into his asylum, because she made repeated efforts to protect her own life and that of her family from any possible danger, he calls insane. (p. 245)

Lathrop takes a minority view here, disagreeing with the almost unanimous public voice that supported Gray and criticized Spitzka (Rosenberg, *Guiteau*, p. 185). By agreeing with Spitzka that Guiteau was largely the victim of heredity and circumstance, she disassociates herself from the insane, the "objects of study" she mentions above. She becomes the observer, the distant narrator of realist fiction, the case of mistaken identity, the sane among the insane. She realigns herself with the insane as a class, however, when she ironically attacks Gray as the expert witness who has not been "brought into constant contact" with the insane, as she has.

In this sense, she also aligns herself with Spitzka's critics and all those who question the authority of the specialist. As Rosenberg points out, in the 1880s, after Guiteau's trial, the expert witness as called by either side came increasingly under attack. Despite her agreement with hereditarian, biological theories of insanity, she questions the validity of the testimony of an expert hired by one side of the case. She might agree with a front-page *New York Times* editorial: "Two men, of equal eminence and equal pretensions, cannot come to diametrically opposite conclusions upon the same data in any branch of knowledge that deserves to be called a science. This has occurred in the examination of Rhinelander, it occurred in the trial of Guiteau. It is tolerably sure to occur in every case where the sanity of a man is in question and each side has money enough to hire witnesses who will swear that they are experts" (*NYT*, Aug. 30, 1884, pp. 1–2).

Lathrop sees the position of the expert witness on insanity as connected more to relations of power than to the conclusions of an objective science. Her words challenge—from inside the asylum—the attempts of both neurologists and asylum superintendents to claim the power to interpret behavior.

For Lathrop, the publication of details of Guiteau's trial was only a mask for the real story of Gray's relations with the insane. She wanted to be granted the moral responsibility that Gray insisted belonged to Guiteau and that Spitzka denied him. In either case, she saw no place being given for her version of her own story.

It was almost as if, in late nineteenth-century American dominant culture, madness, and especially female madness, had become a stage where the Calvinist notion of innate depravity played its last lines opposite neurology's increasingly self-confident positivism. What in the seventeenth century was labeled innate human sinfulness in the nineteenth had become the evil and mysterious secret never quite revealed and almost always represented as feminine. The actors in the drama were never quite sure which parts to play, as discourse identifying the madwoman as evil and unfathomable was interwoven with pronouncements on the deterministic nature of heredity and circumstances. In 1895, Charles Lock wrote of the hysterical woman, "morbid thought and morbid impulse run through the poor, weak, unresisting brain, until all mental control is lost, and the poor sufferer is . . . at the mercy of . . . evil and unrestrained passions, appetites and morbid thoughts and impulses" (quoted in Smith-Rosenberg, p. 205). The hysterical woman was a "poor sufferer," but she was also subject to "evil" passions; she was in a sense possessed, taken over by evil. But, as Carroll Smith-Rosenberg points out, doctors often considered the hysterical woman responsible for her condition in that she had lived a life whose "purpose is too often an indefinite and self-indulgent idea of pleasure" (quoted in Smith-Rosenberg, p. 205).

If the hysteric was evil and mysterious, the institutionalized madwoman was doubly so. It was the mystery of her story that led the *New York Times* to publicize the case of Nelly Bly before they knew she was an impostor, titling their first article "A Mysterious Waif: Bellevue Shelters A Girl of Whom Nothing Is Known" (Sept. 26, 1887, p. 8). While neurologists attempted to explain female insanity in strictly scientific terms, they too often seemed to describe rather than explain, ultimately contributing to the idea that the insane woman was a mystery. For example, in his *Treatise on Insanity*, Hammond gave six extended examples of young girls who went insane after beginning menstruation, elaborating on their strange behavior without really showing its somatic connection to puberty (pp. 105–10). By referring to "the exaggerated desires, the eccentric appetites, the inexplicable aversions, and especially the instinctive perversions" of these girls, he emphasized that their unfathomable behavior could lead to "the perpetration of criminal acts" (p. 105).

When Lathrop objects to John Gray's denial of Guiteau's insanity, she reveals the ambivalence behind Gray's philosophy, an ambivalence that has directly affected her own life. Speaking from a traditional Calvinist belief system, Gray insisted that Guiteau was responsible for his criminal act, but he denied Lathrop responsibility to decide her own life, claiming that as a doctor he could label her insane. The autobiographies of Lathrop and Smith—like that of Packard—foreground the contradictions in scientific discourse that were often obscured in more mainstream writings. While the discourse about mental illness increasingly stressed scientific approaches, Lathrop and Smith experienced not treatment of their illness but punishment of their "bad" behavior, especially when that behavior entailed trying to seize the power of narration. After Lathrop is caught trying to send a letter, she reacts, " 'Oh, Pity me!' I cried. I flew forward, seized the letter from the gentleman's pocket, and seeing an attendant after me, ran and threw it where it could not be found. I then went to my room to ponder over the utter failure of my last attempt, and the consequences that must follow, as I knew some punishment would be inflicted and I naturally dreaded the result. I had not long to wait" (p. 193). Her fear that if caught weeping she would be diagnosed as melancholic also shows that she thinks the label of insanity is a punishment in itself. She experiences the label as chastisement because it denies her own voice.

Lathrop's fear of punishment highlights the conflicts inherent not only in Gray's more old-fashioned religious understanding of insanity but, more important, in the more modern ideas of neurologists who saw mental disease as an inherited ailment that could attack both conscience and intellect. In *Insanity in Its Relation to Crime*, written in 1873, Hammond maintained that while an insane person could not control the disease, he or she must nevertheless be held responsible for crimes, for "even if actual cerebral disease be the cause of the irresistible impulse, it does not materially detract from the right of society to protect itself against injury from those in whom it exists" (p. 73). In a seemingly uncharacteristic assertion that the insane should be able to control any criminal impulses, Hammond tellingly remarked that "every superintendent of a lunatic asylum knows that many of his worst patients can be improved in their conduct, mind, and character, by being rewarded when they deserve commendation, and punished when they have incurred censure" (p. 60).

Hammond's confusion about the nature of moral responsibility points to the fact that while neurologists on the one hand defined those they called insane in physical terms—thus making them other, different, closer to animals than to humans—on the other hand they described them in moral terms, as behaving badly and violating social morality. The punishment that Smith and Lathrop receive thus comes in direct response to their attempt to break out of the definition of femininity that the asylum is trying to enforce as a return to normalcy. They learn to survive by adopting a mask of femininity; they behave submissively, deferentially, passively, industriously—whatever they need to do to survive and avoid punishment. But like Charlotte Perkins Gilman's insane woman character in "The Yellow Wallpaper," who sees herself creeping through the lines of the wallpaper and finally across the open grounds of her house, they clandestinely work within another reality, struggling to escape their imprisonment.

Like the superintendent's demeanor, the surface of asylum life is deceptive. Smith claims that despite the visits of investigative committees, "the outside world knows nothing of the treatment of their insane, of the 'life behind the scenes' " (p. 122). She explains that the doctors show the committees only the best wards and that "it is represented that all the wards are furnished just alike, and that the patients all fare just the same. This is a falsehood to begin with" (p. 123). She claims that in an investigation during the years 1869–70, when charges had been leveled against the institution, thirty physicians visited the asylum, but were shown "just such portions as were fitted up expressly to be seen" (p. 129). They were supposed to speak with every patient, but "when Dr. Palmer showed [two men] through the hall where I was, he went through so fast that the young men had to almost run to keep up with him" (pp. 129–30).[12]

The fear and hatred of deception that Smith experiences lead her to try to read external circumstances to discover their inner meaning. Once she begins to learn what authorities expect of her, she begins to control her own behavior, to present an appearance that will correspond with the expected reality within the asylum. She adopts the double consciousness of the oppressed, in which on the one hand she acts the part required to maintain her own survival and on the other she remains aware of a different reality, a reality made possible largely by her identification and communication with others of the same class—not the insane, necessarily, but the inmates of the asylum. We might say that she becomes the author of her own actions; she no longer lives her life unconsciously but constructs it so that it will be read in a particular way by those around her.[13]

Lydia Smith describes the necessity of acting the part assigned to her in order to gain an advantage. She claims that when questioned by one of the doctors, "I spoke so pleasantly and candidly, and looked so indifferent, as though I thought nothing of the past, so that, with all his skill and penetration, he could not detect the true state of my feelings" (p. 86). Her strategies of self-presentation are continuous with those needed to protect herself physically. Throughout her descriptions of victimization, she focuses on her calculated efforts to control her own life.

She goes on to describe the methods she needed to adopt in order to escape:

> I had to use more strategem than a general would to win many battles, for this reason: I was a prisoner, without the means of defending myself; I possessed no weapons but my hands and my

tongue. I knew those two members were useful. But I must be very careful how I use them. I must be discreet, must be wise, not appearing to be so; must feel my way along carefully, and, more than all, must stoop to do things distasteful to me. I must act a part. I must flatter [the doctor's] vanity. I must seem not to remember the past, or only as an insane freak, and think it all a delusion. I would be cheerful, and even gay, and tell them how much their treatment was helping me, and praise their skill. Every opportunity that presented itself to me I would take advantage of in one way and another, just as the circumstances called for. But above all, I must flatter them. (p. 87)

Smith tries to simulate wellness by "acting a part," adopting the feminine role, in which the woman acts cheerful, praises the male doctor, and seems grateful for the "treatment" she receives. Significantly, her only "weapons" are her hands, which enable her to write, and her tongue, which allows her to speak. Her newly acquired strategies are those of the narrator, who controls—at least to some extent—the discovery and repression of secrets. In this sense, she is like Lady Audley, whose feminine graces are a mask, a strategy for survival. Like Lady Audley, she must suppress her own past reality, her own fears and suspicions because mentioning them will only support the diagnosis of her insanity. While this act of suppression silences her, it also gives her authorial power.

Like Smith, Lathrop writes of the need to maintain a calm appearance in order to confront the expectations of those in charge. She remarks, "I had seen enough to learn that it was not best to allow any one to see me weep, lest it might be said in addition to their former absurd statements, that I was a victim of melancholia. I consequently studied a calm appearance, and said little of my repressed feeling to any one" (p. 125). Lathrop consciously "represses" a part of herself in order to present a surface wellness.

It is through this need for narrative construction of their lives that they come to believe—in differing degrees—that a narrow culturally defined femininity is a mask that they may choose to wear, but that they will not have forced upon them after their release. Smith will speak publicly for the cause of the insane as she could not speak within the asylum. Like many late nineteenth-century reformers, she will redefine her femininity to become a public crusader in the name of maternity and female virtue. Lathrop, on the other hand, will pre-fer the path that Gilman chose, rejecting marriage and motherhood in favor of economic and personal self-sufficiency.

By donning strategically the mask of sanity (which is also, for women, a mask of femininity) and making their readers co-conspira-tors in this deception, they challenge their readers and perhaps them-selves to see sanity as a collection of social codes and posturings read and misread by those with medical and judicial authority. Even as they use the strategies of realism and reporting to establish a reality, their acknowledgment of these masks prevents the reader from forgetting that reality is always described by someone in a particular social posi-tion at a particular time and place. That someone may be wearing a mask—of femininity, sanity, or something else—and shaping reality according to where he or she stands and how he or she perceives the listening audience.

Clarissa Lathrop and Lydia Smith recognize that control over who describes reality potently sustains the social order. Nevertheless, as Lathrop's resolution to "discover what I could" suggests, they work to tell the stories they know. In this sense, both texts represent the point at which social change is possible, the point where someone labeled insane, in this case, calls attention to both the limits of a narrative voice and the power of that voice to shake the ground under the asy-lum.

# Part 3

## The Prescribed Autobiography

# 5

## "A Human Being Had Turned Beast"

Self-alienation and Subjectivity
in Jane Hillyer's *Reluctantly Told*

■ The early twentieth century saw a shift in both the reception and presentation of autobiographies by former inmates in mental institutions. Beginning with Clifford Beers's widely acclaimed autobiography, *A Mind That Found Itself*, these narratives began to appear with introductions and addenda by psychologists and psychiatrists who presented the texts as evidence of both their professional ability to cure the patient and the wonders and terrors of mental illness as experienced from the inside. While the reforming impulse that was primary in Packard's, Smith's, and Lathrop's texts was still present in Beers's autobiography, the primary interest of both lay and professional readers was in Beers's own psychological journey. In a letter that Beers includes in the final pages of his book, William James remarks, "As for contents, it is fit to remain in literature as a classic account 'from within' of an insane person's psychology" (p. 199).

In his introduction to Marian King's 1931 narrative, *The Recovery of Myself*, prominent psychologist Adolf Meyer uses the autobiography to promote expert opinion on the use of confinement for the mentally ill. He claims, "The means of safety for the protection of the patient are being disguised, but the prejudices linger. There are demands to eliminate all the obnoxious features and many efforts to do so, but often enough these accentuate the unpleasantness and hardships for those for whom the protections become finally inevitable" (vii). According to Meyer, King's autobiography is valuable because it shows the public the good in psychiatry and the success of expert ideas, acted out in the course of the narrative. Over the course of her treatment, King "became socialized, a participant in the hospital world, and finally capable of seeing herself as the physician sees her, with a growing sense of proportion and perspective" (x). Her "cure" is enacted in the narrative itself, which ends when King declares, "So from vital experience I can testify to the modern miracles being wrought by the new revelations of psychology and its practical applications in psychiatry" (p. 147).

As her title, *Reluctantly Told*, suggests, Jane Hillyer is more ambivalent than Beers or King about revealing her inner struggle. Hillyer is clearly less allied with those who have institutionalized her. To the extent that her title links her back to earlier women writers who claimed to tell their stories only out of duty or necessity, it suggests that her would-be benefactors in psychiatric publishing have not quite appropriated her story. Her narrative thus moves uncomfortably between self-exploration and social protest.

Nevertheless, as with Beers's and King's autobiographies, Hillyer's is presented to the reading public by professionals in the field of mental illness. In his introduction to Jane Hillyer's well-received work, which was published in 1926, the neurologist Joseph Collins stresses that her book is "a contribution to the understanding and plumbing of mental disorders" and "a contribution to literature" (x). He sees it as useful not only for "the personnel of institutions for the insane," who "will find in it information and encouragement, possibly even a tiny bit of reproach" (x), but for laypersons who "have a vast amount of misinformation" (xii) about insanity. Ignoring the fact that Hillyer's text contains a great deal more than "a tiny bit of reproach" and that the first section focuses on her chagrin at being placed unknowingly behind a locked door, Collins uses her narrative to point out that "it is regrettable that the first step in the proper treatment is to deprive the patient of his liberty and that to accomplish it we have to evoke the law" (xiii–xiv). In other words, he presents her narrative as support for the decisions and practices of psychiatrists, as a kind of tool for mediating between laypersons and professionals in the discussion of insanity.

The use by James, Meyer, and Collins of these autobiographies is more than a public relations effort, however. It reveals psychologists' growing interest in the chronology of a patient's illness. Adolf Meyer claims that a scientific and useful psychology relies not on the structure of a mind but on the "story" of a life. Writes Meyer, "A renewed call for the cultivation of both story and abstraction under the rule of adequate experiential, and finally experimental, enactment of the story is the concerted hope of culture and of science" (*Psychobiology,* p. 33). The story of the mentally ill individual, then, can be both the object of scientific observation and the "experimental enactment" of the patient's cure, the fulfillment of the physician's story about the patient. While the psychologist's "story" helps shape the lives of both male and female patients, it is especially questionable in its application to women's lives given the long history of the scientific and literary objectification and oppression of women.

The new interest in asylum autobiography also reveals the spread of ideas about mental illness beyond the walls of the institution and the domain of pathology into a wider concern about mental health, or, as it was then called, "mental hygiene." Begun by Clifford Beers, psychologist Adolf Meyer, and other laypersons and professionals, the mental hygiene movement stressed that mental illness could be prevented by active attention to laws of mental health, laws promoted by experts who increasingly concerned themselves with the healthy as well as the sick (Rothman, *Conscience,* pp. 305–10; Sicherman, *Quest,* pp. 281–86; Horn, pp. 82–83).

The link between the growth of mental hygiene and its germination and expression in the autobiography of someone institutionalized as insane is crucial because it illuminates a redefinition of the mentally ill as not so different from "normal" people. On the one hand this redefinition further contained women's stories of institutionalization by normalizing the whole topic of mental illness; on the other hand, it enabled women to write narratives about their experiences where fifty years earlier writing itself had been seen as dangerous for the institutionalized woman patient.

The new focus on narratives of mental illness also showed that as both laypersons and professionals came increasingly to question the somaticist explanations of neurologists that described the brains of the insane as constitutionally different and defective, they became more explicitly intrigued with the nature of consciousness and personal identity.

As we have seen, middle-class Americans in the nineteenth century were already preoccupied with the nature of selfhood: the popular concept of the insane woman and the expert's need to control her represented a widespread middle-class fear of a boundaryless self, a self that could lose all sense of autonomy, unity, and social propriety. In the early twentieth century, however, this obsession with the structure and function of consciousness became more self-conscious, more explicit.

In the dissonances between Hillyer's and Beers's narratives, we can hear the anxious preoccupation of early twentieth-century psychologists with childhood, the unconscious, and the nature of identity. William James explicitly rooted the definition of personal identity in the Lockean idea that personality is determined by the connections of memory.[1] The idea of the unconscious, with which James was also fascinated, when brought together with this definition, clearly made identity seem unstable, divided. That James was not the only one perturbed by this unsettling idea is clear in the popular fascination in the late nineteenth- and early-twentieth centuries with multiple personalities.[2] The task of the expert in the popular and medical narrative about the "cure" of this condition was to unify a personality that psychology was increasingly defining as divided by nature.

William James previews the preoccupations of the next generation when he writes in 1895, after surveying the history of "Person and Personality," "All these facts have brought the question of what is the unifying principle in personality to the front again" (p. 320). James was concerned with what he called "The Hidden Self," that part of the mind inaccessible to conscious thought. Attacking the refusal of academic science to confront the seemingly inexplicable mysteries of human consciousness, "the unclassed residuum" ("The Hidden Self," p. 248), James claimed that "if there is anything which human history demonstrates, it is the extreme slowness with which the ordinary academic and critical mind acknowledges facts to exist which present themselves as *wild* facts with no stall or pigeon-hole, or as facts which threaten to break up the accepted system" (p. 249). James saw a need for modern science to explore what it seemed to have been afraid of in the human mind, for "it is clear already that the margins and outskirts of what we take to be our personality extend into unknown regions" ("Person and Personality," p. 321).

The autobiographer Marian King reveals the ambivalence behind the task of unifying the divided self when she writes, "For the first time in human history this new science has turned the searchlight into the depths of human nature. For the first time, through mastery of detailed scientific knowledge, are we able to follow the ancient injunction, 'Know thyself' " (pp. 147–48). Is lack of self-knowledge "human nature," and, if so, how can science hope to help us know ourselves? The nineteenth-century concept of a discernible "true self" survived in the form of this anxiety over the psychiatrist's project. King's words reveal a profound irony in her invocation of "the ancient injunction" to know one's self. As a psychiatric patient, her self-knowledge can only be mediated by the medical and psychological expert, whose "mastery" offers her the promise of a unified, known self that she must then accept as her own. Her own experience of subjectivity falls away before her assumption of a "we" that invites the psychiatric expert to represent the mass of humankind.

In the period during which King offers her tribute to psychiatric science in the form of her own story, the discourses of psychology give conflicting reports on how knowable or unified the individual self is. James's interest in what he calls the "facts" of human consciousness reveals a growing concern among psychologists with functional psychology, with the workings of the mind as manifested in observed behavior rather than with the organic causes behind mental functioning. Meyer explains this shift when he writes in 1908, "As soon as we put ourselves in a dynamic psycho-biological foundation, we make unnecessary the continual yearning for something back of the events, at the expense of the plain facts in evidence. The whole movement of modern thought is one of distrust of the noumena back of things and rather favors a valuation of what is at hand in just the form in which we have to handle it" ("The Problems of Mental Reaction-Types," pp. 259–60). His use of "distrust" here echoes the paranoia, the suspicion about the real self within the person that we saw in nineteenth-century writings. While that paranoia and its associated literary modes continues —detective fiction, sensationalistic journalism, sensation fiction— Meyer's words point toward a gradual release from reliance on real, perceivable root phenomena (which were never quite discoverable) in favor of a belief that reality is made up of dynamic, interactive forces whose importance lies in their function rather than their essence.

Meyer's functionalist model dominated American psychology even after Freud's 1909 lectures at Clark University and the subsequent popularization of ideas about sexuality and the unconscious. Where Freudian psychology relied on the unseen world of the unconscious, Meyer's "psychobiology" focused on observable phenomena in them-

selves. In his influential text *Psychobiology*, Meyer confronts the
question, " 'Yes, but when do you begin to get back of these phenomena?' " (p. 95). He replies,

> I do not start with the subconscious or the unconscious, either
> in the sense of nonawareness or in the specific sense of the re-
> pressed unconscious of Freudian analysis. I do not take the dream
> or the complex or the fundamental instinct as my point of depar-
> ture, but I can respect and use them in their place, in a setting of
> the more obvious and familiar. Should I take myself away from
> the data open to everyone's critical sense, as many analysts do?
> Should I go even "behind the shadows," to quote from one of
> my daughter's puppet plays? Is it evasion to prefer shadows cast
> from at least enough real substance to justify study and general-
> izations? To go directly to the functions of real living bodies—
> *functions which may be more or less conscious?* (p. 95)

Meyer shies away from what he sees as the shadow world of "the repressed unconscious of Freudian analysis," a world perhaps more directly descended than Meyer's own from the "puppet show" secrets
that formed the core of so much nineteenth-century popular fiction.

It was largely the collision between this new reliance on observable
phenomena—including human behavior—and nineteenth-century
expectations of a deeper reality that left Henry Adams baffled and
overwhelmed after his introduction to the dynamo at the Great Exposition in 1900: "Between the dynamo in the gallery of machines and
the engine-house outside, the break of continuity amounted to abysmal fracture for a historian's objects. No more relation could he discover between the steam and the electric current than between the
Cross and the cathedral. The forces were interchangeable if not re-
versible, but he could see only an absolute *fiat* in electricity as in faith"
(p. 381). Adams's attraction to the mysticism behind the dynamo is
the other side of James's belief in scientific method; both try to understand a world that threatens to evade explanation and deny the old
rules of cause and effect, surface and depth, falsehood and reality.

I have discussed in previous chapters the tremendous ambivalence
of nineteenth-century American alienists over their ability to define
or treat mental illness. Even as the study of the human mind became
more scientized into the twentieth century, psychologists and psychiatrists revealed an insecurity, not unlike that of James and Adams,

about how knowable the mind really was. These scientists of the mind described their project—and their ability to carry it through—in strikingly contradictory terms. For example, in his 1916 book *Who Is Insane?* the former New York State commissioner in lunacy Stephen Smith writes, "[This book's] intent and purpose are to illustrate with as few technicalities as possible the illusive nature of insanity, its origin in the derangement of the functions of the brain-cells, the extreme impressibility of these cells and our power to increase or repress their activities. In these facts, which modern science has developed, are found the scientific principles on which the prevention of insanity, and its successful treatment, must be based" (pp. 8–9). Smith describes insanity as "illusive" in the same paragraph in which he praises the ability of modern science to bring it under control.

At several points in his study, Smith voices the popular doubt about whether an expert can really distinguish the sane from the insane. He describes at length an incident in which while he is observing patients at an asylum a young woman asks him, " 'Who is insane, you or I?' " (p. 24) When he replies that she is, she responds with an ironic challenge:

> Taking a small mirror from a stand, she moved it before her face, saying: "Will you be so kind as to teach me how to examine a person's face and discover what may be his mental condition?" She placed herself in different attitudes, holding the mirror in different positions, and making ludicrous grimaces, greatly to the amusement of the by-standers. She continued: "If you will teach me your occult art, I should be delighted to be able to say to anyone I meet: 'Why, of course, you are insane.' If I become as expert as you think you are, and had your assurance, I might even say to you, 'Why, you, of course, are insane.' " (p. 25)

When Smith then claims he knows she is insane because she is an inmate in the asylum, she replies, " 'This whole business of locking people in these prisons for life, because some fool of a doctor says they are insane, is a contemptible and transparent fraud. You admit that if you had met me in the street, or in the cars, or in a hotel, you would have declared me sane, but happening to meet me in this asylum you promptly and audaciously pronounce me insane. On what a slender thread hangs our destiny!' " (pp. 26–27). By presenting this narrative Smith is not only spelling out the distrust of expert authority he might expect from a general reading audience; he is also voicing the insecurity of the psychiatric profession about its own abilities. At first he seems to relate this narrative only to answer the young woman's challenge later. Her ironic regard of her own face in the mirror refers back in time to a dependence on physiognomy for diagnosis that Smith and other experts now see as too simplistic, too divorced from function and behavior.

Yet even as Smith explains the complexities of modern diagnosis, he reaffirms the ability of the psychiatrist-hero to obliterate all doubts and difficulties in identifying insanity. He celebrates the diagnostic talents of Amariah Brigham, superintendent of the Utica Asylum in New York, who, claims Smith, identified an insane man at first sight by "stretching out his long arm and pointing with his finger toward a person on one of the rear tiers of seats" (p. 54).

Through conflicting explanations of insanity, Smith and other theorists expressed a longing for a secured place in the social order and for a unified identity that their own ideas continued to bring into question. As they struggled—consciously or unconsciously—to legitimate the dominance of upper- and middle-class white men, experts balanced a weak faith in their ability to locate insanity in a cynical woman inmate against a suspicion that they really had no answer to the question "Who is insane?"

It may be that early twentieth-century mental hygienists privileged childhood and "child guidance" in response to middle-class Americans' desire to start all over again and reconstruct a unified identity through a social and moral education that, as Henry Adams pointed out, had already become virtually impossible for his generation of the dominant classes. The "normal" child who seemed in the eighteenth century like a blank book to be filled with the help of parents was by the early twentieth endangered by faulty heredity and "maladjustment" to a threatening modern environment.[3]

Of course, one of the most apparent threats to what Adams called a "historian's objects" and what Smith might have called the psychologist's search for a coherent definition of insanity was the New Woman, who in turn-of-the-century America was increasingly demanding equal rights and making her voice heard in the public sphere. She was refusing to be the object of history and science, or—what amounts to the same thing—the virgin or muse who, according to Henry Adams and other male thinkers, should provide the force and inspiration for male productivity. The loss of a source of energy, a source identified as the female, meant for white American men of the dominant classes a loss of origins, of depth, of identity posited on the existence of an other. Middle- and upper-middle-class white women also feared this loss to some extent, as we have seen in the earlier autobiographies, where these writers continually posit their own sanity at the expense of immigrant women, women of color, and poor women. We see this displacement in Charlotte Perkins Gilman, who deftly deconstructs the male psychological establishment in her story "the Yellow Wallpaper," yet expounds on her fear that America will be overrun by immigrants in her 1935 autobiography *The Living of Charlotte Perkins Gilman*. Writes Gilman, "The petty minority of Americans in New York receive small respect from their supplanters. Why should they? What must any people think of another people who voluntarily give up their country—not conquered—not forced out— simply outnumbered and swallowed up without a struggle" (p. 316). This fear of the other is a fear of non-coherence, of self-disintegration that plays itself out most dramatically in the asylum autobiography.

What appeals to the public in Clifford Beers's autobiography is his penchant for self-analysis, his ability to look at his own mental disintegration and rehabilitation while assuring his readers of his normality. While he evokes a fear of the unconscious and its power to rule the self, he ultimately assuages that fear by asserting the victory of a controlled and conscious narrator now able to construct a "realistic" account of his past madness. His book was in a sense perfect for reassuring his readers of their own controlling subjectivity precisely because Beers was more firmly located within hegemonic upper-middle-class culture than many former asylum autobiographers had been. Where Clarissa Lathrop, for example, was not only "insane," but a poor unmarried woman, Beers was a solidly middle-class Yale graduate with strong connections in the business and professional worlds. The reviews of the book, which went through seven editions with numerous reprintings of each, continually stressed that Beers was "a young man, well-born and well-bred, a graduate of Yale" and that his autobiography itself was different from preceding ones in the same genre (Van Dyke, "A Remarkable Human History," p. 647). In an explicit reference to such narratives as those by Packard, Smith, and Lathrop, Adolf Meyer writes in *The Psychological Bulletin*, "it has nothing in common with the frequent attempts at revolutionary disclosures by ex-patients who carry a chip on their shoulder and have had the most detrimental effects on legislation and on the attitude of the legal profession and the public—detrimental to the great majority of patients while perhaps a protection for a few greedy for special rights" (Aug. 15, 1908, pp. 283–84).[4] Where any admission of mental distress Lathrop might have made could have stripped her of what little credibility she had, Beers's self-exposure actually makes him even more acceptable. It is precisely Beers's own expression of the dominant classes' (and gender's) fear of disintegration that made his book so successful. Acknowledging that experts are at a loss for adequate explanations of mental illness, Meyer writes, "Moreover, the book comes at a more opportune time than its futile predecessors. There is a growing demand for more knowledge of mental disorders and mental difficulties among physicians, as well as a growing feeling of responsibility about mental hygiene among people generally" (*North American Review*, April, 1908, p. 63). As an upper-class white male, Beers can bridge the gap between patient and physician, between loss of control and supreme control. More important, he can reassure his readers that control will always be regained.

Beers presents his illness as a battle between two human parts of himself, the rational observer who witnesses and mentally records events and the depressed or manic self who misinterprets the external world. He opens his narrative, "It is an autobiography and more: in part it is a biography; for, in telling the story of my life, I must relate the history of another self—a self which was dominant from my twenty-fourth to my twenty-sixth year. During that period I was unlike what I had been, or what I have been since. The biographical part of my autobiography might be called the history of a mental civil war, which I fought single-handed on a battlefield that lay within the compass of my skull" (p. 1).

Beers perceives his illness as a division between two kinds of human identity, one of which must win while the other loses. The rational self remembers everything and is thus able to narrate events in chronological order, a fact that several reviewers remark upon with relief and admiration. One of his reviewers remarks reassuringly that "as a sane man he had a thorough grasp upon his former insane self, and with a vivid recollection of the latter's career from beginning to end" (*NYT Books*, June 13, 1908, p. 325). Beers's in-control self is thus intimately linked to the ability to produce a realistic chronological narrative with a beginning, middle, and end. The life story that Meyer sees as the focus of modern psychology, as the source of information and symptomology, here shows itself as shaped and constrained by preconceptions of what constitutes a proper narrative. Mental illness, far from unfolding as story to be interpreted, reveals itself to signify instead the disruption of story. Narrative becomes possible only after the cure, which is proved by the ascendancy of coherent narration over disorder, misinterpretation, misreading of the world and self.

Beers's autobiography shows to what extent the male Victorian worship of willpower was struggling with the concept of William James's "hidden self."[5] We can read Beers's illness as a crisis of the will, in which he tries to master his mental illness on the one side and to enact his ambitious projects and enforce his desires at all costs on the other. His ambition to be a business manager, his terror of his brother's epilepsy—with its embodied loss of self-control—his insistence on getting his way in the asylum: all point to this struggle to assert his will under seemingly impossible circumstances. We may attribute the commercial success of his book largely to its enacting the final triumph of his will, much as sensation fiction celebrates the triumph of social order after its threatened destruction.

Beers encapsulates his victory in the first paragraph of his opening statement: "An Army of Unreason, composed of the cunning and treacherous thoughts of an unfair foe, attacked my bewildered consciousness with cruel persistency, and would have destroyed me, had not a triumphant Reason finally interposed a superior strategy that saved me from my unnatural self" (p. 1). The irrational self is also the "unnatural" one, a self that exists within him as a kind of foreign, though human, intruder. The "hidden self" alternately appears as the most "natural," core part of one's subjectivity—in its refusal to be socialized—and the most "unnatural"—in its failure to correspond with an authoritative, controlling sense of identity. It is perhaps not a coincidence that Beers was committed to the asylum in 1900, the year that Henry Adams remarked the failure of his will to unify events, "his historical neck broken by the sudden irruption of forces totally new" (*Education*, p. 382). Beers counters and gives voice to the turn-of-the-century upper- and middle-class male anxiety over the loss of willpower by extolling the ability of his reason to overcome unreason and recollect the tale of the victory.

■

While in *Reluctantly Told* Jane Hillyer follows Beers's emphasis on inner struggle, her story also descends from those of Packard, Smith, and Lathrop, who tried to create a sense of self despite the constraints of the institution. Institutionalized first in a sanitorium, then transferred to an unnamed state facility after she failed to recover, Hillyer describes a battle with dementia praecox. She describes this experience as a struggle between what she experiences as human identity and de-humanizing insanity.

The form of Hillyer's narrative parallels this division as she moves between reconstituting the past and identity through chronological memory and describing the failure of memory to form a coherent story about her life. When the autobiography itself begins, Hillyer as narrator appears disoriented, unable to put together a narrative about where she is or how she has gotten there. We as readers have already anticipated a certain level of disorientation not because of her voice, which is calm and controlled, but because of the context of mental illness and cure that the introduction has already provided for us. However, expecting the controlled perspective of the now-cured narrator, we have not been prepared to be plunged without explanation into a scene devoid of clear social and cultural markers. Rather than giving her reader the expected contextualized memories of her asylum surroundings, she begins with her escape from a place she herself has not identified or recognized as a locked institution: "I walked down the hall; I was going out. At the head of the stairs a door covered with heavy wire netting confronted me. The lock was fastened on the outside. I put my hand, unusually slim just then, through the netting— the wire cut my wrist—slipped the catch and went downstairs" (p. 1). While the reader knows from the introduction that Hillyer is in an asylum of some sort, her refusal to recognize this throws us off guard; where we expected confinement presented as an unfortunate circumstance of the patient's past experience, we get instead her movement and determination: "I was going out."

Hillyer's effort to escape is not only a movement to break out of physical imprisonment, but an action to create story where none seems possible. The move to escape becomes an assertion of subjectivity, which contains and allows the position of narrator. Her subjectivity is reinforced by her refusal to consider herself an object of narration. When she descends the stairs and overhears two nurses discussing her whereabouts, she asks herself, "Who were they talking about, I wondered? Perhaps it was one of the patients in the back of the house. They seemed very queer" (p. 2).

While on the one hand we read these lines from the ironic distance provided us by the now-"cured" narrator, on the other hand her refusal to identify herself as a patient establishes her as a credible subject. By the time she remembers "I was locked in. It was I that the nurses had been discussing" (p. 2), she has brought the reader into her view of the world and led the reader to experience the rush of memory, in which Hillyer as patient becomes suddenly and disturbingly a character in a story as well as its narrator. Unlike Beers, who begins his narrative from the position of already-cured, rational and credible male subject, Hillyer begins her story from a position of disorientation that shows itself as rational subjectivity. Thus from the very beginning she prevents her reader from forming a notion of a rational, coherent, cured and curable subject. As a woman, Hillyer can never speak from Beers's position of coherence and credibility, a position largely founded on the definition of woman as incoherent, in-credible, insane. Her move, then, to make that position of incoherence the location of subjectivity calls into question the dichotomy of sanity and insanity that underlies the expected story of her illness and recovery.

Hillyer's autobiography continually enacts and challenges the possibility of her existence as a subject. Like Beers, Jane Hillyer presents her illness in terms of a battle, but it is less a fight between two human selves than the encroachment of a new self, "a thing," upon her whole being. She returns throughout the autobiography to descriptions of herself as an animal, a thing, a nonhuman. Interestingly enough, this self-perception begins when she regards herself in the mirror while in the sanitorium:

> By a faint light that came from the hall I saw a tall figure reflected in the mirror. It wore a dark blue negligee, dark hair hung down around a white face, dark eyes looked from under knitted brows. I knew definitely that the figure in the mirror was mad. *I* was mad.
>
> I have never learned words with which to describe the sensations accompanying that realization. I seemed dual; struggling against the truth, crying out against fate, pleading, praying; and at the same time, cool and almost surgical in my analysis of

the situation. I probed to find the cause; I reckoned the factor of fatigue, long continued fever, strain, tension; I checked my recent behavior and the accompanying drives and emotions. Yes, that explained it all. I was mad. Again I looked at the mirrored figure. It seemed all eyes. I called it by name. "Do you know," I said, "do you know that you are insane? Do you know what that means? Do you know they won't trust you any more? They can't. You may not work in the fall. You will disappoint them all. Do you know what it is like to be mad? That *thing* will get stronger and stronger. Some day it will *be* you." The figure covered its face. (p. 14)

Shortly afterward, she calmly remarks, "The questioner seemed satisfied and went away. Nothing so cool, so piercingly clear came near the crumpled blue heap on the bed for many years. But the *thing* came closer and closer" (p. 15). Where Elizabeth Packard's mirror was the repository of her sense of self, Hillyer's becomes the source of her destruction. It is the act of beholding herself as a "figure" whom she knows but does not know that leads her eventually into complete self-alienation. At the point when she looks into the mirror, she has a sense of a split self, the analytical one that looks and the one that looks back at her "all eyes." When she sees those eyes, she immediately calls "it" by name—her own name—thereby both identifying herself with it and alienating herself. As the "thing"—the insanity—becomes herself, the rational questioner departs.

From this point on, she becomes increasingly nonhuman in her own recollection. After she has been transferred, the doctor comes to see her and calls her by name:

Again my own name had a magical effect. I had one of those curious experiences in which one sees oneself. I saw what she saw.

A human being had turned beast; its hair was in a mat over its eyes, its face twisted and marred by rage and pain; the upper part of its body was incased in stiff canvas from which a wrecked negligee hung in limp, faded folds. "Is this Jane Hillyer?" she repeated. I made a swift turn and threw myself face downward upon my bed. Yes, this *thing* was "me," the *thing* that had brought me to my feet in the middle of the night months before with its sinister prophecy had indeed ceased to haunt, and had become in-

carnate; it had made its spring and landed full and square. "Yes,"
I answered. "Yes, *this* is "me." (p. 83)

By saying her name, the psychiatrist both recalls her to the familiar and holds up to her the mirror of madness and thus both implies
that she is not quite human and provides her with a human language
with which to describe her beastliness. To say "*this* is 'me' " is simultaneously to announce one's identity in relation to a set of cultural
signifiers and to differentiate oneself—by means of an ironic "me"—
from the possibility of human identity. Through this dialectic and the
dialogue that frames and shapes it, the psychiatrist will help usher her
back to "mental health," but only to the extent that Hillyer herself
agrees to accept the category "human." By continuing to see herself as
an "it," she resists the signifiers of human identity even as she invokes
them to compare herself against. While this resistance is a painful
one for her, it at least gives her a part in the dialogue about her own
identity, a part in which the conscious mind never asserts itself as un-
problematically as it does for Clifford Beers.

Hillyer's narrative suggests that while she, like Beers, struggles
with the power of her will, she often experiences that will as alien-
ated from her, usurped by her own body. Her body often seems to have
taken on a will of its own. At one point she recalls, "I realized the sex
drive had me in hand; apparently it had gone on 'while I was away' "
(p. 72). Her bodily experience as she records it challenges the late
nineteenth-century concept that will inheres in conscious thought
and action. Indeed, these lines reveal an almost parodic fulfillment of
nineteenth-century medical descriptions that located women's will
not in their minds but in their bodies, which could then become split
off from their sense of identity.

Hillyer's representation of her insane self as a nonhuman "it" illuminates the ways in which the "hidden self" was represented as feminine in early twentieth-century America. Medical discourse never
seemed to run out of case histories describing the symptoms of hysterical women whose bodies seemed to take on a will of their own. As
the new psychologies examined what Freud called "the strange and
wonderful phenomena of hysteria," they incorporated the nineteenth-
century association of women with sexuality, animality, flesh, body.
In the narratives of psychiatric discourse the female body could take
over the rational self, becoming the object of both the disconcerted/

disconnected female patient and the doctor hired to rectify the situation. Thus in a note to the Dora case, Freud remarks on "the case of a fourteen-year-old girl who suffered from dangerous hysterical vomiting." After a few sessions with Freud, the girl

> proved . . . to have been a masturbator for many years, with a considerable leucorrhoeal discharge (which had a close bearing upon her vomiting). She had finally broken herself of the habit, but was tormented in her abstinence by the most acute sense of guilt, so that she looked upon every misfortune that befell her family as a divine punishment for her transgression. Besides this, she was under the influence of the romance of an unmarried aunt, whose pregnancy (a second determinant for her vomiting) was supposed to have been happily hidden from her. The girl was looked upon as a "mere child," but she turned out to be initiated into all the essentials of sexual relations (p. 33).

Here the girl's exposure to female sexuality—in the form of masturbation and pregnancy—leads her into a self-revulsion in which, according to Freud's interpretation of her illness, her body tries to get rid of itself through vomiting. She has already learned to "read" her own body and its actions, whether consciously or not, as transgressive. Freud's reading of her reading may give her an explanation for her body's behavior, but it also offers her body once again as something to be read, as reading "material" both for herself and for other psychologists reading Freud's work.

Whatever the motives behind Freud's description, this story presents a diagnosis that then becomes part of the cultural context for women's bodily experience. A diagnosis such as Freud's—or Adolf Meyer's—is never just a description but a prescription not only for how the physician will treat a woman's body but for how she will conceive of her own experience.

■

Hillyer's concept of herself as a beast—a concept largely described and prescribed for women by medical and cultural dictates—may have been informed not only by ideas about female psychology but by wider changes in the lives of early twentieth-century middle-class American women. As the separation of spheres gave way to middle-class women's increased participation in the world of work outside the home and in political decision making, Victorian social mores were coming into conflict with women's belief in their right to sexual fulfillment and a more general loosening of restrictions on sexual behavior (Hale, pp. 259–75). For women born to middle-class Victorian parents, this change was likely to have brought with it conflicting feelings about female selfhood and especially about the newly "liberated" female body. Raised by mothers who had gained freedom by preaching sexual abstinence and who at any rate had been taught that normal women had little sexual appetite, many members of the new middle-class generation would be plagued by guilt. Hillyer suggests this when she remarks, in referring to her uninhibited sexual behavior in the mental hospital, that "this very common sex manifestation had so eaten into my mind that, being in my own consciousness acutely, I thought it must, perforce, be in every one's; it had 'got out,' 'appeared in the papers'; it had contaminated childhood, destroyed those youngsters whose musical education had been entrusted to me" (p. 44).

Jane Hillyer ties her failure to control herself sexually during her illness to a romantic obsession she had as an adolescent in which it was not possible for her to express her passion: "When the brain cells gave way which enable one to eat ashes and so maintain the proprieties I found I had dug a ditch of ignominy before I reached it" (p. 48). The idea that to maintain proprieties is to eat ashes reveals Hillyer's ambivalence about such social regulations; the proprieties seem unreasonable, yet she conceives it is somehow her own moral failure, her own ditch-digging rather than rational choice, that leads her to abandon them. She especially shudders when she imagines what her mother would think of her now. When she recalls her mother, who is no longer living, Hillyer thinks, "There was no place for her in the mind of a craven. She had turned away her face" (p. 21). This is not to say that the only cause of Hillyer's illness was the collective guilt of a generation caught between conflicting sexual values, but that her illness constructed itself within and as part of this wider context.[6]

Hillyer's narrative not only illuminates the confrontation between Victorian women's sexual inhibitedness and early twentieth-century women's expectations that they might express their sexuality more openly; the autobiography also reveals the implications of changing definitions of homosexuality, which Hillyer somewhat confusedly describes as the instigator of her illness. Her self-revulsion is intimately connected to an experience of lesbian love, an experience that was positive until a male "adviser" named it to her as deviant.

As Estelle Freedman and John D'Emilio have pointed out, ideas about sexuality in America have not so much tended toward greater freedom, as is popularly believed, but toward continual redefinition according to the cultural, social, and political demands of a particular period (xi–xii). Thus, at the same time that women were beginning to express heterosexual eroticism more openly, popular and medical discourse was defining same-sex eroticism as deviant. Where until the 1880s female romantic attachments were for the most part tolerated, by the early twentieth century, sexologists such as Richard von Krafft-Ebing, Havelock Ellis, and Auguste Forel had delineated theories of homosexuality that contributed to increasing suspicions about female friendships. As Carroll Smith-Rosenberg and Sheila Jeffries have suggested, opponents of women's struggle for equality saw in female attachments a potential denial of heterosexuality and the social order it supported (*Disorderly Conduct*, pp. 286–87, and *The Spinster and Her Enemies*, p. 112).

Increasingly, then, female same-sex relationships came to be described not only as undesirable but as unnatural (Freedman and D'Emilio, p. 194). Fear of women's exclusivity and domination was displaced from women's behavior onto their bodies; theorists held that the "invert" was a type of person who could be identified by appearance. As Freedman and D'Emilio show, after the 1920s Freudianism influenced theorists and public alike to think of homosexuality as an acquired rather than an innate condition (p. 226). Nevertheless, we have already seen that for Freud an acquired condition was still an embodied one, especially for women, who not only *had* bodies but represented them.

Hillyer's own process of internalizing negative feelings about her body shows itself clearly when she describes the change in her feelings about Miss Winthrop. When she mentions her "pleasure and astonishment" at her feelings for her teacher, her male friend replies, " 'I have been thinking about that. . . . I wonder if your attitude is quite wholesome" (p. 37). When she shows shock at the question, he "told me of an experience he had just seen some one through, a girl who had shown every sign of lover-like adoration to another girl. 'It did not work. I would hate to see you twist a friendship that way . . .

especially just now' " (p. 37). Having not thought of her friendship in the terms her adviser describes, Hillyer now feels "depressed enough to believe the worst of any situation. I hated the thought of the unnatural. I felt somehow soiled even to be considering it" (p. 38). Here, she readily adopts the language of the period that describes such an attraction as "twisted" and "unnatural." In seeing herself as a "beast," she reproduces an ideology that constructed lesbians as a "third sex," a kind of degenerate mutation that had no place (or a beastly place) in a gender system in which the human was marked above all by the duality male-female.[7] In her recounting of her adviser's warning that danger lies ahead "especially just now" she connects her passion to her unstable mental situation.

Her description of her feelings for another woman as "unnatural" reverberate with her sense that her own body is beastly and foreign. As in Beers's narrative, we can see here profound contradiction within the concept of "naturalness." Hillyer inherited one set of contradictions from the tenacious nineteenth-century ideology of separate male and female spheres: Women were thought to be naturally closer to the animal, the bodily, the unconscious, as well as naturally closer to unbodied qualities of purity and passionlessness. This whole set of contradictions came into conflict with what was considered natural for men, whose qualities defined the norm: men were supposedly naturally more in control of themselves and their world.

Given this context, Hillyer can only see her attraction to another woman as unhealthy, linked to her own mental imbalance:

> We continued to see each other, until my adviser, who had been watching me very carefully, said again, "You look so tired and white when you have been with Miss Winthrop." No wonder. I was suffocated, prostrated, poisoned by self-hatred. I knew he was right; my self-possession had been slipping rapidly the last few days. But why had I been singled out for such humiliation, such misery? Nothing like this had ever come near me before though nearly all my friends, like Miss Winthrop, were older than I. The magnetized pull of my thoughts in her direction— when I had other uses for them—the warm, dreamy, stopped, languorous feeling that came upon me sometimes in her presence were all new. No woman or girl had ever been so wrapt in an emotional mist before. What *was* it? Certainly nothing that accorded

either with my real desires or my upbringing. It was humiliating
—and yet it had the quality of a welcome anesthetic. This latter
element was its greatest attraction. "What *what!*" It was to be
many long, long months before I understood that this disturbing
element was but a bit of smoke rising from the volcano burning
within my consciousness. It had nothing to do with the object
of my devotion, everything to do with that all-consuming inner
flame that was about to burst forth and consume me. The outer
crust of reserve, of quiet affection, good-fellowship, was thin and
broken. The fumes of distorted emotionalism, the forerunners of
madness, were pouring forth steadily and insidiously. (pp. 38–39)

What stands out in this segment about Miss Winthrop is the super-
imposition of one discourse upon another. Hillyer's "pleasure and
astonishment"—terms that a mid-nineteenth-century middle-class
woman might have used to describe her romantic friendship with
another woman—give way to terms—"self-hatred," "humiliation,"
"misery"—informed by twentieth-century definitions of homosexuality as an embodied illness. Her definition of the attachment, bracketed by her adviser's perception of it, itself becomes the catalyst of
her illness. The correct form of friendship, which comprises "quiet affection" and "good-fellowship," has been usurped—in her new understanding of the relationship—by "the fumes of distorted emotionalism, the forerunners of madness." Female same-sex passion, which a
generation or two earlier was seen as a more or less healthy and normal
influence on middle-class women, has here become an expression of
insanity, an expression inseparable from physical and emotional self-
hatred.

∎

Hillyer's detachment from her body—reinforced as it is by her belief
that loving another woman's body is wrong and unhealthy—is intimately connected to her failure to constitute her own identity through
memory, a failure that Beers does not remark as part of his experience with mental illness. Memory plays a crucial role in Jane Hillyer's
story. On the one hand, she fails to remember long periods of her illness and loses one year altogether. During one phase, she only recalls,
"a feeling of being lost, lost utterly with no sense of place or time,
no idea as to whom voices belonged, no clear realization of my own

identity, lost in mind and body and soul, lost to light and form and color; a distinct, acid nausea of self-revulsion—all these were in the feeling that swept over me. . . . The emotion became *me*. I went down with it whence it had come, to some far depth beyond the bounds of any remembering" (pp. 71–72). Where Beers retains his analytical self, Hillyer loses all sense of rationality and control; she becomes nothing but a body that continually strives to reject itself. Her later writing self can only partially reconstruct her illness. On the other hand, when her memories do emerge, they do so seemingly without warning; they interfere with the order of her life both in the content of the story she tells and in the structure of that story itself. Thus, her narrative begins in the locked sanitorium, and then takes us back abruptly when Hillyer claims that as she contemplated her imprisonment, "I was swept back to my early childhood in a stream of confused, crowding thoughts" (p. 3). In contrast, while Beers discusses his childhood, he maintains a controlling distance, beginning with his youth and taking us step by step through his incarceration and recovery.

Both Hillyer's and Beers's efforts to explain their illnesses by recounting memories of childhood events coincide with the tendency of early twentieth-century psychological theory to look for signs of an endangered self in a maladjusted childhood. Anxious to reinforce his curability, Beers is torn between finding evidence of mental illness in his past and insisting on his normality. He qualifies his list of fears by saying, "after all, I am not sure that the other side of my nature— the natural, healthy boyish side—did not develop equally with these timid and morbid tendencies, which are not so very uncommon in childhood" (p. 2–3). Beers's insecurity about whether his illness is rooted in inherent deviant character traits reflects the era's ambivalence about the role of heredity, which, as we have seen, had been established as primary in the late nineteenth century and which continued to be seen as an important factor in mental illness. In fact, one reviewer, writing in the Science section of *The Nation*, responded to Beers's book by lamenting,

> To be sure, the melancholic and allied functional states yield more readily to treatment, possibly most readily; but how can one prevent hereditary types, save by marriage restrictions, or the type due to some pre-existing disease such as that which is thought to be responsible for paretic dementia? . . . However

> hopeless the view may seem, one is bound to face the fact that
> insanity is in the majority of cases an unpreventable and an in-
> curable disease, and nothing short of Utopia itself can ever make
> it be much less so. (Mar. 19, 1908, pp. 265–66)

The writer's comments reveal that hereditarian ideas were alive and
well in the early twentieth century. In a 1927 textbook by Daniel Wolford La Rue called *Mental Hygiene,* the author advises students, *"Eu-
genics* aims to get children better born. We are coming to see that we
cannot keep people healthy-minded unless they are well born" (p. 10).

Mental hygienists' ambivalent belief in both the powers of heredity
and environment and experts' ability to affect an individual's life
course revealed a need to trust in willpower and in an ultimately uni-
tary self in the face of increasing psychological evidence that there
existed an "unclassed residuum" in the human mind. A focus on childhood and memory allowed the individual to construct a coherent personal identity.

■

In contrast to this notion of wholeness, Jane Hillyer transforms the
idea of childhood memories. They are not segments of the past that
construct a whole self but disruptive elements that jar her sense of
coherence whenever they enter her consciousness. As they "sweep"
her away, these elements become the evidence not of wholeness but
of the unconscious, of disjuncture. In this sense they are closer to the
beast in her than to the conscious human.

For Hillyer, memory is not a reservoir of incidents that enables the
conscious mind to construct a coherent narrative; on the contrary,
memory calls into question the very nature of the activity of narration. While her story does follow a vague chronological line, it repeatedly turns back upon itself as Hillyer describes past events that never
quite fulfill reader expectations. Unlike Beers's narrative, in which
reason and willpower win out in the end, Hillyer's autobiography, like
the earlier ones I have discussed, leaves us with little sense of resolution. Hillyer begins the last section of her narrative, "The answer to
the question, 'What did your "tomorrow" prove to be; what happened
after all?' is simply: the best I could do was to fit into a very *simple*
pattern, plain and without distinction, the pattern of my Ring. Am I
going to keep on fitting in? I don't know" (p. 204). We are left with

her failure (or perhaps refusal) to be distinctive, with her lowered expectations for her own life, and with her uncertainty about her ability to remain well. She ends not so much with the final triumph of cure as with a suggestion that the narrative will continue itself, moving in circles over memories, over ground already covered.

Yet her "ring" is not only a circle of repetition and containment; it is also a circus ring, into which "I have leaped from my high estate on the tight rope, where I balanced precariously over the depths of re-dissolution" (p. 184). When she describes her current life as a circus, where "as yet I have avoided being led around on a chain or put on exhibition as 'the most dangerous beast in the whole show, the mad elephant'" (pp. 184–85), Hillyer calls into the question the "realism" of her narrative and the very possibility of a narrative, such as Beers's, that gives a chronological account of illness and cure. She suggests that the world of sane relations, as well as the narrative she has written to communicate with that world, are part of a show in which she barely escapes the role of madwoman. It is the tenuous act of narration itself that assures her a place in "the ring." In this last chapter she comes close to unmasking the illusion of realism that both enables her and requires her to be not the "mad elephant" but the recovered autobiographer, freshly returned from the asylum.

# 6

## *Zelda Fitzgerald's* Save Me the Waltz *as Asylum Autobiography*

■   While Jane Hillyer's asylum autobiography to some extent engages in dialogue with the methods and solutions of modern psychiatry, Zelda Fitzgerald's *Save Me the Waltz* challenges and rewrites the
expected descriptions, diagnoses, and definitions of the mentally ill
woman. As this autobiographical novel, which Fitzgerald published
in 1932, takes us from the childhood and marriage of the main character, Alabama Beggs, through her ballet career, physical illness, and
recovery, it both obscures and reveals a fragmented story of mental
turmoil and incarceration. In *Save Me the Waltz*, a narrative about
Alabama's bodily experience is substituted for a suppressed story of
mental illness. Through this substitution, the novel not only avoids
conventional representations of the insane woman—such as the version of Zelda produced in F. Scott Fitzgerald's 1934 novel *Tender Is
the Night*—but exposes those representations and the psychiatric discourse surrounding them as dependent on an appropriation and objectification of female bodies.

In the tradition of twentieth-century asylum autobiographers, such
as Clifford Beers, Jane Hillyer, and Marian King, who were often encouraged to begin their life stories while still in the asylum, Zelda
Fitzgerald finished her autobiographical novel in 1932 while a patient
at Adolf Meyer's Phipps Psychiatric Clinic of Johns Hopkins University Hospital in Baltimore. She had begun to break down emotionally
starting in 1929 and had spent time in institutions in Europe before
returning to the United States for treatment at the Phipps clinic. Her
choice not to tell explicitly the story of her illness and hospitalization

is a strategic one; she writes this novel against the expectations for asylum autobiography, expectations that would shape and constrict her narrative.

Fitzgerald feared that as a woman labeled mentally ill she played a part in a script written for her by husband and doctor, a script that— fulfilling her fears—has played itself out in novel, case history, biography, and review.[1] As Mary Gordon points out, "real labor is required to read her without prejudice of one sort or another, to read her not as a symbol of something but as the creator of works of art" ("Introduction," p. xvii). As she waited in the Phipps Clinic for the publication of *Save Me the Waltz*, Fitzgerald did write an asylum autobiography at the suggestion of her psychiatrists. Showing an acute suspicion of the uses of such a narrative, not only did she refer to this autobiography as a "fairy tale," but she left five blank lines for her psychiatrists to fill in (Milford, p. 252). Even as she described her experience of breakdown in the narrative, she thus undercut its authenticity by presenting it to her doctors as a document they could cowrite, a document shaped by prevailing definitions of femininity, mental illness, and cure.

Zelda Fitzgerald's life and writing are particularly important because her illness served as a focal point for significant early twentieth-century narratives about women and mental illness. Not only was she treated by some of the most noted psychologists of the age— Oscar Forel, Paul Bleuler, and Adolf Meyer—all of whom created stories about her "case"—but her life and illness were described/created within what was to become a canonized American literary classic—F. Scott Fitzgerald's *Tender Is the Night*. Zelda Fitzgerald's own largely unrecognized autobiographical novel directly challenges the version of her life set forth by her husband in the character of Nicole Diver.

When F. Scott Fitzgerald makes Nicole Diver's husband a psychiatrist in *Tender Is the Night*, he evokes connections forged in the nineteenth century between ideologies of marriage and medicine. As the field of medicine—and especially what was to become psychiatry— became increasingly professionalized, middle-class American women became more subject to the advice of "experts" who saw the female body as both delicate and dangerous. Just as women were expected to submit to their husbands' authority in marriage, they were encouraged to yield to the diagnoses and prescriptions of physicians and psychologists who tried to save their sanity by controlling their bodies. As

Foucault points out, nineteenth-century medicine was characterized by "a hysterization of women's bodies: a threefold process whereby the feminine body was analyzed—qualified and disqualified—as being thoroughly saturated with sexuality" (*History*, p. 104). This sexualized body was described and controlled in a discourse that intimately linked physical symptoms and insanity. Thus in a description of "puerperal insanity," nineteenth-century physician and asylum superintendent Andrew McFarland writes that the sufferer "becomes irritable, subject to causeless fits of passion, and jealous of, and estranged from those in whom she had before invested fullest confidence. Sometimes she is merely changed in temperament, and is moody, solitary, and reserved. These symptoms have their aggravation whenever the functions of the uterine system are in action, till a regular monthly fit of spleen, or something worse, becomes habitual" ("Maladies," p. 18).[2] McFarland describes the woman's behavior not in terms of her relations with those around her or with a larger social system, but in terms of the function of her reproductive organs, a function seen less as abnormal than as normally pathological.

While with the advent of psychoanalysis the patient participated more in her own recovery through the "talking cure," medical ideology still required that she remain under the authority of the psychiatrist. In fact, from the point of view of the psychoanalyst, women's language often became one more site of symptomology and thus less a manifestation of subjectivity than an object, like the female body, to be analyzed and discussed. For example, in an early study of Anna O., Josef Breuer writes,

> Some ten days after her father's death a consultant was brought in, whom, like all strangers, she completely ignored while I demonstrated all her peculiarities to him. "That's like an examination," she said, laughing, when I got her to read a French text aloud in English. The other physician intervened in the conversation and tried to attract her attention, but in vain. It was a genuine "negative hallucination" of the kind which has since so often been produced experimentally. In the end he succeeded in breaking through it by blowing smoke in her face. She suddenly saw a stranger before her, rushed to the door to take away the key and fell unconscious to the ground. (*Studies*, p. 27)

Anna O.'s verbal reaction to the demonstration, her laughter, her refusal to acknowledge the observer, and her panicked reaction to the observer's physical intrusion upon her all carry equal weight as symptoms in Breuer's description. He presents the scene not as an interaction among three people but rather as his own supposedly objective record of one person's words and behavior.

F. Scott Fitzgerald's novel takes on these issues around women's sanity by telling a story of complex power relations between Doctor Dick Diver and his young wife Nicole, who struggles with schizophrenia. In some ways the novel deconstructs the conventional relationship between medical authority and patient. As the story becomes less about Nicole's mental illness and more about Doctor Diver's progressive alcoholism, the opening section title, "Case History, 1917–1919," sounds more and more ironic: the "case" of doctor-husband eclipses that of the disturbed young woman. Yet in a sense the application of the title to Nicole's case is never completely erased. Our sense of Nicole as a patient is firmly established in the opening scenes, in which Nicole's psychiatrist discusses her relationship with Dick Diver, who is becoming both lover and doctor through "a transference of the most fortuitous kind" (p. 9).[3] These scenes are chilling if only by virtue of the fact that Nicole's own voice is absent and her person objectified by the two men, even though we infer that the "transference" has been diagnosed based on her own words. The dialogue between psychiatrist and patient that constitutes part of her treatment here gives way to a dialogue about her, or, more specifically, about her physical attractiveness. When Diver remarks, "'The girl was about the prettiest thing I ever saw,'" psychiatrist Franz Gregorovius replies, "'She still is'" (p. 8). He goes on to say, "'I'm intensely proud of this case, which I handled, with your accidental assistance'" (p. 9). The line between doctor and lover blurs here; both men see as their purpose the cure of the female "case," who ideally will remain entirely dependent upon and grateful to them. Her own words become, in a sense, subsumed within the body they see her as, the body that is understood to be the object of treatment despite any discussion of her mental condition.

It is the physical powerlessness of this "scarcely saved waif of disaster" (p. 27) that attracts Dick Diver, who seems to become more interested in her after he hears from Franz that she became ill after being raped by her father at a young age. Indeed, Fitzgerald presents the story of Nicole's rape as a crucial narrative within the larger tale, a narrative that brings the two men together and motivates their continued interest in her:

> "Now about the girl, Dick," [Franz] said. "Of course, I want to find out about you and tell you about myself, but first about the girl, because I have been waiting to tell you about it so long."
>
> He searched for and found a sheaf of papers in a filing cabinet, but after shuffling through them he found they were in his way and put them on his desk. Instead he told Dick the story. (p. 14)

More important than the personal stories of the two friends is this narrative of a girl's rape by her father, a narrative that has stirred Franz so much that he must drop his professional papers and shape the story with his own words. The molding of the incident gives him a power over the rape itself, a power that places him in the position of both sympathetic doctor and rapist. With this story, he offers Nicole up to Dick, hoping for a successful "transference," for a replaying of the father-daughter relationship so that it will come out right. It is this perception of another man's power over her and violation of her that brings Dick to want to marry Nicole. Fitzgerald writes, "The luncheon in Zurich was a council of caution; obviously the logic of his life tended away from the girl; yet when a stranger stared at her from a nearby table, male eyes burning disturbingly like an uncharted light, he turned to the man with an urbane version of the intimidation and broke the regard" (p. 28). The "yet" here implies that despite his reluctance to become attached to her, his own jealousy of her in relation to another man spurs his interest.

While at times the novel upsets husband-wife-psychiatrist power relations by revealing them, it more frequently recreates them. Nicole in her illness remains elusive, undecipherable throughout the narrative. Her illness itself seems mysterious, dangerous—as when she unexpectedly tries to force the family car off the road—and linked often to hatred of men. Franz remarks in describing her progression from rape to madness that "she developed the idea that she had no complicity and from there it was easy to slide into a phantom world where all men, the more you liked and trusted them, the more evil—" (p. 20). In this image of Nicole Diver we see beneath the language of psychoanalysis and modern diagnosis the persistent nineteenth-century picture of madwoman as both completely powerless and potentially all-powerful, the "waif" and the "complicit" seductress. These images appeared throughout nineteenth-century art and literature as representations not only of women who lost their reason but of women living in particular kinds of bodies. Elaine Showalter has traced the history of the both the Crazy Jane figure, who "was a touching image of feminine vulnerability and a flattering reminder of female dependence upon male affection," and the Lucy figure, who "represented female sexuality as insane violence against men" (*Malady*, pp. 13–14). The embodiment of both these figures in Nicole Diver shows that representations of the madwoman are alive and well in Fitzgerald's twentieth-century America.

Given this context, it is not insignificant that Zelda Fitzgerald's autobiographical novel refuses to tell an explicit tale of mental illness. As she neglects the story of her mental breakdown, she parallels and subverts the expected narrative of psychological journey and cure by telling the tale of her career and failure as a ballet dancer. This tale brings into the foreground the cultural construction of women as the material of male art, whether in dance or psychiatry.

Zelda Fitzgerald was aware of the dangers of conventional narratives. In her biography of Zelda Fitzgerald, Nancy Milford shows that while Zelda often cooperated with her husband and the psychologists who treated her, she feared that if she lived the cure written out for her she would lose her creativity. She wrote to well-known alienist Forel: " 'if you cure me whats going to happen to all the bitterness and unhappiness in my heart—it seems to me a sort of castration, but since I am powerless I suppose I will have to submit, though I am neither young enough nor credulous enough to think that you can manufacture out of nothing something to replace the song I had" (Milford, p. 185). She fears that her own creativity will be replaced with something else. Her sense that cure is castration, a loss of power, evokes Scott Fitzgerald's picture of Nicole Diver, who is manipulated and created by doctor, husband, and, ultimately, male author.

Ironically enough, Zelda Fitzgerald rebelled against the possibility that her own life might be material for someone else's story. She wrote to her husband: " 'Momma does know whats the matter with me. She wrote me she did. You can put that in your story to lend it pathos' " (Milford, p. 170). As Milford points out, Zelda was distraught that Scott lifted sections of her intimate personal letters to him for inclusion in

*Tender Is the Night.* The issue of whose writing and whose experience belonged to whom emerged repeatedly in their relationship. Again, this is not just a question of one interesting marriage between colorful figures; Zelda Fitzgerald's disempowerment during the course of her illness and in her characterization as Nicole bears on much wider issues of women's relationship to psychiatric authority, the institution of marriage, and the right to authorship. Milford shows that when Scott Fitzgerald was outraged that *Save Me The Waltz* had gone to the publisher without his permission and that it contained possible references to his personal life unapproved by him, he received an apology from the psychiatrists who had "allowed" Zelda Fitzgerald to send it out (Milford, p. 217). As Judith Fetterley has pointed out, "as husband, professional writer and 'sane,' Scott had the right to play the role of editor and authorizer in relation to Zelda's work" (Fetterley, p. 112). The kind of collusion between author-husband and psychiatrists that *Tender Is the Night* portrays was lived by Zelda Fitzgerald. The agreement between Forel and Scott Fitzgerald to discourage her from dancing is only one example of this control (Milford, p. 165). The infantilization of a mentally ill woman that an astute reader sees in the portrayal of Nicole Diver reverberates in Zelda Fitzgerald's appeal to Scott to help her " 'not as you would a child but as an equal' " (Milford, p. 165).

Given that Zelda suspected both the requirements of asylum autobiography and her husband's representations of her life, we need to read *Save Me the Waltz* as the partly veiled autobiography she wanted to write. Zelda Fitzgerald's story of her career as a ballet dancer runs parallel to the hidden narrative of her diagnosis as schizophrenic. Far from being a story whose main value lies in its appeal to those interested in ballet, as F. Scott Fitzgerald saw it, the novel is an indictment of the self-revulsion and abuse of the body integral to the art of ballet as Zelda Fitzgerald describes it. This reading of the novel has so far gone unacknowledged in what little recent criticism exists on Zelda Fitzgerald's work. Most critics—including feminist critics— have seen Alabama's dancing career primarily as fulfilling expression within an otherwise frustrated life. For example, Sarah Beebe Fryer claims, "Despite her associates' refusal to take her career seriously, Alabama becomes a good dancer—and derives significant personal satisfaction from her ability" (Fryer, p. 324). For Linda Wagner, the pain Alabama suffers is an unfortunate hindrance to her ballet career rather than an expression of self-abuse. She sees Alabama as "defeated (in the fiction) by the very body that was to be her means into the world of art" (Wagner, p. 206).

As readers aware of Zelda's diagnosis of mental illness, we cannot help but see in her story of ballet—a story in which mental illness is never mentioned—the diagnosis and control of the female body enacted in an art form. *Save Me The Waltz* reveals the diagnostic sentencing of women not only within the realm of mental illness— the obscured but always present subject of the novel—but within the wider cultural context of definitions of femininity and of artistic creation and convention. Within these definitions, the female body is the living metaphor for the material of art, the object of the male artist. As Gordon points out, Alabama's flesh is marked as female and thus must be brought under control ("Introduction," p. xxii).[4] The female ballet dancer is both artist and material; her body is shaped both by the male director and by herself. She is thus split from her own body— precisely one of the conditions manifested in both hysteria and schizophrenia. In her history of female insanity, Elaine Showalter claims that "the 'withness' of the flesh, and its proper management, adornment, and disposition, are a crucial and repeated motif in the schizophrenic women's sense of themselves as unoccupied bodies." Showalter further points out that the split between body and mind is reinforced by the treatments of these diseases, treatments that objectify the women diagnosed as mentally ill (*Malady*, p. 212).

Alabama Beggs, the novel's main character, grows up within a world severely circumscribed first by the authority of her father Judge Austin Beggs and later by her husband, painter David Knight. Her father's position as judge makes him a powerful figure in both the home and the community. To Alabama, her "father was a wise man. Alone his preference in women had created Millie and the girls" (*Waltz*, p. 24). Alabama, her sisters, and her mother Millie live within the highly ordered system of Judge Beggs's mind.

Later, Alabama finds in David both an escape from this home and the power of another male authority. From the beginning, David finds himself complete in a way she cannot: "He verified himself in the mirror—pale hair like eighteenth-century moonlight and eyes like grottoes, the blue grotto, the green grotto, stalactites and malachites hanging about the dark pupil—as if he had taken an inventory of himself before leaving and was pleased to find himself complete" (p. 38). It is this ability to verify one's self in the mirror that Alabama increasingly finds beyond her reach. For her, looking into the mirror means losing a sense of herself as a separate being. Love for her is not an experience of completeness but one of dissolution. As she comes to love David, "so close and closer she felt herself that he became distorted in her vision, like pressing her nose upon a mirror and gazing into her own eyes. She felt the lines of his neck and his chipped profile like segments of the wind blowing about her consciousness. She felt the essence of herself pulled finer and smaller like those streams of spun glass that pull and stretch till there remains but a glimmering illusion" (p. 38).

Her inability to retain a sense of herself intensifies as she begins to train under Madame Sirgeva, the fictional counterpart of Zelda Fitzgerald's teacher Egorova. Alabama Knight works unceasingly in the dance studio, despite the Paris heat and the rebellion of her tired body.

> The heat of July beat on the studio skylight and Madame sprayed the air with disinfectant. The starch in Alabama's organdy skirts stuck to her hands and sweat rolled into her eyes till she couldn't see. Choking dust rose off the floor, the intense glare threw a black gauze before her eyes. It was humiliating that Madame should have to touch her pupil's ankles when they were so hot. The human body was very insistent—she passionately hated her inability to discipline her own. Learning how to manage it was like playing a desperate game with herself. She said to herself, "My body and I" and took herself for an awful beating: that was how it was done. (p. 125)

Alabama's separation from her body represents a rejection, a disgust at the body she cannot control. Even as she presents the ballet as Alabama's only outlet for self-expression, Fitzgerald clearly ties the women dancers' self-abuse in ballet training to the demands of their master Diaghilev, a kind of ruling patriarch who, like Judge Beggs, requires the obedience of the dancing daughters who adore him. Writes Fitzgerald, "If they weighed more than 50 kilos, Diaghilev protested in his high screeching voice, 'You must get thin. I cannot send my dancers to a gymnasium to fit them for adagio.' He never thought of the women as dancers, except the stars" (p. 144). In a differential diagnosis of the women's physical condition, he describes them as dancers, as stars, or as overweight nuisances.

Fitzgerald's narrative delineates her internalization of male requirements for the female body, requirements that the body rebels against even as she struggles to bring it under control. She looks at her own body more and more critically, from the outside, as a doctor or a ballet master might see it: "Her work grew more and more difficult. In the mazes of the masterful fouetté her legs felt like dangling hams; in the swift elevation of the entrechat cinq she thought her breasts hung like old English dugs" (p. 154). Alabama here describes her body as split off into different chunks of meat. The narrative calls attention to Alabama's objectification of her body as the narrator remarks, "It did not show in the mirror. She was nothing but sinew" (p. 154). These sentences imply not only that she has a view of her body as detached from her sense of self, but that her body has somehow become invisible.

Obsessed by a sense that her body is muscular, disjointed meat, she has lost a sense of it existing beyond the diagnostic sentence that she herself enforces. The descriptions of her body recall earlier descriptions of Alabama's childhood home dominated as it was by her father: "Winter and spring the house is like some lovely shining place painted on a mirror. When the chairs fall to pieces and the carpets grow full of holes, it does not matter in the brightness of that presentation. The house is a vacuum for the culture of Austin Beggs' integrity" (pp. 6–7). If the imagined mirror here gives back a reflection of her father's ordered world, the mirror at the dance studio shows her a picture detached from her lived bodily experience. The body she lives in cannot be envisioned; it cannot exist in the ordered world of Diaghilev or Judge Beggs. Eventually, as Alabama tries to shape her body according to father Diaghilev and mother Sirgeva's rules, she develops an infection in her foot—caused by glue in her ballet slipper—that leads to hospitalization, blood poisoning, hallucinations, and a permanent leg injury that means the end of her dancing career.

This story of physical defeat and illness, a story that enacts Alabama's objectification of her own body, parallels and evokes a silent narrative of her mental breakdown. Alabama's apparent escape from a conventional life and subsumed identity, an escape through artistic self-expression in dance, leads to a profound sense of separation from herself. Identifying with the artist as male subject (the successful artists in the novel—husband David and master Diaghilev—are men), Alabama has tried to make her own body the material of her art. Physical and mental breakdown become indistinguishable in the novel as she lies with her legs restrained in sliding pulleys, listening to doctors, husband, ballet instructor conspire about her condition. Sirgeva laments, " 'If she had only disinfected,' " voicing Alabama's disgust with the infected nature of her own flesh. Her injury brings her separation from her body to a crisis in which she is alone in her pain, cut off from communication with those who have power over her. She asks,

> Why did the doctor inhabit another world from hers?
> Why couldn't he hear what she was saying, and not stand talking about ice-packs?
> "We will see," the doctor said, staring out of the window impassively.
> "I've got to have some water! Please give me some water!"
> The nurse went on methodically straightening the dressings on the wheel-table. (p. 192)

The body that would not appear in the mirror finally cries out in thirst, only to be ignored by the enforcers of hospital rules. Her felt body manifests itself where the seen body cannot, but the seen body is the only one acknowledged in the medical/epistemological system in which she finds herself. Even her words fail to convey her subjectivity. Offered up as dialogue with no response, they lie like prone objects on the white page, just as her body lies helpless on the hospital bed.

Alabama's isolation in pain and illness here recalls not only Zelda Fitzgerald's own mental illness but her related struggle with a painful recurring eczema condition. The multiple and conflicting meanings given her disease emerge both in her descriptions of Alabama's trapped condition and in Scott Fitzgerald's description of one of Dick Diver's female patients, who suffers and eventually dies from eczema. In Scott Fitzgerald's rendition, Dick Diver attributes his patient's illness largely to the fact that she is too upper class and too delicate to be the artist she would like to be: "The frontiers that artists must explore were not for her, ever. She was fine-spun, inbred—eventually she might find rest in some quiet mysticism. Exploration was for those with a measure of peasant blood, those with big thighs and thick ankles who could take punishment as they took bread and salt, on every inch of flesh and spirit" (p. 201). Scott Fitzgerald's language reverberates with the still vital nineteenth-century American discourse about middle-class women's illnesses, discourse that described middle-class women as frail, dependent, susceptible to debilitating diseases. In this discourse, disease itself is represented as female. (Writes McFarland, "A man can not even exchange his roundabout and boots for a dressing-gown and slippers without being made, in feeling, at least, somewhat effeminate by the act, and what an abatement in his manliness is there when he is reduced—a single garment only excepted—to the original suit in which he made his mundane debut" ["Minor Mental Maladies," 12].)

The etiology of Alabama's condition contrasts markedly with that Scott Fitzgerald describes. The self-revulsion and physical disease that Alabama suffers are connected not to her own weak constitution but to her embattlement with an art form—ballet—largely controlled by men, an art form that parallels medical ideology in the ways that it rigidly prescribes the shape and movement of the female body. The Fitzgeralds' conflicting narratives about an illness diagnosed as psychosomatic reveal to what extent that diagnosis represents an interpretation indistinguishable from gender- and class-related social controls.

In her illuminating discussion of Charlotte Perkins Gilman's "The Yellow Wallpaper," Paula A. Treichler remarks that "diagnosis is a 'sentence' in that it is simultaneously a linguistic entity, a declaration or judgment, and a plan for action in the real world whose clinical consequences may spell dullness, drama, or doom for the diagnosed" (p. 71). Alabama's sickness becomes the point where medical diagnosis has most succeeded in controlling her body—confining it to a sickbed surrounded by doctors. Lost in the pain of her foot while she is in the hospital, Alabama hallucinates a place with "a lake . . . so clear that she could not tell the bottom from the top," a place explosive with lush animality and sensations that seem to run together without order: "Nebulous weeds swing on the current: purple stems with fat animal leaves, long tentacular stems with no leaves at all, swishing balls of iodine and the curious chemical growths of stagnant waters" (p. 194). Out of this landscape stifling in its mixture of sexual physicality and medical imagery, "the word 'sick' effaced itself against the poisonous air and jittered lamely about between the tips of the island and halted on the white road that ran straight through the middle. 'Sick' turned and twisted about the narrow ribbon of the highway like a roasting pig on a spit, and woke Alabama gouging at her eyeballs with the prongs of its letters" (p. 194). The linguistic signifier that emerges from this bodily landscape is the word "sick," the one-word diagnostic sentence that defines her physical being and violates her own seeing, her own subjectivity.

This sickness is also the point, however, where subversion of the diagnostic system becomes possible. In her illness she retreats from the demands of wifehood and of the ballet into her own imaginative world, a world in which language reveals itself as profoundly connected to bodily experience. The authority of the experts' description of her is unmasked as she realizes that the authoritative description is itself the sickness that invades and inhabits her body: The word "sick" itself is what "[gouges] at her eyeballs with the prongs of its letters." At this point she suddenly remembers her father and almost simultaneously imagines his death thinking, "without her father the world would be without its last resource." In the crisis of her illness, to which the diagnoses of husband, physician, ballet master have in a sense driven her, she thus envisions her father's death, then remarks "with a sudden shock, 'it will be me who is the last resource when my father is dead' " (p. 195). Alabama is released from the patriarchal word, the word of her father (the judge, the pillar of his community), the source of her comfort, her dependence, and her own internalized regulatory system. When her father dies, her creativity is no longer ruled in the same way by the interlocking ideologies of daughterhood, wifehood, mental illness, mental health, appropriate feminine art forms.

Released from the hospital, and from her status as father's daughter, the prisoner of medical and judicial authority, Alabama returns to her place of birth and presumably begins the third-person narrative that we have before us. The novel ends not with Alabama's celebration of the cure of her illness—the standard closing of the asylum autobiography—but with her meditation on the power of form and its relation to her own self-expression. As she and her husband David socialize with friends and family after her father's funeral, Alabama notices,

> The cacophony of the table volleyed together and frustrated itself like a scherzo of Prokofiev. Alabama whipped its broken staccato into the only form she knew: schstay, schstay, brisé, schstay, the phrase danced along the convolutions of her brain. She supposed she'd spend the rest of her life composing like that: fitting one thing into another and everything into the rules.
>
> "What are you thinking about, Alabama?"

"Forms, shapes of things," she answered. The talk pelted her consciousness like the sound of hoofs on a pavement. (p. 208)

Later, as the guests are leaving, David chastises her by saying, " 'If you would stop dumping ash trays before the company has got well out of the house we would be happier.' " She replies, " 'It's very expressive of myself. I just lump everything in a great heap which I have labelled 'the past,' and, having thus emptied this deep reservoir that was once myself, I am ready to continue' " (p. 212).

These two passages reveal Alabama's conflicting impulses regarding form: her need to find rules in all things and her desire to "just lump everything in a great heap." In the first passage, she describes her search for order as almost compulsive. It is the latter passage, however, that is the novel's penultimate paragraph. When David chastises her for breaking a social rule, she maintains that just such lumping together at the wrong moment is "very expressive of myself."

The narrative thus presents itself as autobiography in this final description of Alabama's creativity, even as the novel as a whole skirts the details of Zelda Fitzgerald's life. Yet this is not necessarily a contradiction, given that her analogy between self-expression and the ill-timed dumping of ashtrays challenges the notion that she must follow any generic conventions.

Ultimately, the narrative line, which seems to fizzle out at the end of the novel, seems less important than the texture of the language that evolves along the way. It is in the language of the narrative that her body finally reenters the picture. The criticism of the book after its release—that it is too ornate, flowery, exaggerated—comes precisely from this entrance of the body into language. One reviewer complains of "an almost ludicrous lushness of writing" (Brande, p. 735). Several reviewers complain that the language gets in the way of the story itself, which thus loses the realism it needs to make it a good novel. For one critic, the book is marred by "an extremely involved prose style which fails to do anything but clog both the action of the plot and the reader's understanding of the characters. . . . none of its people is more than a pivot about which the author weaves words, words, words" (*Forum*, xi). For another critic, "no phenomenon is too simple for her to obfuscate with the complexities of figure of speech." He goes on to say that "the desperation which prompts Alabama to turn to ballet-dancing with a group of dingy, impoverished people in Paris is anything but convincing on the part of a healthy young woman (which she has been shown to be) who has a husband whom she loves and a young daughter she adores" (Hellman, p. 190). This criticism in particular reveals the expectations of many of Zelda Fitzgerald's readers: Not only did they want the story and characters to be "realistic" in the first place, but their idea of what constituted a "real" story and "real" characters was determined largely by assumptions about what a "healthy young woman" might want and how she might behave.

One reviewer who actually enjoyed her prose style characterized it as having "a masculinity that is unusual; it is always vibrant and always sensitive" (*NY Herald Tribune*, 10x). These comments suggest that objections to her prose may themselves be informed by the readers' idea that a woman's written language should subordinate itself to the story. The word "unusual" above clearly refers to the body of writing by women, since masculinity would hardly be unusual in writing by men.

As Alicia Ostriker remarks, "Male readers, and indeed conservative critics of any stripe, tend to be made uncomfortable by women's body imagery, to feel that it is inartistic, and to take it as evidence of the writer's shallowness, narcissism, and unseemly aggressiveness" (p. 92). Even as Zelda Fitzgerald's narrative tells the story of Alabama's abuse and mastery of her physical self, her prose is thick with sensual imagery that explodes any orderliness imposed on the body of the text. The narrative gives us a virtual litany of flowers, smells, body parts that, as in the hallucination passage above, destroys the categories of disgust and pleasure even as it creates them.

Ostriker, Hélène Cixous, and other feminist theorists have explored the possibility of a "women's writing" based in female bodily experience.[5] I think Zelda Fitzgerald is working—if unconsciously—toward this kind of writing, which challenges the prescriptive sentences of male-generated discourse. Even as her narrative chronicles Alabama's enactment of patriarchal regulation of the female body, her writing brings the body into language. For her language to register itself in this way, it must make itself felt, violating the myth that the language of autobiography must be transparent, that it must allow the reader an illusion of realism. To make itself felt, her language must be, in effect, inappropriate to the conventions of realistic novel and autobiography, conventions that were expected from the female autobiographer even as literary modernism was disrupting the rules of nineteenth-century realism. As the male modernist was beginning to acknowledge his displacement and his inability to know the world, Zelda Fitzgerald wrote against the ever increasing tendency of realistic psychiatric and medical narratives to create worlds in which women's bodies would remain the described, controlled objects of discourse.

In her article "Reading the Slender Body," Susan Bordo analyzes "the contemporary preoccupation with slenderness as it functions within a modern, 'normalizing' machinery of power in general, and, in particular, as it functions to reproduce gender-relations" (p. 85). Bordo shows that in contemporary society conditions that appear as pathology—such as anorexia and bulimia—can actually serve an important normalizing function as they help define and contain female sexuality. Zelda Fitzgerald's writing resists the ordering that Bordo describes, an ordering that Alabama associates with the hospital and the doctor's diagnosis. From her hospital room, Alabama observes that "the streets ran about the tiny grass plots like geometrical calculations—some learned doctor's half-effaced explanatory diagrams on a slate" (p. 192). The controlled rational world reminds her of the diagnosis of her own condition which remains obscured even as it is enacted on her.

*Save Me the Waltz* reveals even as it resists the existence of an expanse of controlled territory—from female body to female activity to female mind—as well as a continuum of controlling discourses in dance, art, medicine, psychiatry. In the place of sickness, the controlling discourse both signals its power and faces the consequences of its violence. The sick woman—Alabama Beggs—is intensely contained and intensely explosive. In her pain and defeat, she recognizes the constructedness of her body and of the medical and marital narratives of her experience.

The image of tiny grass plots takes us back much earlier in the narrative to a point where, as a child, Alabama "is already contemptuous of ordered planting, believing in the possibility of a wizard cultivator to bring forth sweet-smelling blossoms from the hardest of rocks, and night-blooming vines from barren wastes, to plant the breath of twilight and to shop in marigolds" (p. 7). The narrative itself is the work of this wizard cultivator whose language has planted itself in the hard rock of the diagnostic sentence. *Save Me the Waltz* thus subverts the illusion of realism in autobiography in two ways. On the one hand, by substituting the ballet story for the expected schizophrenia story, the novel exposes the expected narrative, bracketed by psychiatrist's introduction, as a diagnosis shaping and controlling female experience. On the other hand, by writing the body into language, it interferes with the reader's impulse to see through language into the "real" story of illness and cure, a story that would keep the female body under control. The "night-blooming vines" of the wizard cultivator thus overrun the "ordered planting" of the female body in a gesture that calls into question any narrative—medical, psychiatric, literary—that describes "woman" and calls that description "real."

# Conclusion

Recently I gave a lecture to a local community group on writings by women in asylums. At the time, I was new in town and had agreed to the lecture partly as a way of meeting people in the community. As I began my talk, I was at least as concerned about my own adjustment to a new job, a new place, new people, as I was about the material I was presenting. I was somewhat unprepared, then, for the reaction—particularly of the women in the audience—to the writings I spoke about. Afterward, woman after woman came up to me, some in tears, to say how much the experiences and words of these writers—some over a hundred years in the past—reverberated either with their own experiences or with those of mothers, daughters, sisters, grandmothers, aunts. Many of these women had at some point read Phyllis Chesler's *Women and Madness* or Marge Piercy's *Woman on the Edge of Time*, had been angered and empowered by the exposure of women's oppression in these books, and were longing to talk about their own experiences with mental illness and its institutions. Hearing these stories helped make visible to me the experiences of women in my own family with mental illness and its treatments, experiences that I only now saw had left an indelible mark on my own life.

What struck me over and over again after the lecture was the sense that the women I spoke with had rarely, if ever, articulated their experiences with psychiatric diagnoses and institutions. I would include myself in this as well, since, I now began to see, while I had spent years reading and writing about women's encounters with these institutions, I had remained silent—even in my own mind—about the ways I had been moved and affected not only by these historical accounts but by the experiences of the many living women I knew (friends, family, co-workers, acquaintances) who had spent time in psychiatric institutions.

As I explored the ways in which certain American women had

raised their voices against a discourse that first disallowed those voices altogether and then encompassed the voices themselves as objects of analysis, I became increasingly aware of my own connection—and that of the women around me—to these courageous writers. I began my study with sympathy for their powerlessness and admiration for their resourcefulness. By the end of the project I also felt both hope and fear for women today who have inherited on the one hand a legacy of objectification and silencing and on the other a legacy of resistance and demand for control over one's own mental health.

I do think that women have increasingly become able to speak out about their experiences with mental illness and psychiatric institutions. However, I think we need to be aware of the conditions under which recent narratives of mental illness and institutionalization have been produced. It is very easy to let a model of medical progress obscure our vision of the mechanisms still at work in mental health systems and discourses, mechanisms that serve to enforce inequalities of race, class, and gender. Our need to believe in medical truths has been made evident to me in a question that has been raised at almost every lecture or paper I've delivered on this subject: "But were these women really crazy?" Behind this question is a desire to separate the "realities" of mental illness from the discourse that permeates it. Such a separation is impossible; there is no "reality" of mental illness outside of a particular historical and cultural context.

In discussing interviews with women institutionalized for schizophrenia in the late 1950s and early 1960s, Carol Warren writes, "the effect of mental health legislation in the 50's was to reinforce the patriarchal authority of the husband and the medical authority of the (usually male) psychiatrist" (p. 15). Her observation suggests that the connection that Elizabeth Packard pointed out between the medical establishment and the institution of marriage was alive and well one hundred years later and may still be so today. In looking at contemporary asylum autobiographies, we would need to consider the ways in which the image of ideal housewife and mother has helped construct the subjectivity of women. We would need to take into account as well the factors of race, class, and religious background that might intersect in the formation of a woman's subjectivity and relation to family and community.

Where the advent of "the talking cure" in the early twentieth century paralleled a shift in the focus of the asylum autobiography from protest to inner journey, the increase of deinstitutionalization and drug therapy in recent years marks another change in the genre. We need to ask whether these two movements have facilitated or hindered women's ability to voice their experiences. Has deinstitutionalization left women on the street without the community support that Elizabeth Packard was able to count on, ironically enough, within the asylum? Has drug therapy enabled women to avoid institutions only to leave them trapped in untenable home situations without the ability to think and feel clearly?

We should also ask how new theories of mental illness and recent diagnostic categories have affected women defined by these new terms. Definitions of schizophrenia that stress chemical imbalances may free women from blame for their own illness, but they also obscure the power relations that may be at work in schizophrenia as both illness and medical category.

For example, the standard handbook on diagnosis of mental illness, *The Diagnostic and Statistical Manual of Mental Disorders—Third Edition Revised* (or *DSM-III-R*), claims that schizophrenia can be recognized by, among other symptoms, "marked impairment in role functioning as wage-earner, student, or homemaker" (p. 194). The manual makes no reference to the fact that each of these "roles" carries multiple meanings that will necessarily affect different subjects differently, depending on their race, class, and gender. The *DSM-III-R Case Book: A Learning Companion to the DSM-III-R* reinforces this lack of contextualization with telling narratives about specific cases and their outcomes. In the "follow-up" to an example of "delusional disorder, erotomanic type," the *Case Book* offers the following reassuring conclusion:

> Mrs. Field readily accepted medication, and primozide, an anti-psychotic drug, was prescribed, eventually in a daily dose of 2 mg. Over a period of three to four weeks, she became much calmer, the delusion became less insistent, and she reduced her alcohol consumption considerably. She developed an episode of depression which responded to a tricyclic antidepressant that was temporarily added to her antipsychotic medication.
>
> Three years later, Mrs. Field remains well and rarely drinks. She and her husband appear content with their marriage, which remains platonic. She occasionally thinks of the physician with

some nostalgia and still believes he loves her but is no longer
distressed about this. She continues to take her antipsychotic
medication. (p. 32)

This narrative reminds us disturbingly of the nineteenth-century discourse on insanity that defined a woman's cure in terms of her ability
to return to home and marriage. Here, Mrs. Field's need for physical
and sexual fulfillment is displaced by treatment through drugs. While
she has not been physically incarcerated in an asylum, as was Clarissa
Lathrop, who manifested similar symptoms, she has clearly been controlled by medication prescribed by a psychiatrist. Behind the claim
that she "readily accepted" this medication lies an important untold
story. How do we know she readily accepted it? What were her options?
Did she feel coerced, helpless, empowered? These questions are not
presented in the *Case Book* as important ones for the psychiatric student to learn.

The disempowerment of women diagnosed as mentally ill spills
over into popular manuals on the subject, just as it did one hundred
years ago. *Mental Illness: A Homecare Guide* counsels family members that when the mentally ill person asks, "How Can I Handle Not
Getting Along Very Well with My Family?" they should answer, "First,
you must understand that your family wants only the best for you.
The illness you have puzzles them as much as it puzzles you. In the
healthiest of families, there are always conflicts. You'll just have to
work together, and you'll have to abide by the household rules. You
give and they'll give. If you can't, you may have to find other living
arrangements" (p. 175). The messages are mixed here about just how
seriously one should take the subjectivity of someone diagnosed as
mentally ill. From the first sentence above, the diagnosed patient is
separated out from the other family members and clearly told she is
the one who must leave if the "arrangements" do not work out. There
is no discussion of who makes the rules or who enforces them. In a
culture where male power is dominant, the above instructions contain an unspoken gender element. How do women fare when these
guidelines are put into practice?

Family systems theories can similarly become apolitical by treating each role in the family "system" equally without considering the
ways that unequal gender, race, and class systems in the larger social
network affect different individuals in the family. Family therapist and

researcher Mara Selvini Palazzoli acknowledges this problem when she remarks, "By stubbornly limiting the scope of our exploration to the here and now and inquiring, for instance, what the wife did just before her husband started beating her, we are obviously being simplistic and reductive" (*Family Games*, p. 160).

Given the changed function of the mental institution, a study of more contemporary narratives would need to reconsider the ways that the sciences of the human mind have developed new methods of controlling women that do not necessarily include confining them in a physical space. In discussing the power of the "medical personage" outside the asylum, Foucault writes that Freud "focussed upon this single presence—concealed behind the patient and above him, in an absence that is also a total presence—all the powers that had been distributed in the collective existence of the asylum; he transformed this into an absolute Observation, a pure and circumspect Silence, a Judge who punishes and rewards in a judgment that does not even condescend to language; he made it the Mirror in which madness, in an almost motionless movement, clings to and casts off itself" (pp. 277–78). While the contemporary American psychiatrist may not be the silent judge Foucault describes here, he may still exercise the power of the asylum, deciding whether his patient needs medication and how much, writing his diagnosis and prescription in her medical records, and shaping the rules of the doctor-patient interaction, rules which are not the less present for being unspoken.

A study of contemporary asylum autobiography would also do well to look at the popularized genre of case study, for wherever a doctor writes a case study of a woman patient a woman's voice has been largely usurped—even if the doctor means well in educating the public. For example, in his popular book *Through Divided Minds: Probing the Mysteries of Multiple Personalities—A Doctor's Story*, Robert Mayer clearly wants his women patients' stories to be told and is careful to say, "I still struggle with my countertransferences" (p. 280), referring to the danger that he might read his own life into theirs. It is largely his ability to listen to their multiple voices that leads him to move outside of conventional diagnostic categories. Yet while their voices come through in his narrative, they do not give it shape; we never see their experience of illness and treatment (not to mention their feelings about their psychologist) through their own eyes. Mayer's inability really to tell their story is apparent in the fact that he introduces virtually every woman patient by describing how much she weighs and how attractive she is. Given that his patients have all been sexually abused and have dissociated from their bodies as a result, it is disturbing that the man who tells their story objectifies them as well. I use Mayer as an example here not so much to point out problems in one particular book as to demonstrate how deeply the sciences of psychology and psychiatry are rooted in the objectification of women. A "case study" will almost inevitably evoke and replay this objectification.

We need to continue to be distrustful of the discourse on mental illness, even as we engage with it or look to it for answers to our own trouble and alienation. Psychiatry and psychology need to continually be reminded of their own history, of their inheritance of an ideology that first says women are inherently irrational and then proposes to cure them of madness, an ideology that conflates difference with deviance. As women, we need to listen to each other's stories of mental illness, institutionaliztion, recovery, fear—stories that can help us gain control of decisions about how to remedy our troubles without losing our voices or denying the voices of others.

# Notes

## Introduction

1. Among the scholars who have called into question the asylum-as-progress view are Elaine Showalter, *The Female Malady*, David Rothman, *Conscience and Convenience* and *The Discovery of the Asylum*, Andrew Scull, "The Social History of Psychiatry in the Victorian Era," and Thomas Szasz, *The Manufacture of Madness* as well as his many other works on the history of madness. Interestingly enough, Szasz, who, like Chesler, most vehemently challenges the motives and methods of psychiatry and gives voice to psychiatric patients, is rarely cited by historians of mental illness. His work may be seen as a little too close to the "inside."

2. Ellen Dwyer, in "A Historical Perspective," presents Gray as more than ordinarily interested in helping overworked women escape from the burdens that led them into melancholy (pp. 23–24, 28).

3. After her release, Clarissa Lathrop joined with some of these lay questioners to form the "Anti-Kidnapping League and Lunacy Reform Union," an organization the *New York Times* reported on January 18, 1891, with tongue very much in cheek.

4. Here, I use the word "psychiatric" provisionally. There really was no psychiatry to speak of before the twentieth century. Nineteenth-century "experts" on mental disease were referred to as "alienists," a term resonant with the nineteenth-century middle-class preoccupation with otherness. For the most part, I use the term "alienist" when discussing the nineteenth-century writers, but "psychiatrist" when discussing the twentieth century or both centuries together.

5. Rothman points out that between 1845 and 1860 at the Worcester state hospital as many as 532 patients occupied rooms meant for 250 inmates. In 1871, at a state asylum in New Jersey, 700 inmates were housed in rooms meant for 500 (*Discovery*, pp. 265–66).

6. See Nancy Tomes, "Historical Perspectives on Women and Mental Illness," pp. 145–46.

7. Grob points out that many alienists argued that use of restraints was not desirable but was practical and unavoidable (*Mental Illness*, pp. 17–18).

8. At least one asylum visitor, Dr. George A. Tucker, "Insane Asylum Superintendent in the Australian colonies," who toured American asylums in 1882, did have access to the "rear wards, usually allotted to supposed chronic

and turbulent patients," and remarked on the "dreary monotony of bare walls, locked doors, and barred windows" compared to the surroundings in the front wards (*NYT*, May 14, 1883, p. 8).

9. With regard to the association of women with madness, Elaine Showalter writes, "While the name of the symbolic female disorder may change from one historical period to the next, the gender assymmetry of the representational tradition remains constant. Thus madness, even when experienced by men, is metaphorically and symbollically represented as feminine: a female malady" (*The Female Malady*, p. 4).

10. The question of whose view is being presented is an important one because it is in the narration of history that ideology can be reconstituted and subversion silenced. As Barbara Harlowe points out in *Resistance Literature* in reference to contemporary resistance movements against colonialism and imperialism, "the struggle over the historical record is seen from all sides as no less crucial than the armed struggle" (p. 7).

11. For example, in his survey of autobiographical literature and criticism, James Olney sees in autobiographies by African American men and women as well as white women "something akin to a paradigm of the situation of autobiography in general" (p. 15), yet he identifies Rousseau and Leiris as the "classic" autobiographers: "As Rousseau was the classic autobiographer of his time, so Leiris seems well on the way to becoming that for our time" ("Autobiography and the Cultural Moment," p. 27).

12. Autobiography theorists have pointed out that the genre of autobiography depends more on a mutually agreed upon relationship between writer and reader than on an identifiable form. Elizabeth Bruss writes, "The syntax of a question does not explain its illocutionary value, in the same way that the style or structure of autobiography cannot explain what is at the heart of its generic value: the roles played by an author and a reader, the uses to which the text is being put" (p. 5). See also Philippe LeJeune, *Le pacte autobiographique.*

13. A good example of this eclectic form is *A History of Mary Prince, A West Indian Slave*, published in 1831 in London, the first published slave narrative by a woman. It included a preface by the white editor, a "Supplement" comprising facts about the author's life and authenticating letters from "respectable" citizens, and another brief slave narrative, "The Narrative of Asa-Asa, a Captured African."

14. Feminist critic Nina Baym makes a useful distinction between the sentimental novels of Richardson and the domestic novel, or what she calls "woman's fiction," in which the heroine occupies a more powerful position. I think Packard draws on both versions of this tradition.

15. Grob points out the roots of psychiatry in the asylum when he remarks that private practice among "alienists" emerged only after 1875. Before that, their work was almost always tied to institutions (*Mental Institutions*, p. 42).

16. Autobiographical experiments have a different set of meanings for male writers than they do for women writers. For example Henry Adams' experiments with exposing the secure "I" of conventional nineteenth-century autobiography differ from Zelda Fitzgerald's liberties with autobiographical fiction. Adams's use of third-person narration and parody of the idea of the self-made man take place in the light of his privileged access to the male "I" of literature with all its history, tradition, and power. Zelda Fitzgerald's experimentation emanates from an "I" that must first be created before it can be questioned or discarded.

## Chapter 1: Elizabeth Packard and Versions of Sanity

1. Himelhoch and Shaffer point out that until recently, most historians accepted the case history of Andrew McFarland, the Jacksonville Asylum superintendent at the time Packard was an inmate, as the best account of Packard's story. Himelhoch and Shaffer undertake "a comprehensive review of her contributions" to legislative reform. As they point out, Dorothea Dix received both praise from contemporaries and a place in history for supporting the supposedly benevolent asylum system. In contrast, Packard was villified by the medical profession of her era and was virtually unheard of until her reform work was rediscovered by historian Albert Deutsch in the 1930s (Himelhoch and Shaffer, p. 346). Since then, Packard has also been discussed by Thomas Szasz, in *The Manufacture of Madness*, and Phyllis Chesler, in *Women and Madness*, pp. 33–34. Packard published several versions of her autobiography, which she sold primarily by subscription (Himelhoch and Shaffer, p. 359).

2. Many nineteenth-century American advice writers and physicians saw the acquisition of knowledge or any kind of intellectual activity as dangerous for women. See Haller and Haller, *The Physician and Sexuality*, pp. 37, 38, and Smith-Rosenberg, *Disorderly Conduct*, pp. 187–92, on the nineteenth-century concept that education was dangerous to women's reproductive systems. Also see Showalter, *Female Malady* (p. 55) and Scull, "Psychiatry in the Victorian Era" (pp. 23–24), on insanity and women's reproductive systems.

3. On Andrew McFarland's term as superintendent of the state asylum at Jacksonville, see Hurd, *The Institutional Care of the Insane*, p. 453.

4. See Smith-Rosenberg, *Disorderly Conduct*, pp. 197–216, on physicians' perceptions of their female patients. See also Douglas, "The Fashionable Diseases," p. 7, on doctors' common belief that women pretended illness, and Barker-Benfield, "Spermatic Economy," pp. 355–56, on the use of female castration to control rebelliousness later in the century.

5. See Elaine Showalter, "Victorian Women and Insanity": "as the Victorian asylum became more overtly benign, protective, and custodial, it also

became an environment grotesquely like the one in which women normally functioned. Such factors of asylum life as strict chaperonage, restriction of movement, limited occupation, enforced sexlessness, and constant subjugation to authority were closer to the 'normal' lives of women than of men" (p. 169). See also *The Female Malady,* pp. 17, 28, on the "homelike" nature of the asylum.

6. The Utica crib was not only infamous among patients (it is mentioned by all three nineteenth-century autobiographers in this study) but was an object of debate among alienists themselves. In an 1885 study of American asylums, noted British alienist Daniel Tuke writes that, despite some of the crib's uses, it "inevitably suggests, when occupied, that you are looking at an animal in a cage. Moreover it is so temptingly facile a mode of restraint, and is on that account so certain to be abused, that I hope it will not be introduced into this country among the useful American inventions we are so glad to possess. That whatever its occasional utility may be, it may be abused, will be admitted when I say I counted fifty in use in a single asylum, and that a very good institution in most respects. At the celebrated Utica Asylum, under Dr. Gray, where a suicidal woman was preserved from harm by this wooden enclosure, my companion, Dr. Baker, of the York Retreat, allowed himself to be shut up in one of these beds, but preferred not remaining there" (p. 55).

7. William L. Andrews discusses the way that slave narratives developed within the context of a particular rhetorical situation in which African-American writers needed to persuade white readers of their selfhood (p. 17). While Packard is writing within a context of power relations connected to defining sanity and insanity, rather than within the context of race relations, she adopts strategies of persuasion modeled in slave narratives. Whether or not she actually read these narratives, which is unclear from her writing, they emerge in her own narrative. Her numerous references to the abolitionist movement suggest that she was at least familiar with such stories.

8. In her reading of Bacon's "Masculine Birth of Time" (1602–3), Evelyn Fox Keller shows that Bacon separated the inquiring mind from the objectified body and used a language of sexual domination to describe the masculine scientist's analysis of his always feminized object of study. According to Bacon, the scientist must enact " 'a chaste and lawful marriage between mind and Nature' " in which Nature was perceived as a subduable feminine object. At the same time that Bacon denied "that truth is, as it were, the native inhabitant of the human mind and need not come in from outside to take up its abode there," he characterized the object of scientific inquiry as female; truth was both separated from the (male) scientific mind and feminized (Keller, pp. 44–59, 36, 39).

9. This rendering of madness and the mad into object is nowhere more evident than in alienists' use of photography in their practice. British psychiatrist

Hugh Diamond celebrated the use of photography in the observation and cure of the mad in his 1856 paper, "On the Application of Photography to the Physiognomic and Mental Phenomena of Insanity." He writes, "I may particularly refer to the four portraits which represent different phases of the case of the same young person commencing with that state of Mania which is marked by the bustled hair, the wrinkled brow, the fixed unquiet eye, and the lips apart as if from painful respiration, but passing, not to a state in which no man could tame her, but happily through less excited stages to the *perfect* cure—In the third portrait the expression is tranquil and accompanied with the smile of sadness instead of the hideous laugh of frenzy—the hair falls naturally and the forehead alone retains traces, tho' slight ones, of mental agitation. In the fourth there is a perfect calm—the poor maniac is cured. This patient could scarcely believe that her last portrait representing her as clothed and in her right mind, would even have been preceded by anything so fearful; and she will never cease, with those faithful monitors in her hand, to express the most lively feelings of gratitude for a recovery so marked and unexpected" (quoted in Gilman, pp. 164–65). Here the photograph is truly the "perilous mirror" that Packard seeks to destroy. Diamond links the photographic proof and record of her cure to his own fear that she might have worsened, might have regressed "to a state in which no man could tame her."

10. On the contradictory role conflicts experienced by nineteenth-century American women, see Smith-Rosenberg on the hysterical woman, *Disorderly Conduct*, esp. pp. 198–208.

11. Interestingly enough, in her later version of this work, *Modern Persecution*, Packard reasserts her claim to motherhood, stating, "To my mind the claims of the public are secondary at least to those of maternity. Never primary when her children's training is at stake. Could I have prevented it my children would never have been separated from their mother" (p. 381). I think at this point, Packard had come to see maternal rights as inseparable from the other reforms she sought. Even here, however, she continues to support her family by selling her books, "which took me from them about three months in a year" (p. 381).

12. McFarland later returned this manuscript to Packard. She continued to work on it after she left the asylum and published it as *The Prisoner's Hidden Life* in 1868, including, among other added sections, the appended narrative of Sophie Olsen. *Modern Persecution*, which she published in 1873, was another expanded version of her original story, including more testimony by friends and acquaintances and a general revision of the previous work. She published *The Great Drama* in book form in 1892. While this shows some differences from *The Prisoner's Hidden Life*, I'm not sure whether it reflects completely the earlier manuscript that she composed primarily from within the asylum.

13. On women reformers' use of the rhetoric of maternity and domesticity, see Ryan, p. 208.

14. Linda Kerber has described the ways the "republican mother" was supposed to use her domestic function in the early United States to create virtuous citizens for the new republic. See Kerber, *Women of the Republic.*

## Chapter 2: Elizabeth Packard and Sophie Olsen

1. While Olsen does not identify her preasylum class position, her writing, with its references to Greek mythology and other literary sources, suggests she received a middle-class education. I'm not sure whether Packard solicited Olsen's written narrative or transcribed it from an oral recitation or whether Olsen volunteered it; in any case, the voice of the narrator seems different than that of Packard in the main body of the text.

2. David Rothman points out that in the second half of the nineteenth century, the majority of patients in state asylums were foreign-born and/or working class (*Conscience,* p. 24).

3. As Ann Braude points out, it is difficult to determine exactly how large of a movement Spiritualism was given that Spiritualists resisted official organizations and that believers ranged from active practitioners to those who had attended one or two seances. We can get some idea from the fact that the 1890 census, taken after the movement had largely declined and reporting only on those in organizations, listed forty-five thousand Spiritualists in thirty-nine states and territories. Braude reports also that the 1871 *American Booksellers Guide* claimed Spiritualist publications sold at the rate of fifty thousand books and fifty thousand pamphlets annually (Braude, pp. 25–26).

4. Ann Braude points out that "mediumship gave women a public leadership role that allowed them to remain compliant with the complex of values of the period that have come to be known as the cult of true womanhood" (*Radical Spirits,* p. 82). According to Braude, the delicate sensibilities that true women were supposed to have allowed them to claim that they could sense spirits. On the political subversiveness of women Spiritualists, see Mary Farrell Bednarowski, "Women in Occult America." On tendency of Spiritualism to undermine orthodoxies of various kinds, see Ernest Isaacs, "The Fox Sisters and American Spiritualism."

5. Judith Walkowitz has shown that for famous medium Georgina Weldon, Spiritualism offered access to the public realm in a time when middle-class women were expected to stay within the domestic sphere. See "Science and Seance."

6. Locke wrote, "I admit that all people are by nature endowed with reason,

and I say that natural law can be known by reason, but from this it does not necessarily follow that it is known to any and every one. For there are some who make no use of the light of reason but prefer darkness and would not wish to show themselves to themselves. . . . Who, as I might almost say, is there in a commonwealth that knows the laws of his state, though they have been promulgated, hung up in public places, are easy to read and to understand, and are everywhere exposed to view? And how much less will he be acquainted with the secret and hidden laws of nature? hence, in this matter, not the majority of people should be consulted but those who are more rational and perceptive than the rest (*Law of Nature*, p. 115).

7. Other reform victories by Packard included her "Bill to equalize the rights and responsibilities of husband and wife," whose main provisions passed the Illinois Senate in 1871 (*Modern Persecution*, p. 373), and an "Act to Protect the Insane by Law," guaranteeing asylum patients rights of free correspondence and ensuring regular asylum inspection. This law passed in Iowa in 1872 (*Modern Persecution*, p. 328).


## Chapter 3: Lydia Smith and Clarissa Lathrop

1. Tuke reports that in 1884 the Utica asylum held 600 patients, 309 male and 291 female (p. 119). Sophie Olsen reports 300 at the Jacksonville asylum (*Modern Persecution*, p. 324).

2. As Nancy Armstrong has argued, nineteenth-century genres were gendered. Genres, such as domestic fiction or sensation novel, that represented a personal, inner life were marked as "feminine," while those that considered philosophical questions in essay form were marked as "masculine." These genre divisions coincided with the middle-class separation of spheres into public (masculine) and private (feminine) (*Desire*, p. 41).

3. On women and neurasthenia in the nineteenth-century United States, see Showalter, *Female Malady*, pp. 121–44, and Haller and Haller, *The Physician and Sexuality*, pp. 24–41. The diagnosis of neurasthenia in women served several purposes. It supported the notion that women should not read or write too much, since the disease supposedly signified that the brain was being overtaxed and the reproductive organs starved. It supported the idea as well that the urban middle and upper classes were suffering from their superior mental powers. This suffering was seen as a necessary, if unfortunate, stage in evolution, which helped mark the difference between white middle- and upper-class men and women and African Americans, immigrants, and the poor.

4. On the contradictory role conflicts experienced by nineteenth-century American women, see Smith-Rosenberg on the hysterical woman, *Disorderly*

*Conduct,* esp. pp. 198–208. On the real-life responsibilities of middle-class Victorian women, see Branca, "Image and Reality," in Hartman and Banner, *Clio's Consciousness Raised.*

5. See Rush McNair, *Medical Memoirs of Fifty Years in Kalamazoo* (1938), pp. 51–52. I owe enormous thanks to Catherine A. Larson, Local History Specialist at Kalamazoo Public Library, for pointing out the Newcomer case to me and for bringing to my attention both the above book and "Sensational Civil Case, that of Nancy Newcomer vs. Dr. E. H. VanDeusn, Tried 50 Years Ago," *Kalamazoo Gazette,* Oct. 26, 1929. The now standardized spelling of the superintendent's name appears to be VanDeusen. Smith spells it both Vandussen and Vandusen.

6. Many single working women such as Lathrop were not the "social mothers" that Jane Addams was and could not honestly employ the rhetoric of women's piety and maternity as they strove for reform. For a specific discussion of Jane Addams, see Barker-Benfield, " 'Mother Emancipator.' "

7. For good explanations of separate male and female spheres in nineteenth-century America, see Ryan, pp. 113–19, and Barker-Benfield, "The Spermatic Economy," pp. 336–37.

8. English alienist Daniel Tuke remarks, on his 1884 visit to American asylums, that American state asylums included paying patients "mixed with the others who are supported by the State or County. It is strongly urged that this helps to raise the tone of the institution" (p. 91). Tuke reports that at Utica "one-fifth to one-fourth of the inmates are pay patients." Their privileges included a special attendant and private room, both available at extra cost (Tuke, p. 120).

9. In early Calvinist New England, physical disease had corresponded with the natural sinfulness inherent in the whole human race. The body spoke a spiritually symbolic language. While Protestantism was elemental in the rise of the individual because it posited an individual relationship between believer and God, Calvinists nevertheless saw themselves as imbued with a common sinfulness that softened the borders of each individual self. Everyone was a part of Adam in his sinfulness, so that a person experienced illness not because of the failings of his or her own individual body but because that person took part in the communal bond of sin.

10. On the differences between and among neurologists and asylum superintendents, see Sicherman, pp. 35–74; Blustein; Grob, *Mental Illness;* and Rosenberg, *Guiteau,* pp. 70–74.

11. The problem of defining the line between sanity and insanity plagued the writings of neurologists, even though, for example, Hammond could write that "there is no middle ground between sanity and insanity" (p. vi).

12. Foucault describes the family as "a network of pleasures and powers linked together at multiple points and according to transformable relation-

ships. The separation of grown-ups and children, the polarity established between the parents' bedroom and that of the children (it became routine in the
course of the century when working-class housing construction was under-
taken), the relative segregation of boys and girls, the strict instructions as to
the care of nursing infants (maternal breast-feeding, hygiene), the attention
focused on infantile sexuality, the supposed dangers of masturbation, the importance attached to puberty, the methods of surveillance suggested to parents,
the exhortations, secrets, and fears, the presence—both valued and feared—of
servants; all this made the family, even when brought down to its smallest di-
mensions, a complicated network, saturated with multiple, fragmentary, and
mobile sexualities" (*History of Sexuality*, p. 46).

13. In *The Corporeal Self: Allegories of the Body in Melville and Hawthorne*, Sharon Cameron shows convincingly that in nineteenth-century
American literature "the problem of human identity [is] considered explicitly
as a bodily problem, a problem that revolves around knowing the boundaries
of the body" (p. 6). However, her study ignores the extent to which the issue of
corporeal identity was conceived in gendered terms, with women representing
both the body itself and the threat to bodily and spiritual integrity.

14. For a discussion of the importance of willpower in Victorian culture, see
Richard Sennett, pp. 182–83. For a more specific analysis of male willpower in
nineteenth-century America, see Barker-Benfield, "The Spermatic Economy."

15. On the "dangers" of female education, see Haller and Haller, pp. 38–39.
William Hammond clearly expresses his fear of the effects of female education
on future generations when he writes, "There is scarcely a woman belonging to
the upper classes of society who is not more or less irregular in her menstrual
discharges, and this, too, from causes which are the result entirely of an artifi-
cial and abnormal mode of existence. Exposure to cold and damp when thinly
clothed or shod, late hours in exciting society, the reading of modern works
of fiction, which too frequently excite unduly and unhealthily the feelings of
a sensitive girl, the avoidance of the duties and obligations of maternity, the
cramming of the mind at school with subjects such as civil engineering, differential and integral calculus, and other mathematical studies, which it grasps
with difficulty, influence materially the nervous system primarily, and second-
arily the generative organs. These, again, react upon the brain, the spinal cord,
and the sympathetic ganglia, and hysteria, hypochondria, and other forms of
*quasi* insanity are produced, to say nothing of neuralgia, spinal irritation, epilepsy, chorea, nervous dyspepsia, and a dozen other diseases as bad or worse"
(*Treatise*, p. 105).

16. In *The Madwoman in the Attic*, Gilbert and Gubar emphasize the negative impact that monstrous images of women had on the Victorian woman
writer, who had to learn to kill "the 'monster' in the house, whose Medusa-face
also kills female creativity" (p. 17). As other feminist criticism has suggested

(for example, Nine Auerbach's *Woman and the Demon*), that monster could rather be a source of subversive creativity. In *The Female Malady*, Showalter stresses the Victorian woman writer's subversiveness by looking at female insanity in works by Florence Nightingale, Charlotte Brontë, and Mary E. Braddon (pp. 61–73). While it is vital to recognize the subversive nature of these texts—their rebellion against standard psychiatric discourse—I think Showalter underplays the impact of the "madwoman" image on the female characters' self-perception. The woman writer's relationship to monstrous images of female insanity was a complex one which she both feared and looked to as a source of power. I am more inclined to look at it this way than to accept Jonathan Loesberg's assertion that Braddon's novel *Lady Audley's Secret*, like other sensation fiction, "can be read either as subversive or as conventional" (136n).

Chapter 4: "The Hidden Things of Darkness Shall Be Brought to Light"

1. In chapter 1, I discussed Nancy Armstrong's view that gender and genre are intimately connected in the nineteenth century. Writing that is "about" the personal and that refers to subjectivity was marked as feminine, while writing that attached itself to the political realm was marked as masculine.

2. Freedman and D'Emilio discuss the important role of advice literature in shaping appropriate behavior within the family. See *Intimate Matters*, pp. 66–73.

3. Mary Kelley writes of nineteenth-century women writers, "Thinking as private domestic women that they could not enter the wide world, the literary domestics thought to make woman's private domestic world wider, and the thought was that woman would shape society by influencing and controlling man. The man living in the world by woman's ethics testified to the higher moral and spiritual sphere of the woman's life in the home" (p. 308). Even for these women, however, the line between public and private was becoming harder to discern. As Kelley points out, they conducted business with publishers and developed public selves, even as they continued to define themselves as within the domestic sphere.

4. In her "Address to the Legislature of New York on Women's Rights" on February 14, 1854, Elizabeth Cady Stanton said, "Gentlemen, in republican America, in the nineteenth century, we, the daughters of the revolutionary heroes of '76, demand at your hands the redress of our grievances—a revision of your State Constitution—a new code of laws" (DuBois, p. 44). Of course, like most white feminists of the period, she partly based her claim of equality on her race, complaining, "We are moral, virtuous, and intelligent, and in all respects quite equal to the proud white man himself, and yet by your laws we

are classed with idiots, lunatics, and negroes" (DuBois, p. 45). Here she reproduces the hierarchy of being that the asylum autobiographies themselves both repeat and expose.

5. The asylum investigations she refers to are discussed in *NYT*, Dec. 7, 1880, p. 12.

6. On the movement for antebellum female reformers to discuss publicly such formerly taboo subjects as adultery and prostitution, see Smith-Rosenberg, *Disorderly Conduct*, pp. 109–28.

7. For example, the following articles, among others, appeared in the *NYT* from 1880–83: "Insane Asylum Methods: Alleged Abuses Laid before the Senate Committee," Dec. 2, 1880, p. 8; "Ward's Island Asylum Answers to Charges against Its Management," Dec. 5, 1880, p. 2; "Investigating Asylums, Witnesses Tell of Insane People Who Died in Cribs," Dec. 7, 1880, p. 2; "The Reverend Mr. French heard Telling the Senate Committee about Abuses in the Insane Asylum," Dec. 10, 1880, p. 3; "A Long Island Asylum: An Investigation by Queens County Supervisors," Aug. 23, 1882, p. 8; "Stories of Cruel Treatment: Serious Charges against A Pennsylvania Hospital for the Insane," Feb. 24, 1883, p. 1; "Pleas for the Insane," June 7, 1883, p. 2.

8. Daniel Borus connects literary realism to the rising social sciences of the late nineteenth century: "Although literary realism did not fashion the claims to scientific precision that sociology did, it was an essential component of the intellectual movement of the late nineteenth century. Steeped in the intellectual environment of the period and drawing upon many of the same sources as the new or revitalized disciplines, realists brought to literature the same concern for the mapping of society and its behavioral rules and the same method of observing the concrete rather than replicating the abstract" (p. 14).

9. This is not to say "the non-expert voice" is a unified one. As Christopher Wilson points out, the "exposure" of the newspapers was often a planned manipulation of public opinion that actually covered up and contributed to deeper corruption (p. 47).

10. For a wonderful discussion of Mrs. Weldon's "case," see Walkowitz, "Science and Seance."

11. Thomas Szasz has discussed the ways that moral policing disguised as medical diagnosis informed turn-of-the-century psychiatry. He considers "Kraepelin, Bleuler, and Freud the conquistadors and colonizers of the mind of man. society, their society, wanted them to extend the boundaries of medicine over morals and law—and they did so; it wanted them to extend the boundaries of illness from the body to behavior—and they did so; it wanted them to disguise conflict as psychopathology, and confinement as psychiatric therapy—and they did so" (*Schizophrenia*, p. 22).

12. When Smith and Lathrop express the suspicion that investigators have not probed deeply enough into asylum secrets, they echo a similar fear com-

mon in the courts, legislatures, and press in mid-to late-nineteenth-century America. For example, in 1882, when the Queens County Board of Supervisors began an investigation of New York's Mineola Asylum, the *NYT* reported, "The questioning by Supervisor Brinckerhoff and the construction put upon the answers of witnesses in the written testimony did not tend toward an impartial and searching investigation" (Aug. 23, 1882, p. 8). In a later report on this investigation, the same paper reported that one of the supervisors complained that newspapers gave the impression the committee would not make a thorough investigation (Aug. 29, 1882, p. 8).

13. This observing mind itself becomes an object of fear if its power becomes too threatening. The all too clever head of Melville's character Babo, an ex-slave who takes over a slave ship in "Benito Cereno," must be severed from the body in relation to which it plays the role of mind. Babo's severed and displayed head, like that of the Medusa, is thus the mind made into body, made into object of observation. Its gaze continues, however, to remind the observer of its power.

## Chapter 5: "A Human Being Had Turned Beast"

1. See James, "The Hidden Self," 258, and "Person and Personality," pp. 317–19, both in *Essays in Psychology*.

2. See James, "The Hidden Self." See also Nathan G. Hale, Jr., *Freud and the Americans*, pp. 117–21, on the well-publicized case of Miss Beauchamp.

3. On the education of the eighteenth-century child, see Jay Fliegelman, *Prodigals and Pilgrims*, pp. 9–35. On the dangers to the child in the early twentieth century, see Margo Horn, *Before It's Too Late*, pp. 78–86, 99–102.

4. On Beers's difference from his predecessors, see also Adolf Meyer, *North American Review*, Apr. 1908, *187*, pp. 611–14; Henry Van Dyke, "A Remarkable Human History," *Yale Review*, 1921–22, *11*, pp. 646–48; and *The Nation*, Mar. 19, 1968, *86*, pp. 265–66. Van Dyke writes, "I suppose it stands quite alone in literature as a clear, vivid, and sane narrative of the moving adventures of a human mind, passing through the dark territory of insanity, and coming out on the other side, not only with the power to tell of its wanderings and sufferings, but also with the purpose to make that experience a source of help to others and benefit to the world."

5. In describing the phenomenon of automatic writing, James remarks, "the writing hand becomes sometimes anaesthetic, sometimes not; and there are all degrees of detachment of the principal consciousness from what is written. In no case, however, is the subject's 'will' felt to be concerned" (James, "Person and Personality," p. 320).

6. It is very suggestive to read Hillyer's words in the light of recent studies

of incestual abuse and its effects on incest survivors. Hillyer's shame, self-blame, and disocciation from her body suggest that there may be another unspoken narrative buried in the one I have been discussing. See Judith Herman, *Father-Daughter Incest*, pp. 96–108.

7. According to early twentieth-century sexologist Havelock Ellis, both the "active" female invert and her "inactive" lover were physiologically and genetically different from the "normal" female. The women to whom the active invert is attracted "differ, in the first place, from the normal, or average, woman in that they are not repelled or disgusted by lover-like advances from persons of their own sex. They are not usually attractive to the average man, though to this rule there are many exceptions. Their faces may be plain or ill-made, but not seldom they possess good figures: a point which is apt to carry more weight with the inverted woman than beauty of face. . . . The actively inverted woman usually differs from the woman of the class just mentioned in one fairly essential character: a more or less distinct trace of masculinity. She may not be, and frequently is not, what would be called a 'mannish' woman, for the latter may imitate men on grounds of taste and habit unconnected with sexual perversion, while in the inverted woman the masculine traits are part of an organic instinct which she by no means always wishes to accentuate" (*Studies in the Psychology of Sex*, p. 222). Both these categories of women are "beastly" in that they "invert" the rules of human interaction. Where they should be "repelled or disgusted" they are not or where their "organic instinct" should give them feminine traits it gives them masculine ones.

## Chapter 6: Zelda Fitzgerald's *Save Me the Waltz* as Asylum Autobiography

A version of this chapter first appeared in *Tulsa Studies in Women's Literature* (Fall 1992): 247–64. Reprinted with permission of the Journal.

1. Despite efforts at objectivity and fairness, for the most part the biographies of the Fitzgeralds (with the exception of Milford's) follow the lead of Oscar Forel (one of her therapists) and F. Scott Fitzgerald in casting Zelda as an unbalanced, jealous, frustrated wife. Writing of her "consuming spiritual passion" about dance, Andre LeVot maintains, "A stubborn ardor fed the flame that raised her and set her spinning, a burning intoxication that charred anything that came near it," in *F. Scott Fitzgerald: A Biography*, p. 251. Sara Mayfield reports on Forel's view of Zelda Fitzgerald as if his opinion is an objective, scientific one. Forel saw Fitzgerald as "a very difficult patient" whose "prismatic moods appealed to him as an intrinsic part of her charm," cited in Mayfield, *Exiles from Paradise*, p. 153. Both James R. Mellow and Scott Donaldson refer to Fitzgerald's attitude toward ballet as an "obsession" and describe

her work accordingly. To Donaldson she was "an inspired amateur," and for Mellow, her writing produced "horrible couturier versions of the natural," in Donaldson, *Food for Love*, p. 79, and Mellow, *Invented Lives*, pp. 399–400. Reviewers responded similarly. Dorothea Brande remarks that "Mrs. Fitzgerald should have had what help she needed to save her book from the danger of becoming a laughing-stock," in *Bookman*, 75, no. 7 (1932): 735.

2. See also Smith-Rosenberg, *Disorderly Conduct*, pp. 182–216; Haller and Haller, *The Physician and Sexuality in Victorian America*, pp. 24–87; and Showalter, *The Female Malady*, pp. 145–64.

3. F. Scott Fitzgerald published two versions of *Tender Is the Night*. The first, published in 1934, begins with the character Rosemary. Fitzgerald revised the novel after it had come out, preferring in the end to change the chronology. The 1951 version, published by Malcolm Cowley after Fitzgerald's death, begins with Dick Diver in Book One, entitled "Case History: 1917–1919." I chose to use this later edition since Fitzgerald ultimately favored it. For a discussion of the two versions and the critical debate surrounding them, see Milton R. Stern, "*Tender Is the Night:* The Text Itself," in Stern, *Critical Essays on F. Scott Fitzgerald's Tender Is the Night*.

4. Writes Gordon, "Flesh belongs to the mother, and, like everything female, for Alabama, it is inferior. The aloof father-judge is replaced by the implacable ideal of pure art; the female, growing in the middle, can only be starved into madness" ("Introduction," p. xxii).

5. Cixous writes to women, "Write your self. Your body must be heard. Only then will the immense resources of the unconscious spring forth. Our naphtha will spread, throughout the world, without dollars—black or gold—nonassessed values that will change the rules of the old game" ("The Laugh of the Medusa," p. 25).

# Works Cited

Abel, Elizabeth. "(E)merging Identities: The Dynamics of Female Friendship in Contemporary Fiction by Women." *Signs* 6 (1981): 413–35.

Adams, Henry. *The Education of Henry Adams*. Boston: Houghton Mifflin Company, 1961.

Andrews, William L. *To Tell a Free Story: The First Century of Afro-American Autobiography, 1760–1865*. Urbana: University of Illinois Press, 1986.

Auerbach, Nina. *Woman and the Demon: The Life of a Victorian Myth*. Cambridge: Harvard University Press, 1982.

Barker-Benfield, G. J. *The Horrors of the Half-Known Life*. New York: Harper and Row, 1976.

———. "'Mother Emancipator': The Meaning of Jane Addams' Sickness and Cure." *Journal of Family History* 4 (1979): 395–420.

———. "The Spermatic Economy: A Nineteenth-Century View of Sexuality." In *The American Family in Social-Historical Perspective*. Ed. Michael Gordon. New York: St. Martin's Press, 1973. Pp. 336–72.

Baym, Nina. *Woman's Fiction: A Guide to Novels by and about Women in America, 1820–1870*. Ithaca: Cornell University Press, 1978.

Beard, George. "The Psychology of Spiritism." *North American Review* 129 (1879): 65–80.

Bednarowski, Mary Farrell, "Women in Occult America." In *The Occult in America: New Historical Perspectives*. Ed. Howard Kerr and Charles L. Crow. Urbana: University of Illinois Press 1983. Pp. 177–88.

Beers, Clifford Whittingham. *A Mind That Found Itself*. 1921. Pittsburgh: University of Pittsburgh Press, 1981.

"Best Books for Summer Reading." *New York Times*, June 13, 1908. Books, p. 335.

Blustein, Bonnie Ellen. "'A Hollow Square of Psychological Science': American Neurologists and Psychiatrists in Conflict." In *Madhouses, Mad-Doctors, and Madmen: The Social History of Psychiatry in the Victorian Era*. Ed. Andrew Scull. Philadelphia: University of Pennsylvania Press, 1981. Pp. 241–70.

Bordo, Susan. "Reading the Slender Body." In *Body/Politics: Women and the Discourses of Science*. Ed. Mary Jacobus, Evelyn Fox Keller, and Sally Shuttleworth. New York: Routledge, 1990. Pp. 83–112.

Borus, Daniel H. *Writing Realism: Howells, James, and Norris in the Mass Market.* Chapel Hill: University of North Carolina Press, 1989.

Braddon, Mary Elizabeth. *Lady Audley's Secret.* 1862. New York: Dover Publications, 1974.

Branca, Patricia. "Image and Reality: The Myth of the Idle Victorian Woman." In *Clio's Consciousness Raised: New Perspectives on the History of Women.* Ed. Mary Hartman and Lois W. Banner. New York: Harper Colophon Books, 1974. Pp. 179–91.

Brande, Dorothea. Rev. of *Save Me the Waltz. Bookman* 75 (Nov. 1932): 735.

Braude, Ann. *Radical Spirits: Spiritualism and Women's Rights in Nineteenth-Century America.* Boston: Beacon Press, 1989.

Breuer, Josef, and Sigmund Freud. *Studies on Hysteria, Complete Psychological Works of Sigmund Freud, Vol. 11.* Trans. James Strachey. London: Hogarth Press, 1962.

Bruss, Elizabeth. *Autobiographical Acts: The Changing Situation of a Literary Genre.* Baltimore: Johns Hopkins University Press, 1976.

Budd, Louis J. "Color Him Curious about Yellow Journalism: Mark Twain and the New York City Press." *Journal of Popular Culture* 15 (1981): 25–33.

Cameron, Sharon. *The Corporeal Self: Allegories of the Body in Melville and Hawthorne.* Baltimore: Johns Hopkins University Press, 1981.

Chesler, Phyllis. *Women and Madness.* New York: Avon Books, 1972.

Christ, Carol. "Victorian Masculinity and the Angel in the House." In *A Widening Sphere: Changing Roles of Victorian Women.* Ed. Martha Vicinus. Bloomington: Indiana University Press, 1977. Pp. 146–62.

Cixous, Hélène. "The Laught of the Medusa." Trans. Keith Cohen and Paula Cohen. *Signs* 1 (1976): 875–93.

Collins, Wilkie. *The Woman in White: A Novel.* 1865. New York: G. P. Putnam's Sons, 1917.

Dain Norman. *Clifford W. Beers, Advocate for the Insane.* Pittsburgh: University of Pittsburg Press, 1980.

———. *Concepts of Insanity in the United States, 1789–1865.* New Brunswick: Rutgers University Press, 1964.

Davis, David Brion. *Homicide in American Fiction, 1798–1860: A Study in Social Values.* Ithaca: Cornell University Press, 1957.

Diner, Hasia R. *Erin's Daughters in America: Irish Immigrant Women in the Nineteenth Century.* Baltimore: Johns Hopkins University Press, 1983.

Donaldson, Scott. *Food for Love: F. Scott Fitzgerald.* New York: Congdon and Weed, Inc., 1983.

Douglas, Ann. " 'The Fashionable Diseases': Women's Complaints and Their Treatment in Nineteenth-Century America." In *Clio's Consciousness Raised: New Perspectives on the History of Women.* Ed. Mary Hartman and Lois W. Banner. New York: Harper Colophon Books, 1974. Pp. 179–91.

Duffey, Eliza B. *What Women Should Know: A Woman's Book about Women.* 1873. New York: Arno Press, 1974.

Dwyer, Ellen. "A Historical Perspective." In *Sex Roles and Psychopathology.* Ed. Cathy Spatz Widom. New York: Plenum Press, 1984. Pp. 19–48.

Fetterley, Judith. "Who Killed Dick Diver? The Sexual Politics of *Tender Is the Night.*" *Mosaic: A Journal for the Interdisciplinary Study of Literature* 17 (1984): 111–28.

Fitzgerald, F. Scott. *Tender Is the Night.* New York: Charles Scribner's Sons, 1951.

Fitzgerald, Zelda. *Save Me the Waltz.* 1832. Carbondale: Southern Illinois University Press, 1967.

Flax, Jane. "Political Philosophy and the Patriarchal Unconscious: A Psychoanalytic Perspective on Epistemology and Metaphysics." In *Discovering Reality: Feminist Perspectives on Epistemology, Metaphysics, Methodology, and Philosophy of Science.* Ed. Sandra Harding and Merrill Hentikka. Boston: D. Reidel, 1983. Pp. 245–81.

Fliegelman, Jay. *Prodigals and Pilgrims: The American Revolution against Patriarchal Authority, 1750–1800.* Cambridge: Cambridge University Press, 1982.

Foucault, Michel. *The History of Sexuality, Vol. I: An Introduction.* New York: Random House, 1980.

———. *Madness and Civilization.* London: Tavistock Publications, 1967.

Freedman, Estelle, and John D'Emilio. *Intimate Matters: A History of Sexuality in America.* New York: Harper and Row, 1988.

Freeman, Ruth, and Patricia Klaus. "Blessed or Not? The New Spinster in England and the United States in the Late Nineteenth and Early Twentieth Centuries." *Journal of Family History* 4 (1984): 394–410.

Fryer, Sarah Beebe. "Nicole Warren Diver and Alabama Beggs Knight: Women on the Threshold of Freedom." *Modern Fiction Studies* 31 (1985): 318–26.

Gardiner, Judith K. "On Female Identity and Writing By Women." *Writing and Sexual Difference.* Ed. Elizabeth Abel. Chicago: University of Chicago Press, 1982. Pp. 177–91.

Garner, Shirley Nelson. "'Women Together' in Virginia Woolf's *Night and Day.*" In *The (M)other Tongue: Essays in Feminist Psychoanalytic Interpretation.* Ed. Shirley Nelson Garner, Clair Kahane, and Madelon Sprengnether. Ithaca: Cornell University Press, 1985. Pp. 318–33.

Gilbert, Sandra M., and Susan Gubar. *The Madwoman in the Attic.* New Haven: Yale University Press, 1980.

Gilman, Charlotte Perkins. *The Living of Charlotte Perkins Gilman.* New York: Appleton-Century, 1935.

———. *The Yellow Wallpaper.* Old Westbury, N.Y.: Feminist Press, 1973.

Gilman, Sander L. *Seeing the Insane.* New York: John Wiley and Sons, 1982.

Gordon, Mary. "Introduction." In *Zelda Fitzgerald: The Collected Writings.* Ed. Matthew Bruccoli. New York: Charles Scribner's Sons, 1991.

Grob, Gerald N. *Mental Illness and American Society, 1875–1940.* Princeton: Princeton University Press, 1983.

———. *Mental Institutions in America: Social Policy to 1875.* New York: Free Press, 1973.

———, ed. *The National Association for the Protection of the Insane and the Prevention of Insanity.* New York: Arno Press, 1980.

Gray, John P. "The Dependence of Insanity on Physical Disease." *American Journal of Insanity* 28 (1871): 377–405.

———. "Insanity and Its Relations to Medicine." *American Journal of Insanity* 25 (1868): 160–68.

———. "Mental Hygiene." *American Journal of Insanity* 34 (1878): 303–14.

———. "Thoughts on the Causation of Insanity." *American Journal of Insanity* 29 (1872): 271–82.

Hale, Nathan G., Jr. *Freud and the Americans: The Beginnings of Psychoanalysis in the United States, 1876–1917.* New York: Oxford University Press, 1971.

Haller, John S., Jr., and Robin M. Haller, *The Physician and Sexuality in Victorian America.* Urbana: University of Illinois Press, 1974.

Hammond, William A. *Insanity In Its Relation to Crime.* New York: D. Appleton and Co., 1873.

———. "The Physics and Physiology of Spiritualism." *North American Review* 110 (1870): 233–61.

———. *A Treatise On Insanity in Its Medical Relations.* New York: D. Appleton and Co., 1883.

Hart, James D. *The Popular Book: A History of America's Literary Taste.* New York: Oxford University Press, 1950.

Hellman, Geoffrey. Untitled. *Saturday Review of Literature* (Oct. 22, 1932), 190.

Herman, Judith Lewis. *Father-Daughter Incest.* Cambridge: Harvard University Press, 1981.

Higham, John. *From Boundlessness to Consolidation: The Transformation of American Culture, 1848–1860.* Ann Arbor, Mich.: William L. Clements Library, 1969.

Hillyer, Jane. *Reluctantly Told.* 1926; New York: MacMillan, 1935.

Himelhoch, Myra Samuels, with Arthur H. Shaffer. "Elizabeth Packard: Nineteenth-Century Crusader for the Rights of Mental Patients." *American Studies* 13 (1979): 343–75.

Hogeland, Ronald W. "The Female Appendage: Feminine Life Styles in America, 1820–1860." In *Our American Sisters.* Ed. Jean E. Friendman and William G. Shade. Boston: Allyn and Bacon, Inc., 1976. Pp. 133–48.

Holmes, Oliver Wendell. "The Contagiousness of Puerperal Fever." *The Medical Essays*. Boston: Houghton Mifflin Company, 1911. Pp. 103–72.

———. "Doings of the Sunbeam." *The Atlantic Monthly* 12 (1863): 1–15.

———. *Elsie Venner: A Romance of Destiny*. 1861. Boston: Houghton, Mifflin and Co., 1891.

———. "The Medical Profession in Massachusetts." *The Medical Essays*. Boston: Houghton Mifflin Company, 1911. Pp. 312–69.

———. "The Stereoscope and the Stereography." *Atlantic Monthly* 3 (1859): 738–48.

Horn, Margo. *Before It's Too Late: The Child Guidance Movement in the United States, 1922–1945*. Philadelphia: Temple University Press, 1989.

Hughes, Winifred. *The Maniac In the Cellar: Sensation Novels of the 1860s*. Princeton: Princeton University Press, 1980.

Hunter, Richard, and Ida MacAlpine. *Three Hundred Years of Psychiatry, 1535–1860*. London: Oxford University Press, 1963.

Henry M. Hurd. *The Institutional Care of the Insane in the United States and Canada, Vol. IV*. New York: Arno Press, 1973.

"Illinois Legislation Regarding Hospitals for the Insane." *American Journal of Insanity* 26 (1869): 213–23.

Isaacs, Ernest. "The Fox Sisters and American Spiritualism." In *The Occult in America: New Historical Perspectives*. Ed. Howard Kerr and Charles L. Crow. Urbana: University of Illinois Press, 1983. Pp. 79–110.

Jacobs, Harriet Brent. *Incidents in the Life of a Slave Girl*. Detroit: Negro History Press, 1969.

James, Henry. "The Art of Fiction." In *Henry James: Literary Criticism, Vol. 2 (Essays on Literature, American Writers, English Writers)*. Ed. Leon Edel. New York: Literary Classics of the United States, 1984. Pp. 44–65.

James, William. "The Hidden Self." In *Essays in Psychology*. Ed. Frederick H. Burkhardt, Fredson Bowers, and Ignas K. Skrupskelis. Cambridge: Harvard University Press, 1983. Pp. 247–68.

———. "Person and Personality: From *Johnson's Universal Cyclopaedia*." In *Essays in Psychology*. Ed. Frederick H. Burkhardt, Fredson Bowers, and Ignas K. Skrupskelis. Cambridge: Harvard University Press, 1983. Pp. 315–21.

Jameson, Fredric. *The Political Unconscious: Narrative as a Socially Symbolic Act*. Ithaca: Cornell University Press, 1981.

Jardine, Alice A. *Gynesis: Configurations of Women and Modernity*. Ithaca: Cornell University Press, 1985.

Jeffries, Sheila. *The Spinster and Her Enemies: Feminism and Sexuality, 1880–1930*. London: Pandora, 1985.

Jelinek, Estelle. "Introduction: Women's Autobiography and the Male Tradition." In *Women's Autobiography*. Ed. Estelle Jelinek. Bloomington: Indiana University Press, 1980.

Kaplan, Amy. *The Social Construction of American Realism*. Chicago: University of Chicago Press, 1988.

Keller, Evelyn Fox. *Reflections on Gender and Science*. New Haven: Yale University Press, 1985.

Keller, Evelyn Fox, and Christine Grontkowsky. "The Mind's Eye." In *Discovering Reality: Feminist Perspectives on Epistemology, Metaphysics, Methodology, and Philosophy of Science*. Ed. Sandra Harding and Merrill Hentikka. Boston: D. Reidel, 1983. Pp. 207–24.

Kelley, Mary. *Private Woman, Public Stage: Literary Domesticity in Nineteenth-Century America*. New York: Oxford University Press, 1984.

Kerber, Linda. *Women of the Republic: Intellect and Ideology in Revolutionary America*. Chapel Hill: University of North Carolina Press, 1980.

King, Marian. *The Recovery of Myself: A Patient's Experience in a Hospital For Mental Illness*. New Haven: Yale University Press, 1931.

Kobre, Sidney. *Development of American Journalism*. Dubuque, Iowa: Wm. C. Brown Company Publishers, 1969.

La Rue, Daniel Wolford. *Mental Hygiene*. New York: MacMillan Co., 1927.

Lathrop, Clarissa Caldwell. *A Secret Institution*. New York: Bryant Publishing Co., 1890.

Lears, Jackson. *No Place of Grace: Antimodernism and the Transformation of American Culture, 1880–1920*. New York: Pantheon Books, 1981.

Lejeune, Philippe. *Le pact autobiographique*. Paris: Seuil, 1975.

LeVot, Andre. *F. Scott Fitzgerald: A Biography*. Trans. William Byron. New York: Warner, 1983.

Locke, John. *An Essay Concerning Human Understanding*. Oxford: Clarendon Press, 1975.

———. *Essays on the Law of Nature*. Ed. W. von Leyden. Oxford: Clarendon Press, 1954.

———. *The Second Treatise of Government*. Oxford: Basil Blackwell, 1956.

Loesberg, Jonathan. "The Ideology of Narrative Form in Sensation Fiction." *Representations* 13 (1986): 115–38.

Masson, Jeffrey M. *The Assault on Truth: Freud's Suppression of the Seduction Theory*. Toronto: Farrar, Straus and Giroux, 1984.

Mayer, Robert. *Through Divided Minds: Probing the Mysteries of Multiple Personalities—A Doctor's Story*. New York: Doubleday, 1980.

Mayfield, Sara. *Exiles from Paradise: Zelda and Scott Fitzgerald*. New York: Delacorte Press, 1971.

McFarland, Andrew. "Annual Meeting of the Association." *American Journal of Insanity* 27 (1860): 51–61.

———. "Minor Mental Maladies." *American Journal of Insanity* 20 (1863): 10–26.

McGovern, Constance. "The Myths of Social Control and Custodial Oppression: Patterns of Psychiatric Medicine in Late Nineteenth-Century Institutions." *Journal of Social History* 20 (1986): 3–21.

McNair, Rush. *Medical Memoirs of Fifty Years in Kalamazoo*. Kalamazoo: Rush McNair, 1938.

Mellow, James R. *Invented Lives: F. Scott and Zelda Fitzgerald*. Boston: Houghton Mifflin Co., 1984.

Meyer, Adolf. "The Problems of Mental Reaction-Types, Mental Causes and Diseases." *The Psychological Bulletin* 5 (1908): 245–66.

———. *Psychobiology: A Science of Man*. Springfield, Ill.: Charles C. Thomas, 1951.

———. Rev. of *A Mind That Found Itself*, by Clifford W. Beers. *The Psychological Bulletin* 5 (1908): 283–84.

Melville, Herman. "Benito Cereno." *Great Short Works of Herman Melville*. New York: Harper and Row, 1969.

———. *Pierre, or the Ambiguities*. New York: E. P. Dutton, 1929.

Milford, Nancy. *Zelda: A Biography*. New York: Harper and Row, 1970.

Miller, D. A. "*Cage aux folles:* Sensation and Gender in Wilkie Collins's *The Woman in White*." *Representations* 13 (1986): 107–36.

Mitchell, S. Weir. *Doctor and Patient*. 5th ed. Philadelphia: J. B. Lippincott Company, 1904.

Moore, R. Laurence. *In Search of White Crows: Spiritualism, Parapsychology, and American Culture*. New York: Oxford University Press, 1977.

Mott, Luther. *American Journalism, A History: 1690–1960*. 3d ed. New York: MacMillan, 1963.

Newhall, Beaumont. *The History of Photography from 1839 to the Present Day*. New York: Museum of Modern Art, 1949.

Olney, James. "Autobiography and the Cultural Moment: A Thematic, Historical, and Bibliographical Introduction." In *Autobiography: Essays Theoretical and Critical*. Ed. James Olney. Princeton: Princeton University Press, 1980. Pp. 3–27.

Olsen, Sophie. "Mrs. Olsen's Narrative of Her One Year's Imprisonment at Jacksonville Insane Asylum." Appended to *The Prisoner's Hidden Life or Insane Asylums Unveiled*. Elizabeth Packard. Chicago: Author, 1868.

O'Neill, William. "Divorce in the Progressive Era." In *The American Family in Social-Historical Perspective*. Ed. Michael Gordon. New York: St. Martin's Press, 1973. Pp. 336–72.

Ostriker, Alicia. *Stealing the Language: The Emergence of Women's Poetry in America*. Boston: Beacon Press, 1986.

Packard, Elizabeth Parsons Ware. *The Exposure on Board the Atlantic and Pacific Car of the Emancipation for the Slaves of Old Columbia . . . or, Christianity and Calvinism Compared, with an Appeal to the Government to Emancipate the Slaves of the Marriage Union*. Chicago: Author, 1864.

———. *Great Disclosure of Spiritual Wickedness!! In High Places, with an Appeal to the Government to Protect the Inalienable Rights of Married Women.* Boston: Author, 1865.

———. *The Great Drama; or, the Millenial Harbinger.* Hartford: Author, 1892.

———. *Marital Power Exemplified in Mrs. Packard's Trial . . . or, Three Years Imprisonment for Religious Belief.* Hartford: Author, 1867.

———. *Modern Persecution, or Insane Asylums Unveiled.* Hartford: Author, 1873.

———. *The Mystic Key; or, The Asylum Secret Unlocked.* Hartford: Author, 1878.

———. *The Prisoner's Hidden Life; or, Insane Asylums Unveiled.* Chicago: Author, 1868.

Palazzoli, Mara Selvini. *Family Games: General Models of Psychotic Processes in the Family.* New York: W. W. Norton, 1989.

Papashvily, Helen Waite. *All the Happy Endings: A Study of the Domestic Novel in America, the Women Who Wrote it, the Women Who Read it, in the Nineteenth Century.* New York: Harper and Brothers Publishers, 1956.

Perceval, John. *Perceval's Narrative: A Patient's Account of His Psychosis, 1830–1832.* Ed. Gregory Bateson. Stanford: Stanford University Press, 1961.

Peterson, Dale. *A Mad People's History of Madness.* Pittsburgh: University of Pittsburgh Press, 1981.

Pinel, Philippe. *Treatise on Insanity.* Tr. D. D. Davis. New York: Hafner Publishers, 1962.

Prince, Mary. "The History of Mary Prince, a West Indian Slave." In *The Classic Slave Narratives.* Ed. Henry Louis Gates, Jr. New York: New American Library, 1987. Pp. 185–242.

Reade, Charles. *Hard Cash.* 1863. London: Chatto and Windus, 1908.

Rev. of *A Mind That Found Itself*, by Clifford W. Beers. *The Nation* 86 (Mar. 19, 1908): 265–66.

Rev. of *Save Me the Waltz. Forum*, 88 (Dec. 1932), xi.

Rev. of *Save Me the Waltz. New York Herald Tribune Books* (Oct. 30, 1932), 10x.

Rittenhouse, Mignon. *The Amazing Nelly Bly.* New York: E. P. Dutton, 1956.

Rosenberg, Charles E. "Sexuality, Class and Role in Nineteenth-Century America." *American Quarterly* 25 (1973): 131–53.

———. *The Trial of the Assassin Guiteau: Psychiatry and Law in the Gilded Age.* Chicago: University of Chicago Press, 1968.

Rothman, David J. *Conscience and Convenience: The Asylum and Its Alternatives in Progresive America.* Boston: Little, Brown, 1980.

———. *The Discovery of the Asylum: Social Order and Disorder in the New Republic.* Boston: Little, Brown, 1971.

Rush, Benjamin. *Medical Inquiries and Observations upon the Diseases of the Mind.* 1812. New York: Hafner, 1962.

Rush, Florence. *The Best Kept Secret: Sexual Abuse of Children.* Englewood Cliffs, N.J.: Prentice-Hall, 1980.

Ryan, Mary P. *Womanhood in America.* New York: Franklin Watts, 1983.

Said, Edward. *Orientalism.* New York: Vintage Books, 1978.

Sakolow, Jayme A. *Eros and Modernization: Sylvester Graham, Health Reform, and the Origins of Victorian Sexuality in America.* Rutherford, N.J.: Fairleigh Dickinson University Press, 1983.

Scott-Smith, Daniel. "Family Limitation, Sexual Control, and Domestic Feminism in Victorian America." In *Clio's Consciousness Raised.* Ed. Mary Hartman and Lois W. Banner. New York: Harper and Row, 1974. Pp. 119–57.

Scull, Andrew. "The Social History of Psychiatry in the Victorian Era." In *Madhouses, Mad-Doctors, and Madmen: The Social History of Psychiatry in the Victorian Era.* Ed. Andrew Scull. Philadelphia: University of Pennsylvania Press, 1981. Pp. 5–32.

Sennett, Richard. *The Fall of Public Man.* New York: Alfred A. Knopf, 1977.

Shea, Daniel B. "The Prehistory of American Autobiography." In *American Autobiography: Retrospect and Prospect.* Ed. Paul John Eakin. Madison: University of Wisconsin Press, 1991. Pp. 25–46.

Shortt, S. E. D. "Physicians and Psychics: The Anglo American Medical Response to Spiritualism, 1870–1890." *Journal of the History of Medicine and Allied Sciences* 39 (1984): 339–55.

Showalter, Elaine. *The Female Malady: Women, Madness, and English Culture, 1830–1980.* New York: Pantheon Books, 1985.

———. "Victorian Women and Insanity." *Victorian Studies* 23 (1979): 157–82.

Sicherman, Barbara. *The Quest for Mental Health in American, 1880–1917.* New York: Arno Press, 1980.

Skultans, Veida. *Madness and Morals: Ideas on Insanity in the Nineteenth Century.* London: Routledge, 1975.

Smith, Lydia A. *Behind the Scene; or, Life in an Insane Asylum.* Chicago: Culver, Page, Hoyne and Co., 1879.

Smith, Stephen. *Who Is Insane?* New York: MacMillan, 1916.

Smith-Rosenberg, Carroll. *Disorderly Conduct: Visions of Gender in Victorian America.* New York: Oxford University Press, 1985.

Southworth, E. D. E. N. *The Curse of Clifton.* 1886. New York: Ams Press, 1970.

Spitzka, Edward C. *Insanity: Its Classification, Diagnosis and Treatment.* New York: Arno Press, 1973.

Stepto, Robert Burns. "I Rose and Found My Voice: Narration, Authentication, and Authorial Control in Four Slave Narratives." In *The Slave's Narrative.* Ed. Charles T. Davis and Henry Louis Gates, Jr. Oxford: Oxford University Press, 1985.

Stern, Milton R. "The Text Itself." In *Critical Essays on F. Scott Fitzgerald's*

*Tender Is the Night.* Ed. Milton R. Stern. Boston: G. K. Hall and Co., 1986. Pp. 21–31.

Szasz, Thomas. *The Manufacture of Madness.* New York: Harper and Row, 1977.

Tomes, Nancy. *A Generous Confidence: Thomas Story Kirkbride and the Art of Asylum-Keeping, 1840–1883.* New York: Cambridge University Press, 1984.

———. "Historical Perspectives on Women and Mental Illness." In *Women, Health, and Medicine in America: A Historical Handbook.* Ed. Rima D. Apple. New York: Garland Publishing, 1990. Pp. 143–71.

Treichler, Paula A. "Escaping the Sentence: Diagnosis and Discourse in 'The Yellow Wallpaper,'" In *Feminist Issues in Literary Scholarship.* Ed. Shari Benstock. Bloomington: Indiana University Press, 1987. Pp. 62–78.

Tuke, Daniel Hack. *The Insane in the United States and Canada.* Repr. London: H. K. Lewis, 1885. New York: Arno Press, 1973.

Turner, James. *Without God, without Creed: The Origins of Unbelief in America.* Baltimore: Johns Hopkins University Press, 1985.

Van Dyke, Henry. "A Remarkable Human History." *Yale Review* 11 (1921–22): 646–48.

Veith, Ilza. *Hysteria: The History of a Disease.* Chicago: University of Chicago Press, 1965.

Wagner, Linda. "*Save Me the Waltz:* An Assessment in Craft." In *Journal of Narrative Technique,* 12 (1982).

Walkowitz, Judith R. "Science and the Seance: Transgressions of Gender and Genre in Late Victorian London." In *Representations* 22 (1988): 3–29.

Warren, Carol A. B. *Madwives: Schizophrenic Women in the 1950s.* New Brunswick: Rutgers University Press, 1987.

Wilson, Christopher P. "The Era of the Reporter Reconsidered: The Case of Lincoln Steffens." *Journal of Popular Culture* 15 (1981): 41–49.

# Index

ness, 74, 158–59, 177n; female public identity, 77, 104, 180n; and heredity, 85–86; and otherness, 171n; and scientific ambivalence, 132; and self-hood, 127–28; and sexuality, 140–41; single women, 77, 178n. *See also* Female sphere; Paranoia

Milford, Nancy, 149, 153–54, 183n

Miller, D. A., 95

*Mind That Found Itself, A* (Beers), 19, 125, 182n; divided self in, 134–35; and memory, 144, 145–46; reason in, 144, 146; self-exposure in, 133–34; subjectivity in, 137

Mirrors, 56; and dual selfhood, 137–38; and fight for sanity, 48, 60, 175n; and loss of selfhood, 155–56, 157; and sanity/insanity distinction, 48, 73; and secret writing, 25–26, 73

*Modern Persecution* (Packard), 28, 34; motherhood in, 45, 175n

Moore, R. Laurence, 53, 54

Motherhood, 42–46, 175n; and reform, 14, 17, 45, 176n; and self-dependence, 43–44; Smith's dedication to, 70–71; undermining of, 45–46. *See also* Family; Female sphere

Mott, Luther, 108

Multiple personalities, 128, 169–70

National Association for the Protection of the Insane and the Prevention of Insanity (NAPIPI), 8–9, 111

Neurasthenia, 70, 177n

Neurologists. *See* Scientific views of insanity

Newcomer, Nancy, 74

New Woman, 132–33

New York Neurological Society, 110, 111

Nightingale, Florence, 180n

Occupational therapy, 6

Olney, James, 172n

Olsen, Sophie, 49, 176n. *See also* Olsen's narrative

Olsen's narrative, 16, 28, 62; anonymous resistance in, 51–52, 64; fight for sanity in, 59–61; legitimizing strategies in, 4, 10; and morality, 55; Packard's distancing from, 49, 50–51, 57; and Spiritualism, 54

O'Neill, William, 104

Ostriker, Alicia, 162

Packard, Elizabeth, 25; reform work of, 63, 177n. *See also Modern Persecution; Prisoner's Hidden Life, The*

Packard, Theophilus, 25

Palazzoli, Mara Selvini, 169

Papashvily, Helen Waite, 91–92

Paranoia, 17–18, 80–81; and causes of insanity, 82–84, 85–86; and class, 70, 79–80, 86–87; as diagnostic category, 70, 74–75, 96; and family, 84–85, 88, 96–97; and gender, 70, 86, 87–92; and male willpower, 86, 135; and potency, 93–94, 97–99; and selfhood, 129; in sensation novels, 95–96, 98; and spinsters, 90–92

Photography, 174–75n

Pierce, Marge, 165

*Pierre* (Melville), 99

Pinel, Philippe, 5

*Prisoner's Hidden Life, The* (Packard), 25–47; association with officials in, 50, 68–69; censorship in, 25–26, 28–29, 31, 41, 47, 58; as challenge to female sphere, 29–30; Christian rhetoric in, 10, 36–37; distancing from other inmates in, 49–50, 55, 59; and domestic novel, 15–16, 27, 30–35; family in, 6, 33–35; fight for sanity in, 61; fragmented form in, 27–28, 67; hiding of, 25–26; legitimizing strategies in, 10, 39–40; mirror in, 26, 138, 175n; motherhood in, 14, 42–46; and official record, 4, 29; rebellion in, 57, 61–62, 63–64; rediscovery of, 173n; reform motive of, 11; science in, 37–42, 48; secret writing in, 25–26, 47, 58; self-dependence in,

Spiritualism, 52; and use of asylum autobiographies, 13–19, 125–27; and violence, 8, 171n; and women's anger, 62–63

Scull, Andrew, 110

*Secret Institution, A* (Lathrop), 17–18; censorship in, 117–18; class divisions in, 50, 67, 70, 78–80, 115; Guiteau trial in, 114–16, 117; and journalism, 10, 18, 101; lack of closure in, 94–95, 99; legitimizing strategies in, 4, 10; masculine voice in, 18, 101; and official record, 4; paranoia in, 17, 70, 74–75, 89, 90–92, 96, 98–99; piety in, 76–77; powerlessness in, 92, 93, 95, 100; public identity in, 100–101, 103–6; publicity in, 107–8; and realist fiction, 18, 101; reform motive in, 11; self-doubt in, 67–69; and sensation novel, 17–18, 20, 69–70; violence in, 8. *See also* Lathrop, Clarissa

Seguin, Edward, 110

Selfhood, 127–28, 137–38; loss of, 155–56, 157

Sensation novel, 17–18, 88–96; closure in, 94–95; and family, 96–99; female conflict in, 91–92; paranoia in, 95–96, 98; powerlessness in, 94; subversive creativity in, 179–80n; women as poisonous in, 88–93

Sentimental novel. *See* Domestic novel

Sex roles, 3

Sexuality, 19, 140–44, 163, 182–83n. *See also* Body

Shaffer, Arthur H., 63, 173n

Shaw, J. C., 9

Shortt, S. E. D., 112–13

Showalter, Elaine, 7, 84, 153, 155, 172n, 180n

Sicherman, Barbara, 110, 127

Silkman, James B., 75, 107

Slave narrative, 14–15, 31, 35–36, 172n, 174n

Smith, Lydia: life of, 70–71; reform work of, 102, 104–5, 109–10, 113, 120–21. *See also Behind the Scenes* (Smith)

Smith, Sidonie, 12

Smith, Stephen, 131–32

Smith-Rosenberg, Carroll, 14–15, 105, 107, 116, 117, 142

Southworth, E. D. E. N., 30

Spinsterhood, 91, 92

Spiritual autobiography, 10, 16–17, 20, 46, 56–59

Spiritualism, 52–57, 67, 77; and female sphere, 53–54, 176n; and science, 53–54, 56, 112–13

Spitzka, Edward, 8, 82, 84, 88, 96, 110, 112, 113, 114

Stanton, Elizabeth Cady, 64, 180–81n

Stepto, Robert Burns, 14–15, 36

Stevens, Jane, 9

Stowe, Harriet Beecher, 17, 57, 64

Szasz, Thomas, 171n, 181n

*Tender Is the Night* (Fitzgerald), 19, 149; alternate versions of, 184n; illness in, 158–59; invasion of privacy in, 153–54; rape in, 151–52; traditional representations of madwoman in, 148, 152–53

*Through Divided Minds: Probing the Mysteries of Multiple Personalities —A Doctor's Story* (Mayer), 169–70

Tocqueville, Alexis de, 32

Tomes, Nancy, 7, 33

*Treatise on Insanity* (Hammond), 117

Treichler, Paula A., 159–60

Tucker, George A., 171–72n

Tuke, Daniel, 63, 174n, 177n, 178n

Turner, James, 113

Utica asylum: class divisions in, 80, 178n; reform movements, 75, 110; size of, 68, 177n; violence in, 8, 75, 174n. *See also Secret Institution, A* (Lathrop)

Utica crib, 34–35, 75, 174n

Van Dyke, Henry, 133, 182n

MARY ELENE WOOD is an associate professor of English at the University of Oregon. She has written articles on women and psychiatry, turn-of-the-century American immigrant autobiography, and gender and sexuality in American narrative and scientific discourse.